TREATY CONFLICT AND THE EUROPEAN UNION

Jan Klabbers questions how membership of the European Union affects treaties concluded between the Union's member states and third states, both when it concerns treaties concluded before EU membership and treaties concluded after joining. Following a discussion of the public international law rules on treaty conflict, the author analyses the case-law of the European Court of Justice and examines how such conflicts are approached in state practice.

JAN KLABBERS studied international law and political science at the University of Amsterdam, before teaching international law and EU law at the same university. Since 1996 he has taught international law at the University of Helsinki. He was visiting professor at Hofstra University (New York) in 2007 and at the Graduate Institute of International Studies and Development (Geneva) in 2008. He also directs the Academy of Finland Centre of Excellence in Global Governance Research.

TREATY CONFLICT AND THE EUROPEAN UNION

JAN KLABBERS

CAMBRIDGE
UNIVERSITY PRESS

CAMBRIDGE UNIVERSITY PRESS
Cambridge, New York, Melbourne, Madrid, Cape Town, Singapore, São Paulo, Delhi

Cambridge University Press
The Edinburgh Building, Cambridge CB2 8RU, UK

Published in the United States of America by Cambridge University Press, New York

www.cambridge.org
Information on this title: www.cambridge.org/9780521728843

© Jan Klabbers 2009

First published 2009

Printed in the United Kingdom at the University Press, Cambridge

A catalogue record for this publication is available from the British Library

ISBN 978-0-521-45546-6 hardback
ISBN 978-0-521-72884-3 paperback

CONTENTS

PREFACE

This book aims to address treaty conflict in international law, and to illuminate in particular the situation with respect to the EU. The relationship between international law and EU law is a source of great confusion, yet is, despite its importance, analysed and discussed only relatively rarely. The present monograph (or 'duograph', if you will) aims to contribute to the study of this relationship by concentrating on one small, highly specialised, aspect thereof: the relationship between obligations arising under treaties concluded by EU member states, and those member states' obligations under EU law.

The interest is this: treaties are, under general international law, binding upon the parties to them, and not capable of creating rights or obligations for third parties. Should conflicting treaties be concluded, either by design or – more likely perhaps – as a result of ignorance, then ideally a conflict rule kicks in. International law does indeed have such a conflict rule; in fact, it has several, but none of these seems to work to great satisfaction. The EU has its own conflict rule as well, one which appears at first sight to be rather generous towards international law and which is often indeed held to be so. Yet, its scope is limited: it applies only to treaties concluded by member states before they joined the EU (and, as we shall see, the Court of Justice has been less than fully generous in its interpretation). Hence, it remains an open question what happens to treaties concluded by member states after they join the EU: are these by definition – and by exclusion – governed by Community law, as the Court of Justice would seem to think? Are they instead governed by general international law? Is, indeed, the relationship best seen as one of conflict between treaty obligations, or should other views be adopted?

This study originated in an invitation by Pieter Jan Kuijper, my one time law professor at the University of Amsterdam and then Director of the External Relations division at the Legal Service of the EU Commission, to conduct a seminar with his staff on the topic of 'successive treaties', in March 2005. While preparing my presentation, I noticed that I had read much of the relevant work. Moreover, having written a few smaller pieces on the topic, I always had the frustration of not being able to approach the topic in all its richness. When writing on EU law, I would usually have to sacrifice most of the international law background; and while writing on international law, some of the EU aspects would have to remain unmentioned. With this in mind, I started to wonder whether it would not be possible to write a short monograph on treaty conflict and the EU, and whether it should not be possible to do so in six months or so. That was almost three years ago . . .

For, while writing, it dawned on me that while it was all very well to know what I wanted to write about, I didn't have a clue yet as to what message I wanted to send out. I had a topic, but not yet a thesis. What I did have, however, was an intuition: the intuition that the EC Court usually makes things too simple for itself by ignoring the international law aspects. This study then aims to test this intuition and make some sense of it. It makes the general point that there is no readily available mechanism to solve the difficult treaty conflicts (as opposed to the easy ones), and that the ECJ's insistence that there is such a general formula when EC law is concerned may well be understandable from the EC's point of view, but is bound to do an injustice to treaty partners and to natural and legal persons, on occasion.

The book has benefited enormously from the feedback received during that seminar in Brussels, in March 2005. Apart from substantive points, the feedback also made clear to what extent the Commission's lawyers have adopted the EU law perspective as paradigmatic; if nothing else, this sent a forceful message that I would have to make a strong effort to convince them of the availability (and perhaps even plausibility or desirability) of other perspectives.

I have also benefited from the privilege of teaching various classes on the topic, or aspects thereof, to groups of students at the University of Helsinki and at Hofstra University, and to the faculty at Hofstra as well: many thanks to my ever generous host there, Jay Hickey. In addition, a seminar with the interdisciplinary group assembled in the Centre of Excellence on Global Governance Research at the University of Helsinki proved illuminating. A special word of gratitude is also due to those students who have adopted my fascination for the law of treaties and have written masterful LLM dissertations on the topic, involving lengthy and thought-provoking discussions. This applies to Thomas Henning and in particular to Andrius Mamontovas, with whom I have had many useful discussions on the topic. More generally on the law of treaties, if a bit further removed from the topic *per se*, the same applies to my current doctoral students Rain Liivoja and Varro Vooglaid as well. I also had the good fortune that the person in the office next to mine happens to be Martti Koskenniemi, who was more or less simultaneously working on fragmentation for the International Law Commission: our topics coincided to a considerable extent, and while our discussions tend to be brief, they also tend to be very to the point: for a while, insights and reading tips were shared on an almost daily basis. Discussions with Anja Lindroos, herself rapidly becoming a recognised authority on fragmentation and treaty conflict, proved immensely valuable as well, and I owe a debt of gratitude to Ilona Nieminen for allowing me to use the materials she compiled on the so-called disconnection clause. The book would also have looked rather different (and worse) without the comments of the two anonymous reviewers for Cambridge University Press.

At home, Marja-Leena and Johan provided the regular stability and distractions necessary to function well in an ever-changing academic world where, sadly, the pressures of administration (much of it silly and pointless) are taking over from the pleasures of teaching and research. They made sure that, when confronted with conflicting obligations between work and home, I would have an incentive to have private life prevail.

Cases

European Court of Justice

EC Court of First Instance

Permanent Court of International Justice

International Court of Justice

European Commission of Human Rights

European Court of Human Rights

Materials

EC/EU Documents

ILC Documents

Miscellaneous

Websites

TABLE OF TREATIES AND INSTRUMENTS

As this is a study of, in essence, two treaty provisions, it would seem pointless to have separate entries relating to those two provisions in this table. Hence, there will be no separate entries for article 30 of the Vienna Convention on the Law of Treaties and for article 307 of the Treaty establishing the European Community. By the same token, there are no separate entries for generic references to the EC Treaty and the Vienna Convention, as they are mentioned on well-nigh every single page. There will, however, be separate entries for specific provisions of those treaties other than article 30 VCLT or article 307 TEC.

In particular in Chapter 9, moreover, a number of treaties are mentioned in the footnotes but not discussed as far as their contents go: my main interest has resided in their conclusion, not in their contents. As a result, such treaties are also not referred to in this table, except those that are discussed in some detail in the text. A few final notes: first, the titles of treaties can be fairly long-winded; I have taken the liberty to refer to shorthand titles below. Thus, the Agreement between Italy and the Socialist Federal Republic of Yugoslavia on Mutual Administrative Assistance for the Prevention and Suppression of Customs Fraud, mentioned in a footnote but by no means pivotal to the central argument, is referred to as Italy-Yugoslavia Agreement on Customs Fraud. I have generally done this with treaties, except those that are of more central importance. Second, treaties concluded by the EC or EU are listed under the heading bilateral treaties, not multilateral (benignly neglecting the possibility of mixity), while treaties concluded initially outside the EC framework (such as the two Schengen Agreements) are treated as multilateral treaties rather than EC/EU documents.

Multilateral

Vienna Convention

EU Instruments

Bilateral

PART I

Setting the scene

1

Introduction

Opening words

The parking lot next to a sports hall in the Herttoniemenranta area of Helsinki presents a puzzling sight. The lot has some forty demarcated parking places which, in itself, is no cause for surprise: this is what one would expect in a parking lot. What is cause for surprise, however, is that next to one of the parking spaces, there is a 'no parking' sign: a typical example of conflicting instructions. As an example of conflicting instructions, it is of course not all that uncommon: legislators, at whatever level of governance, may on occasion not realise that instruction A is incompatible with instruction B, or rule A is in conflict with rule B. What makes the case of the parking lot and the 'no parking' sign all the more curious, however, is that the norms do not exist merely in abstract form, as words on paper, but have also met with physical implementation: someone had to build the parking lot and paint the stripes demarcating one parking space from the next, and someone had to put up the 'no parking' sign.

This is not a book about parking signs, or conflicting norm-setting at the local level. It is, instead, a study of the topic of conflicting norms on the international level, where two of the elements characterising the parking problem are usually lacking: international norms do not result from a single norm-setting agency,[1] and typically with international norms, they exist first and foremost as words on paper.

To be more specific, this is a book about treaty conflict in international law with special emphasis on a particular class of conflicts: conflicts between the EC Treaty, and treaties concluded between member states of the EC either with third parties or with each other. It is not a study of

---

[1] Then again, I am not sure whether this applied in the parking sign example. It is possible that the parking space was created by the parking authority of the city of Helsinki, while some agency at the lower sub-municipality level of Herttoniemenranta bears responsibility for putting up 'no parking' signs. Or *vice versa*.

norm-conflict more generally; it will not address conflicts between treaties
and customary norms, or treaty provisions and general principles of law.
Nor does it deal with conflicts between EC law and the national laws of
its member states. The scope of this study, in other words, is limited to
studying the way conflicts between obligations owed under EC law, and
obligations owed under some other international treaty, are addressed.

The immediate inspiration for writing this book resides in a string of
cases decided by the Court of Justice of the EC. In late 2002, the EC Court
came up with its long-awaited judgments in the so-called *Open Skies*
cases. During the second half of the 1990s, a generous handful of the EU's
member states had concluded bilateral agreements with the US relating to
air traffic issues. The Commission, unhappy with this go-it-alone attitude
of so many of the EU's member states, initiated proceedings before the
Court of Justice, claiming in essence that, when concluding these bilateral
agreements with the US, the member states had acted in violation of
their obligations under the TEC. Moreover, their bilateral treaty-making
with the US had been rather counterproductive for, as the Commission
suggested, together the EU member states could boast a far stronger
negotiating position towards the US than any of its member states could
possibly hope to achieve on its own.

The judgments by the Court largely followed the Commission's position: in concluding the agreements, the Court held, the member states had
violated EU law, most notably rules relating to the freedom of establishment, and the general catch-all provision of article 10 TEC, under which
the member states agree to act in a spirit of loyalty to the Community –
the 'fidelity principle' as it sometimes referred to, or *Gemeinschaftstreue*,
in good German.

While scenarios such as those of the *Open Skies* cases do not come about
every day, they seem to be recurring with increasing frequency: indeed,
at the time of writing, a handful of cases are pending before the EC
Court involving the conclusion of bilateral investment treaties by several
member states with third parties. Again, the main argument seems to be
that these bilateral agreements may interfere with internal Community
rules (in this case, the rules on free movement of capital), and with the
ubiquitous notion of *Gemeinschaftstreue*.

In addition, ever since the ending of the Cold War helped re-activate
the Security Council of the United Nations, issues have arisen before the
EC courts concerning the relationship between UN law and EU law;
the notorious decisions of the Court of First Instance in cases involving
sanctions imposed on Swedish citizens are merely the most recent in

an impressive line of cases – and more cases are pending. On several occasions, the relationship between the EC and the European Convention on Human Rights has reached the courts in Europe, with both the EC Court and the Human Rights Court, for the time being, testing the waters rather than burning any bridges. And a general string of cases involving anterior treaties (treaties concluded by a member state before joining the EC) would seem to suggest that although such treaties are protected under the EC Treaty, the protection offered is really marginal: in the summer of 2000, the EC Court rendered judgment in cases against Portugal for failure to take sufficient steps to terminate several anterior treaties.

The curious thing about most of these decisions is what the Court leaves unsaid: it says not a word on the possible role of international law, despite the fact that the agreements at issue were valid international agreements, creating rights and obligations both for each of those member states and for the treaty partners. The Court remains silent about the possible conflict of norms created by concluding those agreements, yet it is this conflict which will be central to this study.

As noted, the *Open Skies* cases do not represent the first time that the EC Court has decided a case without considering possibly applicable international law.[2] Nor is the EC Court the only international tribunal that tends to look at international cases purely from its own internal perspective, thereby possibly (if not always actually) disregarding international law. In 1989, in its famous *Soering* decision,[3] the European Court of Human Rights did much the same in a case involving the question whether extradition of a criminal suspect from the UK to the US, while possibly envisaged under the bilateral extradition treaty, ran counter to the UK's obligations under the European Convention. While the Court's decision was no doubt justifiable also in terms of general international law, given the terms of the extradition treaty at issue,[4] it is nonetheless surprising to see that the international law context was by and large ignored.[5]

[2] See already F. E. Dowrick, 'Overlapping International and European Laws', *International & Comparative Law Quarterly*, 31 (1982), 59–98.

[3] See *Soering* v. *United Kingdom*, European Court of Human Rights application no. 14038/88, judgment of 7 July 1989, *Publications of the European Court of Human Rights*, vol. 161 (1989).

[4] See also Colin Warbrick, 'Coherence and the European Court of Human Rights: The Adjudicative Background to the *Soering* Case', *Michigan Journal of International Law*, 11 (1989–90), 1073–96, at 1093–4.

[5] For a general comment, see Stephan Breitenmoser and Gunter E. Wilms, 'Human Rights v. Extradition: The *Soering* Case', *Michigan Journal of International Law*, 11 (1989–90), 845–86.

And a decade and a half later, the ECtHR suggested that it has retained that basic approach in a case involving a possible conflict between the European Convention and a bilateral Latvia–Russia treaty on withdrawal of Russia's troops from Latvia's territory: once the Court had found that the bilateral treaty did not affect its jurisdiction (in that Latvia had made no reservation in regard to the treaty upon ratifying the Convention), it paid no further attention to it.[6]

Likewise, as is well-documented,[7] the WTO's dispute settlement bodies have shown a marked reluctance to look beyond WTO law proper in deciding disputes.[8] The International Tribunal for the Law of the Sea held, in deciding upon a request for provisional measures in the *Mox Plant* case, that even though provisions in other treaties might be similar or identical, the request could be captured solely in terms of the 1982 Law of the Sea Convention, excluding other relevant norms.[9] An ICSID panel, confronted with a possible environmental justification for an expropriation, noted that for its decision, the international source of the environmental obligation made 'no difference'.[10]

Only the International Court of Justice seems relatively open to all sorts of norms, not surprisingly perhaps given the fact that it is a court of general jurisdiction. But even the ICJ's openness is limited: the Court did its very best (and succeeded brilliantly) to avoid saying anything with finality on the relationship between the UN Charter and other treaties in the *Lockerbie* cases,[11] and felt the need, in *Oil Platforms*, explicitly to

---

[6] See *Slivenko* v. *Latvia*, European Court of Human Rights application no. 48321/99, judgment of 23 January 2002 (admissibility), ECtHR *Reports of Judgments and Decisions* (2002-II) 467.

[7] See, e.g., Joost Pauwelyn, *Conflict of Norms in Public International Law: How WTO Law Relates to Other Rules of International Law* (Cambridge: Cambridge University Press, 2003).

[8] As good an example as any is the panel decision in *European Communities – Measures Affecting the Approval and Marketing of Biotech Products*, WT/DS291.292.293, 21 November 2006.

[9] See ITLOS, *The Mox Plant case* (Ireland v. United Kingdom), request for provisional measures, order of 3 December 2001, paras. 50–2.

[10] See ICSID, case no. ARB/91/1, *Compañía des Desarrollo de Santa Elena, S.A.* v. *Costa Rica*, final award of 17 February 2000.

[11] It underlined, in its 1992 order on provisional measures, that its discussion of Security Council Resolution 748 and the legal effects thereof was preliminary only, leaving the door open for further reflections and ruminations. These, however, would never come about. See *Case concerning Questions of Interpretation and Application of the 1971 Montreal Convention Arising from the Aerial Incident at Lockerbie* (Libya v. USA), provisional measures, [1992] *ICJ Reports* 114, esp. paras. 42–5.

justify interpreting a treaty between Iran and the US in light of general international law.[12]

Treaty conflict and fragmentation

As the brief enumeration of recent court decisions above already suggests, treaty conflict is one of the more hotly debated topics among international lawyers at present. In the literature this is reflected in the appearance of numerous studies on treaty conflict generally,[13] sometimes with special reference to the WTO as the focal point for linking issues,[14] as well as studies on more specific instances of conflict related to trade norms: trade versus human rights;[15] trade versus environmental protection[16] and health;[17] trade versus labour protection;[18] trade versus culture.[19] Some

---

[12] See *Case Concerning Oil Platforms* (Islamic Republic of Iran v. USA) judgment of 6 November 2003, para. 41. Arguably, the Court felt the need to justify this in explicit manner in order to respond to the US argument that the Court's jurisdiction was limited to interpreting and applying the bilateral Iran-US Treaty. *Ibid.*, para. 39.

[13] For the last decade or so alone, see Jan Mus, *Verdragsconflicten voor de Nederlandse rechter* (Zwolle: Tjeenk Willink, 1996); Wilhelm Heinrich Wilting, *Vertragskonkurrenz im Völkerrecht* (Cologne: Carl Heymans Verlag, 1996); Seyed Ali Sadat-Akhavi, *Methods of Resolving Conflicts between Treaties* (Leiden: Martinus Nijhoff, n.y.).

[14] See Pauwelyn, *Conflict of Norms*; José E. Alvarez, 'The WTO as Linkage Machine', *American Journal of International Law*, 96 (2002), 146–58.

[15] See in particular Gabrielle Marceau, 'WTO Dispute Settlement and Human Rights', *European Journal of International Law*, 13 (2002), 753–814; Ernst-Ulrich Petersmann, 'Human Rights and the Law of the World Trade Organization', *Journal of World Trade*, 37 (2003), 241–81; Ernst-Ulrich Petersmann, 'Time for a United Nations "Global Compact" for Integrating Human Rights into the Law of Worldwide Organizations: Lessons from European Integration', *European Journal of International Law*, 13 (2002), 621–50; Hoe Lim, 'Trade and Human Rights: What's at Issue?', *Journal of World Trade*, 35 (2001), 275–300.

[16] A fairly early example is Scott N. Carlson, 'The Montreal Protocol's Environmental Subsidies and GATT: A Needed Reconciliation', *Texas International Law Journal*, 29 (1994), 211–30.

[17] See, e.g., Sabrina Safrin, 'Treaties in Collision? The Biosafety Protocol and the World Trade Organization Agreements', *American Journal of International Law*, 96 (2002), 606–28; Patrick J. Vallely, 'Tension between the Cartagena Protocol and the WTO: The Significance of Recent WTO Developments in an Ongoing Debate', *Chicago Journal of International Law*, 5 (2004–05), 369–78.

[18] See, e.g., Christopher McCrudden and Anne Davies, 'A Perspective on Trade and Labor Rights', *Journal of International Economic Law* 3 (2000), 43–62; Hilary K. Josephs, 'Upstairs, Trade Law; Downstairs, Labor Law', *George Washington International Law Review*, 33 (2000–01), 849–72.

[19] See, e.g., Mary E. Footer and Christoph Beat Graber, 'Trade Liberalization and Cultural Policy', *Journal of International Economic Law*, 3 (2000), 115–44; Tania Voon, 'UNESCO and the WTO: A Clash of Cultures?', *International and Comparative Law Quarterly*, 55 (2006), 635–52.

work discusses the conflict between investment protection and environ-mental regulation,[20] while various studies have been devoted to treaty conflict within specific branches of public international law, most notably environmental law.[21] Asylum lawyers have started to worry about the pos-sibility that so-called 'diplomatic assurances' (agreements between states that extradited persons will not be subject to human rights violations) may end up eroding earlier, more robust human rights commitments.[22] And, as far as the EU is concerned, the links between Community law and the European Convention have attracted particular attention,[23] as well as (albeit to a lesser extent) the connections between Community and United Nations law.[24]

Partly, the reason for this can be found in the subject's relationship with the broader topic of the fragmentation of international law,[25] something which inspired even the International Law Commission to devote further study to treaty conflict, despite the fact that the topic does not lend itself for a codification convention.[26] Fragmentation, after all, might mean that various sub-disciplines or sub-régimes of international law lose track of one another and end up creating norms which may be in conflict: norms

---

[20] See Philippe Sands, *Lawless World: America and the Making and Breaking of Global Rules* (London: Allen Lane, 2005), ch. 6.

[21] See especially Rüdiger Wolfrum and Nele Matz, *Conflicts in International Environmental Law* (Berlin: Springer, 2003); see also Malgosia Fitzmaurice and Olufemi Elias, *Contemporary Issues in the Law of Treaties* (Utrecht: Eleven, 2005), ch. 9.

[22] See in particular Gregor Noll, 'Diplomatic Assurances and the Silence of Human Rights Law', *Melbourne Journal of International Law*, 7 (2006), 104–26; Martin Jones, 'Lies, Damned Lies and Diplomatic Assurances: The Misuse of Diplomatic Assurances in Removal Proceedings', *European Journal of Migration and Law*, 8 (2006), 9–39.

[23] See, e.g., Rick Lawson, *Het EVRM en de Europese Gemeenschappen* (Deventer: Kluwer, 1999); Päivi Leino-Sandberg, *Particularity as Universality: The Politics of Human Rights in the European Union* (Helsinki: Erik Castrén Institute, 2005).

[24] A useful recent contribution is Jan Wouters, Frank Hoffmeister and Tom Ruys (eds.), *The United Nations and the European Union: An Ever Stronger Partnership* (The Hague: TMC Asser Press, 2006).

[25] On fragmentation generally, see Martti Koskenniemi and Päivi Leino, 'Fragmentation of International Law? Postmodern Anxieties', Leiden *Journal of International Law*, 15 (2002), 553–79; also very useful is Matthew Craven, 'Unity, Diversity and the Fragmentation of International Law', *Finnish Yearbook of International Law*, 14 (2003), 3–34.

[26] The ILC established a study group, and appointed its then member Martti Koskenniemi as chairperson. The study group has produced two hefty reports on the fragmentation of international law, paying much attention to treaty conflict. The final report is published as UN Doc. A/CN.4/L.682, dated 4 April 2006, under the title *Fragmentation of International Law: Difficulties Arising from the Diversification and Expansion of International Law*. A convenient book version was published in 2007 by the Erik Castrén Institute of the University of Helsinki.

emerging from the trade régime may be difficult to reconcile with norms created within the environmental régime, or within the human rights regime.[27] As a result, diverging norms may end up applying to a single state. As international law does not have a central legislature, there is no one to guard the unity of the system, and no one to make sure that the norms the system generates are always compatible with each other. Consequently, the identification of a trend towards fragmentation has spawned concern about treaty conflict, as well as about competing courts[28] and normative conflict more generally.[29] In addition, it has generated a heated debate on whether the sub-disciplines of international law can in any meaningful way be regarded as 'self-contained'.[30]

This study aims to focus on a small, under-analysed part of the question: conflicts between the EC Treaty and treaties concluded between the member states *inter se* and between member states and third parties.[31] That is a small part of the larger question of conflicting treaty norms, and

[27] This may owe much to what Slaughter refers to as the 'disaggregated state': states are no longer unitary actors on the international scene; instead, their agencies and departments operate to some extent on their own. See Anne-Marie Slaughter, *A New World Order* (Princeton University Press, 2004).

[28] Vaughan Lowe has sensibly observed that some jurisdictional conflicts 'may be approached *via* the Law of Treaties'. See Vaughan Lowe, 'Overlapping Jurisdiction in International Tribunals', *Australian Yearbook of International Law*, 20 (1999), 191–204; see generally also Yuval Shany, *The Competing Jurisdictions of International Courts and Tribunals* (Oxford: Oxford University Press, 2003).

[29] See already W. Czaplinski and G. Danilenko, 'Conflict of Norms in International Law', *Netherlands Yearbook of International Law*, 22 (1991), 3–42. A novel manifestation of conflict is identified in Yuval Shany, 'Contract Claims vs. Treaty Claims: Mapping Conflicts between ICSID Decisions on Multisourced Investment Claims', *American Journal of International Law*, 99 (2005), 835–51.

[30] The *locus classicus* is Bruno Simma, 'Self-contained Regimes', *Netherlands Yearbook of International Law*, 16 (1985), 112–36; a recent discussion is Anja Lindroos and Michael Mehling, 'Dispelling the Chimera of "Self-contained Regimes": International Law and the WTO', *European Journal of International Law*, 16 (2005), 857–77.

[31] I am aware of only three published papers addressing the topic of treaties concluded between member states *inter se*. Two of these have been written by De Witte: see Bruno de Witte, 'Old-fashioned Flexibility: International Agreements between Member States of the European Union', in Gráinne de Búrca and Joanne Scott (eds.), *Constitutional Change in the EU: From Uniformity to Flexibility?* (Oxford: Hart, 2000), pp. 31–58; and see Bruno de Witte, 'Internationale verdragen tussen lidstaten van de Europese Unie', in Ramses Wessel and Bruno de Witte, *De plaats van de Europese Unie in het veranderende bestel van de volkenrechtelijke organisatie* (The Hague: TMC Asser Press, 2001; Mededelingen van de Nederlandse Vereniging voor Internationaal Recht, no. 123), pp. 79–131. For a third, and very useful, paper see Robert Schütze, 'EC Law and International Agreements of the Member States – An Ambivalent Relationship?', *Cambridge Yearbook of European Legal Studies*, 9 (2006–07), 387–440.

is usually treated in a few paragraphs, or a few pages, in textbooks on the EU's external relations[32] or essays or articles dealing with the connections between international law and EU law.[33] Usually, moreover, the question is studied primarily from the perspective of Community law, with the result that much is made of as general a principle as that of *Gemeinschaftstreue*,[34] or that international law considerations are simply ignored. I am not aware of any monograph on the precise topic of this study; and the number of articles devoted to it is fairly limited as well.[35]

Article 307 TEC and international law

Article 307 TEC is the only article in the entire edifice of the EU relating to the status of treaties concluded by the EU's member states vis-à-vis EU law. Article 307 provides that treaties concluded by member states before the EC came into being or, as the case may be, before the accession of a member state to the EU, shall be immune from the working of EU law. However, as the Court has consistently held, this is not in order to protect the rights of those member states, but rather to protect the rights of others.[36] Moreover, article 307 also entails an admonition that any incompatibilities be terminated as soon as possible, although it fails to prescribe exactly how this termination of incompatibilities should come about.

Still, article 307 is limited only to treaties concluded before the creation of the EC, or a state's accession thereto. That leaves untouched a host of other agreements: those concluded after the member state joined or after the EC was established (I will refer to these as posterior agreements).

---

[32] See, e.g., I. MacLeod, I. D. Hendry, and Stephen Hyett, *The External Relations of the European Communities* (Oxford: Oxford University Press, 1996), pp. 228–31; Dominic McGoldrick, *International Relations Law of the European Union* (London: Longman, 1997), pp. 123–4; Piet Eeckhout, *External Relations of the European Union: Legal and Constitutional Foundations* (Oxford: Oxford University Press, 2004), pp. 333–42. Most generous is Koutrakos, who devotes an entire chapter to 'pre-membership agreements' concluded by the member states. See Panos Koutrakos, *EU International Relations Law* (Oxford: Hart, 2006), ch. 8.

[33] See, e.g., Koen Lenaerts and Eddy de Smijter, 'The European Union as an Actor under International Law', *Yearbook of European Law*, 19 (1999–2000), 95–138, pp. 114–22.

[34] See generally de Witte, 'Old-fashioned Flexibility'.

[35] See above all Ernst-Ulrich Petersmann, 'Artikel 234', in H. von der Groeben, Jochen Thiessing and Claus-Dieter Ehlermann (eds.), *Kommentar zum EWG-Vertrag*, 4th edn (Baden-Baden: Nomos, 1991), pp. 5725–53.

[36] Which others precisely is open to debate; this will be addressed in Chapter 6.

Usually, it is supposed that here Community law simply prevails, and has to prevail by its very nature: if it is indeed the new (and separate) legal order the Court has held it to be, it would seem to follow that its provisions prevail over everything else. After all, any other solution might come to affect the uniformity of Community law; it would provide member states with the possibility of escaping from their obligations under Community law by means of creating conflicting agreements with third parties.

This is, as far as EC law goes, standard fare. The seminal *ERTA* case was already decided on this basis (and not, as is sometimes held, on the basis of the implied powers doctrine): the Court derived a power for the EC to conclude treaties with third parties in the field of road transport from the necessity to safeguard the uniformity of EC law. It was not the case, necessarily, that the founding fathers had intended to provide the Community with such a power; nor was it the case that such a power would have been implied.[37] Indeed, the Court could well have found that EC law was perfectly compatible with treaty-making powers remaining with the member states on the understanding that they would not be allowed to violate their obligations under Community law. Yet the Court found no such thing: instead, it held that the uniformity of EC law warranted the finding of an external power for the EC.[38]

Thus put, it should come as no surprise that article 307 has always been rather restrictively interpreted; the uniformity of EC law permits of no other options. And perhaps for the same reason, it should come as no surprise that the Court tends to ignore (as in the above-mentioned *Open Skies* cases) any possible international law consideration, both when it comes to posterior treaties concluded by the EC's member states, but also (more surprising, given the existence of article 307 TEC) in respect of anterior treaties. To paraphrase Binder, the Court 'conjures up a world without treaty conflict'.[39] Which is, of course, a more polite way of saying that when treaty conflict is at issue, the Court adopts the proverbial[40] ostrich's stance: by putting its head in the sand, the ostrich can see no problems, and if it can't see any problems, they don't exist.

[37] A useful discussion in Dutch is Christine Denys, *Impliciete bevoegdheden in de Europese Economische Gemeenschap* (Antwerp: MAKLU, 1990), pp. 122–32.
[38] See Case 22/70, *Commission* v. *Council (ERTA)* [1971] ECR 273.
[39] See Guyora Binder, *Treaty Conflict and Political Contradiction: The Dialectic of Duplicity* (New York: Praeger, 1988), p. 33. Binder blames ILC Special Rapporteur Fitzmaurice for conjuring up a world without treaty conflict.
[40] At least the Dutch language has the wonderful word '*struisvogelpolitiek*' to denote a policy of simply ignoring problems.

The argument of this book

The argument of this book will be fairly straightforward, and in a nutshell goes as follows. Treaty conflict is, typically, conflict about higher values; indeed, where it is not about values but merely about coordination problems, it can usually easily be solved. Treaty conflict may not originate in a clash of values (many conflicting obligations may result from ministries working, unbeknown to each other, at cross-purposes), but it will typically end up that way. Should trade be encouraged (giving effect to a trade agreement) even at the expense of the environment (giving effect to an environmental obligation)? Should orderly diplomatic cooperation in criminal matters be given credence (giving effect to an extradition treaty) or should, instead, the human rights of the person whose extradition is requested be placed in the foreground (giving effect to a human rights treaty)? Should a person's rights under a labour agreement be protected, even if this were to conflict with the notion of equal treatment? Et cetera. Conflict of treaties is rarely about mundane matters; it is rarely the result of coordination problems. Instead, it is typically the result of a clash of values.

What further typifies this clash of values is that it is often a consequence of (for want of a better term) a non-holistic approach. That means, that the clash of values cannot be detected (or is unlikely to be detected) at the moment a treaty is being negotiated. Chances are that those who negotiate a trade agreement are so focused on trade, that possible environmental ramifications or human rights ramifications do not enter their minds – something which will be strengthened by the fact that, typically, trade agreements will be the work of trade experts. Bureaucratic segmentation, characteristic of the modern state, thus prevents the timely realisation of possible conflicts.[41] Hence, the treaty (or treaties) concerned will typically be silent on possible conflicts, and will also hardly be equipped to deal with possible conflict, for example by stimulating the provision of conflict clauses or providing for mechanisms of coordination. Moreover, such conflict clauses as do exist tend merely to shift the problem.

---

[41] Earlier writers such as Lauterpacht and McNair distinguished between conflict in which the parties were aware of existing commitments, and those where they were unaware. It is telling, perhaps, that this discussion has lost much of its relevance and is all but ignored in today's literature. See Hersch Lauterpacht, 'Report on the Law of Treaties', in *Yearbook of the International Law Commission*, II (1953), 90–166, at p. 156, and Lord McNair, *The Law of Treaties* (Oxford: Clarendon, 1961), p. 222.

It is here, then, one would expect, that general international law comes in. Surely, one would expect, the law of treaties, with its centuries of tradition, must have developed rules to deal with precisely such a circumstance? The answer will be disappointing: yes, the Vienna Convention on the Law of Treaties contains a few rules, but these are typically only helpful when what is at issue is a problem of coordination. Thus, the rules are also fairly useful when state A promises to sell a piece of territory to B, but reneges on its commitment by selling it to C instead. The rules are also fairly useful when treaties are dealing with the same issue, as may be the case in trade relations: a treaty to open up the market for products from A does not really conflict with a similar treaty to open up the market for products from B; a multilateral tax treaty providing for a VAT rate of maximum 20 per cent on, say, academic books, does not clash with a bilateral treaty between some of the parties to the multilateral one providing for a standard VAT rate of, say, 12 per cent. In this sort of case, one may well speak of a coordination problem, and here the rules of the Vienna Convention are quite useful, to the extent that they are necessary to begin with.

When, instead, what is at issue is a clash of values, the Vienna Convention's rules are less helpful; when the clash is between a trade treaty and an environmental treaty, or a trade agreement and a human rights agreement, or a labour agreement and a disarmament treaty, the Vienna Convention offers fairly little guidance. And, crucially, that was only to be expected, precisely because the issue involves a clash of values, a clash of conceptions as to what constitutes the good life. That is not to glorify values: elsewhere, I have written that international lawyers' insistence that values are somehow capable of underpinning the entire international legal order and turning it into a constitutional or quasi-constitutional order is unhelpful:[42] people can, and do, change their values overnight, and tend to be in fundamental disagreement over values: what some hold dear may leave others cold; values that are cherished by some may be repugnant to others. So an insistence that some values are capable of bringing the global community together[43] is bound to remain illusory, or turn into a fig leaf for specific political projects. But that is not to deny that much international politics (and international law, by extension) takes place so as to

---

[42] See, e.g., Jan Klabbers, 'The Commodification of International Law', in Emmanuelle Jouannet and Hélène Ruiz-Fabri (eds.), *International Law: Do We Need It?* (Oxford: Hart, forthcoming); see also Jan Klabbers, 'Possible Islands of Predictability: The Legal Thought of Hannah Arendt', *Leiden Journal of International Law*, 20 (2007), 1–23.

[43] The most vocal proponent of such a value-based view is Erika de Wet, 'The International Constitutional Order', *International and Comparative Law Quarterly*, 55 (2006), 51–76.

promote certain values over others: indeed, for that very reason, sometimes fairly innocent treaty conflicts come to be recast as value clashes,
and become unsolvable as a result, as will be discussed extensively in the
next chapter.

Since the Vienna Convention's rules offer little guidance, it may well
be helpful if guidance can be sought and found elsewhere: in a clause laid
down in a treaty itself on what to do in case of conflict. With article 103
of the UN Charter being a special case (it is the only treaty provision in
force which claims priority for the treaty which contains it), the leading
example of such a provision is article 307 TEC, and it is the analysis
of that provision that will be the point of departure to the third part
of this study. Article 307 regulates, albeit not with finality, the relations
between EU member states and other states. From the perspective of the
EU member state, article 307 tells it what to do in case an obligation under
EU law is incompatible with an obligation under another treaty. There is
a limit though: this only applies to treaties concluded before the member
state joined the EU, or (in case of founding members) concluded before
the creation of the EU. With respect to later treaties, the TEC remains
silent.

And thus, one would expect, the same rules from the Vienna Convention would be activated – yet those have already proven to be less than
helpful.[44] In the end, then, when it comes to a clash of values, there is little
the law has to offer. Instead, such conflicts ought to be resolved (if at all)
in the body politic.

In short, the central argument of this book is that neither the law of
treaties nor EU law will have much to say about certain treaty conflicts.
In making the argument, two bodies of rules will be analysed in some
detail. First, I will have a close look at what the law of treaties says about
conflicting obligations. This will occupy the second part of the book, and
will be made to serve the main thesis. The third part will be devoted to
the analysis of EC law and treaty conflict, and a number of related things
(such as the EC Court's stand on posterior treaties, and the state practice
of the EC's member states). On one level, then, this book can simply,
unassumingly, be read as a 'duograph' (as opposed to monograph) on
conflict of treaties in international law and EC law. On another level, it can
be taken as a study on the relative indeterminacy of a crucial international

---

[44] Boyle and Chinkin suggest much the same; see Alan Boyle and Christine Chinkin, *The
Making of International Law* (Oxford: Oxford University Press, 2007), p. 248 (listing the
various disparate elements governing treaty conflict).

legal institution; the theoretical foundation will be laid in the first part of this study, in particular in the next chapter.

An assumption and a caveat

Throughout the book, I will employ one fundamental assumption, and that is the assumption that the EU is, eventually, subject to international law, at least when it concerns dealings with the outside world.[45] On one level, this is no cause for great controversy: few would ever argue that a bilateral treaty between, say, Belgium and Japan would be governed by EU law rather than international law, or that a treaty between the EU and the US would be governed by anything other than international law.

The point itself is not all that controversial. Indeed, many would agree that the EU is subject to public international law, and is characterised by being open and receptive towards international law. Admittedly, as the standard narrative goes, the EU may have been forced first to put its relative autonomy in place, but once this was accomplished, the way would be paved for an open and mature relationship.[46]

The one problem with this rosy picture, however, is that it is not entirely borne out by practice. As will be shown extensively in part III of this study, at least from the perspective of the international lawyer the attitude of the EC courts has not so much been open and receptive, but rather protective of the European project. The courts have tended to protect EC law and European integration, if necessary at the expense of international law considerations.[47]

The EC Court, for one, has the tendency to keep as much distance between EU law and international law as it possibly can. Some of its decisions on article 307 are fine examples of this, but there are other indications as well. One is that the EC Court, typically, when applying

[45] The seminal articles on this point would include Derrick Wyatt, 'New Legal Order, or Old?', *European Law Review*, 7 (1982), 147–66; Bruno de Witte, 'Retour à Costa: La primauté du droit communautaire à la lumière du droit international', *Revue Trimestrielle de Droit Européen*, 20 (1984), 425–54; Trevor C. Hartley, 'International Law and the Law of the European Union – A Reassessment', *British Yearbook of International Law*, 72 (2001), 1–35.
[46] This standard narrative, complete with the analogy of the child having to become independent from the parent, is lucidly phrased in Christiaan Timmermans, 'The EU and Public International Law', *European Foreign Affairs Review*, 4 (1999), 181–94.
[47] See also Andrea Ott, 'Thirty Years of Case-law by the European Court of Justice on International Law: A Pragmatic Approach towards its Integration', in Vincent Kronenberger (ed.), *The EU and the International Legal Order: Discord or Harmony?* (The Hague: TMC Asser Press, 2001), pp. 95–140, at p. 136.

UN sanctions, applies the EU instrument incorporating those sanctions rather than the original UN Security Council itself, and would probably give preference to the EU instrument in cases of a divergence between the two texts.[48] By the same token, the Court has never adopted wholesale the European Convention on Human Rights as such,[49] and has developed rather sophisticated mechanisms to avoid having to apply WTO law.[50] While all this may be explained as prudent dualism, there is but a fine line between prudent dualism and neglect of international law – as early observers of the Community court already realised.[51]

The assumption, then, is that the EU is bound by international law. That has no bearing on the EC's proudly proclaimed distinct legal order: internally, the EU can set whatever rules it wants, and can dissociate itself as much from international law as it likes. International law does not prohibit this; if anything, it has explicitly accepted as much, for example in article 5 of the Vienna Convention on the Law of Treaties.[52]

The sometimes implicit argument that being a distinct legal order isolates the EU from international law is simply untenable, largely for two reasons. As noted, one is in almost Kelsenian fashion,[53] that international law grants EU law the freedom to develop itself, for instance by means

---

[48] See, e.g., Jean-Pierre Puissochet, 'The Court of Justice and International Action by the European Community: The Example of the Embargo against the Former Yugoslavia', *Fordham International Law Journal*, 20 (1997) 1557–76. This will be further discussed in Chapter 7 below.

[49] For a general critique, see Leino-Sandberg, *Particularity as Universality*.

[50] See Jan Klabbers, 'International Law in Community Law: The Law and Politics of Direct Effect', *Yearbook of European Law*, 21 (2002), 263–98.

[51] See e.g. Christoph Sasse, 'The Common Market, between International and Municipal Law', *Yale Law Journal*, 75 (1966), 695–753. In Schermers' words: 'There is no acceptable reason why the member Governments of the Communities when bound to a rule of international law should be allowed to make or keep conflicting rules of Community law.' See H. G. Schermers, 'Community Law and International Law', *Common Market Law Review*, 12 (1975), 77–90, p. 84.

[52] Article 5 singles out the internal law of international organisations as being protected against unwanted intervention by the law of treaties: 'The present Convention applies to any treaty which is the constituent instrument of an international organization and to any treaty adopted within an international organization without prejudice to any relevant rules of the organization.' On the relations between international organisations and the law of treaties, see generally Catherine Brölmann, *The Institutional Veil in Public International Law: International Organizations and the Law of Treaties* (Oxford: Hart, 2007).

[53] Kelsen famously argued that states are subordinate to international law because they owe their existence to international law and can be characterised as organs of the international legal community. See Hans Kelsen, *Introduction to the Problems of Legal Theory* (Oxford: Clarendon Press, 1992, Litschewski Paulson and Paulson trans.).

of article 5 of the Vienna Convention. The second, more relevant, consideration is that isolating the EU from international law would entail lawlessness: it would result in an actor being above the law. And this seems simply untenable. It only adds an ironical element to realise that the one actor above the law would itself be a creation of that law.[54]

Partly as a result of this assumption, I will look at things from the viewpoint, and with the sensitivities, of an international lawyer rather than an EU lawyer. I will address some issues which would quite possibly be left unaddressed by EU lawyers working on the same topic, and conversely I will ignore some issues that EU lawyers would typically address. That is not necessarily a bad thing – although taken to the extreme, there is a certain discomfort in the thought that the paradigms of international law and EU law have drifted so far apart that I feel the need even to make this caveat to begin with. Be that as it may, though, at least I might be able to offer the EU lawyer a different, and hopefully helpful, perspective.

---

[54] As Trevor Hartley, among others, has pointed out repeatedly, the EC is itself based on a treaty, and thus initially a creature of international law. See Hartley, 'A Reassessment'.

2

Understanding treaty conflict

Introduction

The idea behind this chapter is to discuss various ways in which the problem of treaty conflict has been addressed, against the background of the law of treaties and in light of a more generally theoretical approach to the law of treaties. More specific emanations of thought on treaty conflict will be reserved for later chapters; the present chapter aims to sketch a more general framework. One important conclusion will be that the law of treaties remains silent precisely when it concerns the most difficult treaty conflicts: these are conflicts involving treaties the parties to which are only partially overlapping (often labeled AB:AC conflicts: A has an engagement with B, and a conflicting one with C). In order to gain some understanding, the chapter will address the ways in which legal theory – jurisprudence – addresses normative conflicts; the insights this discussion yields will be further elaborated and subjected to closer scrutiny.

The thesis I develop in this chapter is that treaty conflicts tend to be fairly unproblematic when limited to coordination problems: two agreements on double taxation can easily be reconciled, in the normal course of events, as can two agreements on extradition. Things become far more difficult, however, when there is a clash of values, real or manufactured, underlying the different commitments. Where values clash, typically the political positions harden, resulting in the practical impossibility of finding a way out. As a result, the law, too, cannot decide in the abstract what to do: all that is left is to hope to find a modus vivendi, to find some way to accommodate incommensurable values. This chapter will prepare the jurisprudential groundwork. The subsequent three chapters will discuss how this has resulted in what is often referred to as the principle of political decision: when confronted with conflicting commitments, the state finding itself in that position simply has to choose which commitments it deems to be more relevant.[1]

Theory in international law

International lawyers (lawyers generally, perhaps) usually quickly run for cover whenever the word 'theory' is mentioned. Partly, this is no doubt the result of a specific vision on the task of the lawyer. Theory is often juxtaposed to practice, with the task of the lawyer often considered limited to either thinking of practical advice for their clients, or to solving practical conflicts. In short, for the lawyer who sees their task as eminently practical, the very term 'theory' will not be immediately persuasive.

That is based on a misconception, in that the split between theory and practice is a false dichotomy: practice ought to inform theory, and theory inescapably informs practice. Matters are not helped, of course, if those in leading academic positions publish diatribes against theory – and therewith influence many generations of international lawyers. A prime example is that of Ian Brownlie, who used a commemorative study of the work of his predecessor at Oxford, Sir Humphrey Waldock, to ventilate anger at theory in general (too general, indeed, as Brownlie refused to specify his charges[2]) and political science ('that most vacuous of spheres') in particular.[3]

To the extent that Brownlie aimed his arrows at bad theory, he had a point, of course. Bad theory ought to be simply dismissed. But that raises obvious questions as to how to separate bad theory from good theory, and it is here that an additional concern, perhaps specific to legal studies, comes in. As the legal theorist Kaarlo Tuori puts it, the scientific or academic study of law possesses 'dual citizenship': legal studies are typically both (aiming to be) explanatory and normative. In Tuori's words: 'legal science is not only a scientific but also a legal practice, which participates in the reproduction and modification of the legal order – its own object

---

[1] Sinclair, with a keen eye for understatement, must have had much the same in mind when he noted, with respect to the Convention's rules on treaty conflict, that '[p]erhaps little harm has been done so long as the Convention rules are regarded as residuary in character'. See Sir Ian Sinclair, *The Vienna Convention on the Law of Treaties*, 2nd edn (Manchester: Manchester University Press, 1984), p. 98.

[2] See Ian Brownlie, 'The Calling of the International Lawyer: Sir Humphrey Waldock and his Work', *British Yearbook of International Law*, 54 (1983), 7–74, e.g. pp. 36, 73.

[3] *Ibid.*, p. 63.

of research.'[4] Studies typically proclaim that article X of treaty Y is best interpreted as meaning this rather than that; or that a customary right typically leaves states free to do this or perhaps prohibits them from doing that. And, typically, such findings are written with a welcoming mindset; as a result, the explanatory and the normative are often difficult to disentangle.

With this in mind, it is perhaps useful to clarify my own position. In this book, I am not particularly concerned with putting forward a normative theory. I am not trying to sell a certain conception of article 30 of the Vienna Convention to states and other actors in the hope that they will henceforth apply article 30 in the manner prescribed by me. Indeed, I am fairly convinced that no single prescription is open, and my main interest in the first part of the book is to try to figure out why precisely that is the case: why is it that, in certain cases, the Vienna Convention does not offer a solution to treaty conflict. Hence, my aim is academic (coming to understand the world around me) rather than normative (coming to influence the world around me). Having said that, however, immediately something normative creeps in again: to my mind, and for reasons set out below, in Chapter 5, it is not such a bad thing that the Convention does not offer a single, one-size-fits-all solution to treaty conflicts. As this suggests, the academic and the normative are not completely separable.

By the same token, I will attempt to draw out a reading of article 307 TEC, which is based on the case-law (in particular), without the overtones that therefore it is also the most proper interpretation of article 307 TEC. Quite the opposite, in fact (re-enter normativity): I will be fairly critical of the attitudes of the two EC courts in applying article 307 TEC and, in passing, of the Commission as well (for it is often the Commission's guidance that is followed). While I might think the Court is mistaken, however, it nonetheless does lay down the most authoritative interpretation, and that alone is sufficient ground to try and describe and analyse what the Court says about article 307.

A single general theory?

The great British contract law specialist Patrick Atiyah once remarked that it was probably impossible to capture the entire law of contract in a single

[4] See Kaarlo Tuori, *Critical Legal Positivism* (Aldershot: Ashgate, 2000), p. 285.

overarching principle.[5] Likewise, it may well be impossible to capture the entire law of treaties in a single overarching theory.

Traditionally, much of the law of treaties is explained with the help of notions such as intent and consent.[6] Thus, as the Permanent Court of International Justice stipulated in the 1923 *Wimbledon* case, treaties are based on the free will of sovereign states; indeed, treaty-making is an attribute of sovereignty.[7] By the same token, most of the grounds for invalidity of treaties, as addressed in the Vienna Convention, have to do with defects in expressing consent to be bound, and termination of treaties and suspension of their regimes are also treated first and foremost as emanating from the intentions and consent of the parties.

There are, however, limits to what this approach can explain. Thus, the ICJ has suggested that international commitments may also be the result of estoppel or good faith acceptance, unrelated to the consent of one the parties.[8] Or, perhaps more accurately, what matters is manifest intent (the intent as it manifests itself to the outside world) rather than real intent.[9] Not all grounds of invalidity can be traced back to the will of the parties: surely, the very idea behind article 53 (laying down the *jus cogens* provision) is that invalidity results from the operation of international law, not from state will; and stipulating that coercion of a state or its representative renders a treaty void also suggests that the Vienna Convention leaves the realm of *voluntas* behind. Moreover, provisions on material breach or a fundamental change of circumstances are supposed to be applicable precisely in those situations where the parties cannot agree on the wisdom of terminating an agreement, most likely because one of them refuses to consent to termination.

Thus, without wishing to downplay the role of intent and consent, these notions cannot explain the entire law of treaties. Indeed, they are not

---

[5] See Patrick S. Atiyah, review of Charles Fried, Contract as Promise, *Harvard Law Review*, 95 (1981), 509–28. The same point runs as a red thread through the excellent study by Stephen A. Smith, *Contract Theory* (Oxford: Clarendon Press, 2004).

[6] See, e.g., Ian Brownlie, *Principles of Public International Law*, 4th edn. (Oxford: Clarendon Press, 1990), p. 606: 'The manner in which treaties are negotiated and brought into force is governed by the intention and consent of the parties.'

[7] See *Case of the S.S. Wimbledon* [1923] Publ. PCIJ, Series A, no. 1, p. 25.

[8] Most instrumental here are the *Nuclear Tests* cases: see, e.g., *Nuclear Tests Case* (Australia v. France), [1974] ICJ Reports 253. In *Qatar* v. *Bahrain*, the World Court purposively ignored the expressed intentions of Bahrain: see *Maritime Delimitation and Territorial Questions between Qatar and Bahrain* (Qatar v. Bahrain), Jurisdiction and Admissibility, [1994] ICJ Reports 112, esp. para. 27.

[9] See also Jan Klabbers, *The Concept of Treaty in International Law* (The Hague: Kluwer, 1996).

very useful in explaining treaty conflict either. As treaty conflicts entail typically two treaties, both of which happen to be in force and both of which are generally considered valid, both of them can be traced back to the intent and consent of the parties to them. The problem then becomes one of preferring one common expression of intent over another one, and this, needless to say, cannot be done by reference to intent without more.[10]

If the notion of intent then has some bearing on the law of treaties but cannot explain everything, the same applies to other notions. Thus, Rosenne has famously suggested that underlying the Vienna Convention (which is not exactly the same as saying: 'underlying the law of treaties') is the choice of regarding treaties as instruments, rather than as collections of rights and obligations. As instruments, treaties may be signed; a right or obligation, however, as such, cannot be signed, except and until it is rendered in the form of an instrument.[11]

This had the additional advantage, when drafting the Vienna Convention, of allowing the law of treaties to remain separate from the law of state responsibility. Trying to incorporate the law of state responsibility into the law of treaties would have delayed the latter's codification for many years, no doubt – perhaps for decades. It does mean, however, that the codified law of treaties has but a limited focus, and this limited focus (on the treaty as instrument) is unable to assist in explaining all aspects of the law of treaties. Most obviously, it has no bearing on those points where the law of treaties and the law of responsibility intersect – such as in case of a breach.[12]

---

[10] Unless, as McNair observed, the parties are identical: 'Where the parties to the two treaties said to be in conflict are the same, an allegation of conflict raises a question of interpretation rather than a question of a rule of law; the parties are masters of the situation and they are free to modify one treaty by a later one.' See McNair, *The Law of Treaties*, p. 219.

[11] See Shabtai Rosenne, 'Bilateralism and Community Interest in the Codified Law of Treaties', in Wolfgang Friedmann, Louis Henkin and Oliver Lissitzyn (eds.), *Transnational Law in a Changing Society: Essays in Honor of Philip C. Jessup* (New York: Columbia University Press, 1972), pp. 202–27, esp. p. 205: 'the work of codification was to be focused upon the instrument embodying the international obligation, the treaty, and not upon the international obligation itself'.

[12] Having said that, practice suggests that the law of treaties and the law of responsibility are to some extent converging: the distinction between a material breach of treaty and an ordinary breach has proved less than workable. Anticipating this development was Bruno Simma, 'Reflections on Article 60 of the Vienna Convention on the Law of Treaties and its Background in General International Law', *Österreichische Zeitschrift für öffentliches Recht und Völkerrecht*, 20 (1970), 5–83.

More to the point, it also means that there is no way to assess the relative weight, if any, of obligations, precisely because the choice has been for the treaty as instrument instead of obligation. While it might be possible to argue that, substantively, some norms or obligations are more important than others, it is more difficult to argue that some instruments are more important than others. In other words, the choice for the treaty as instrument entailed that it became impossible to establish, within the four corners of the Vienna Convention, a hierarchy among instruments; it became impossible to argue coherently that, under the Vienna Convention, an instrument containing the obligation not to commit genocide is hierarchically superior to an instrument containing an obligation not to raise tariffs, or an instrument containing an obligation to forward properly stamped postcards. Instead, all the Vienna Convention suggests is that all instruments, once entered into, are binding upon the parties: *pacta sunt servanda*, regardless of the topic those *pacta* address or regulate, regardless also of the moral or political weight to be attached to their contents.

Applied to treaty conflict, this entails that the gravity of the topic cannot be decisive as to which treaty to prefer, at least not under the Vienna Convention itself. Since both a genocide convention and a trade agreement are instruments to which the maxim *pacta sunt servanda* applies, the Vienna Convention's focus on instruments prevents values from entering the picture in any direct matter.[13]

In short, while the distinction between treaties as instruments and treaties as obligations contributes to understanding on some points, it is by definition not capable of explaining the entire law of treaties: at its very best, the conception of treaties as instruments may help explain the Vienna Convention, but it has little to offer on the law outside the Vienna Convention context. And this is acknowledged in the Vienna Convention itself, for instance when it specifies that its terms shall not affect the legal force of oral agreements.[14] Moreover, it would seem fair to posit that, on many issues, the codified law of treaties and the customary law of treaties have become identical, so that the very distinction between treaties as instruments and treaties as obligations may have lost some of its applicability.

---

[13] But see below, though, where it will be suggested that values indirectly exercise great influence, to the extent that the unsolvable conflicts tend to emerge from value clashes.

[14] See article 3 VCLT.

Another distinction often made (and often made with force) is that between contractual and law-making exercises. This is indeed a relevant distinction, however difficult it may be to apply it. It would seem that much of the Vienna Convention was based on a contractual conception: the rules on reservations, for example (however counter-intuitive it may sound) might work best on a contractual conception.[15] Likewise, the interim obligation between signature and ratification or, when appropriate, between ratification and entry into force, has a more obvious applicability in case of contractual treaties than in case of conventions aiming to lay down rules of general application, for it will often be implausible to argue, as the Vienna Convention would seem to demand, that a single violation of such a rule of general application undermines the treaty's object and purposes. In more concrete terms, a single case of torture committed before entry into force of a treaty outlawing torture does not render that treaty superfluous; instead, it only underlines how necessary the treaty may still be.[16]

And while it is possible to argue that the contractual conception also influenced the drafters when it came to creating rules on conflict of treaties, the contractual analogy has fairly limited applicability here as well. As we will see in more detail later on, the typical contractual solutions to conflicting norms would be twofold: either produce more of the good so as to satisfy a multitude of buyers, or compensate those who lose out. While in particular the latter option is fairly prevalent among international lawyers (and has untapped potential), it does not provide a solution within the framework of the law of treaties – quite the opposite, the compensation option is more closely associated with the law of responsibility,[17] and this branch of international law was intentionally not included in the Vienna Convention.

Normative conflict in jurisprudence

If the law of treaties offers no ready-made theory to deal with treaty conflict, neither does jurisprudence. Analytical legal theory, the branch

---

[15] See Jan Klabbers, 'On Human Rights Treaties, Contractual Conceptions and Reservations', in Ineta Ziemele (ed.), *Reservations to Human Rights Treaties and the Vienna Convention Regime: Conflict, Harmony or Reconciliation* (Leiden: Martinus Nijhoff, 2004), pp. 149–82.

[16] See Jan Klabbers, 'How to Defeat a Treaty's Object and Purpose Pending Entry into Force: Toward Manifest Intent', *Vanderbilt Journal of Transnational Law*, 34 (2001), 283–331.

[17] Watson puts the general point succinctly: 'Treaty is slowly being reabsorbed into an international law version of Tort.' See Geoffrey R. Watson, 'The Death of Treaty', *Ohio State Law Journal*, 55 (1994), 781–853, p. 849.

of jurisprudence most obviously occupying itself with the properties of rules, has shown fairly little interest in conflicting rules. Typically, rules are either studied in complete togetherness, as an entire legal system or, more often perhaps, studied in isolation, so as to lay bare and analyse the properties and characteristics of rules on their own, unclouded by intervening issues. Thus, H. L. A. Hart's favourite example, explored at length, was the rule 'No Vehicles in the Park',[18] while Frederick Schauer also made much mileage out of a single rule, to wit the rule 'No Dogs Allowed'.[19] In both cases, the normative universe surrounding those rules is rather empty: the rules are not embedded in systems of rules, nor competing with any other rules, let alone being in conflict with such other rules. The furthest both Hart and Schauer go is to acknowledge that there can be reasons for departing from rules, be it in the form of exceptions or in the form of overriding justifications, in that, for example, the speed limit (another perennial jurisprudential favourite) may be breached when transporting a sick child to hospital.[20]

In those rare cases where conflicting norms are taken as the central problem to be studied, typically the choice of perspective is that of the judge who, confronted with two conflicting norms, will have to figure out how to solve the conflict. While this sometimes gives rise to useful insights (e.g., that conflict can lapse into a gap in the law: the absence of a rule to solve conflicts), typically the emphasis will be on techniques for conflict resolution and, equally typically, those techniques will first and foremost include interpretation.[21]

There are exceptions, of course. Hans Kelsen devotes some attention to conflicting norms valid at different levels, the obvious way to solve them being the application of a hierarchically superior norm.[22] Other than that, Kelsen was, as Lon Fuller somewhat disapprovingly

---

[18] See H. L. A. Hart, 'Positivism and the Separation of Law and Morals', *Harvard Law Review*, 71 (1958), 593–629, p. 607, and H. L. A. Hart, *The Concept of Law* (Oxford: Clarendon Press, 1961), e.g. pp. 123–6.

[19] See Frederick Schauer, *Playing by the Rules: A Philosophical Examination of Rule-Based Decision-making in Law and in Life* (Oxford: Clarendon Press, 1991).

[20] Beitz suggests that this sort of abstraction is typical also for political theory: the very use of 'ideal theory' obscures the awareness of conflicting obligations which only become visible in the 'non-ideal' world. See Charles R. Beitz, *Political Theory and International Relations* (Princeton, NJ: Princeton University Press, 1999, first published 1979), p. 171.

[21] A fine example is Chaim Perelman (ed.), *Les antinomies en droit* (Brussels: Bruylant, 1964). The point on conflict lapsing into lacuna is made by Perelman himself, in his essay 'Les antinomies en droit: essai de synthèse', in *ibid.*, pp. 392–404, p. 400.

[22] See Hans Kelsen, *Introduction to the Problems of Legal Theory* (Oxford: Clarendon Press, 1992, trans. Litschewski, Paulson and Paulson, first published 1934), esp. pp. 71–5.

put it, more interested in positing the problem of conflict (holding that one cannot claim simultaneously that A is, and not-A is), than in resolving it.[23]

Fuller himself devoted some attention to the matter, but mainly within the context of domestic legislation, and in such cases one can typically work on the assumption that the legislator does not want to contradict himself (which would suggest a reconciliatory interpretation of conflicting provisions), or that later legislation may set earlier legislation aside to the extent that the two are incompatible.[24]

Dworkin, for his part, has habitually shown a greater interest in conflicting rights than in conflicting norms,[25] but that is, as a problem, of a radically different nature: my right to be free from racial hatred might limit your right to express yourself freely, but it does not make free speech impossible; my right to play the trumpet in my own house may be limited by my neighbour's right to study algebra in peace, but again, there is no logical (if that is the proper term to use) contradiction between the two unless both of us wanted to exercise our rights to the extreme: only if I wanted to play the trumpet 24 hours a day, seven days a week, and my neighbour would insist on studying algebra in peace and quiet full time, would a 'logical' problem emerge.

Still, while not concentrating too much on conflicting norms, and while the domestic setting often at the heart of jurisprudential work does not quite encompass the salient aspect of treaty conflict (with partly different parties being subjected to conflicting norms[26]), the jurisprudence literature offers at least three useful insights for present purposes. The first

---

[23] *Ibid.*, p. 112. For Fuller's commentary (on another of Kelsen's works where he makes the same point), see Lon L. Fuller, *The Morality of Law*, rev. edn (New Haven, CT: Yale University Press, 1969), pp. 111–2: Kelsen never 'discusses a single problem of the sort likely to cause difficulties in actual practice'. Instead, the whole discussion deals with such abstractions as that 'it is logically impossible to assert both "A ought to be" and "A ought not to be" – a proposition certainly not likely to help a judge struggling with a statute that in one section seems to say Mr. A ought to pay a tax and in another that he is exempt from it'.

[24] See Fuller, *Morality of Law*, at pp. 65–70. Earlier, Fuller briefly touched upon normative conflict when discussing legal fictions, and suggested (without spelling it out) that conflicts between rules owe much to the fiction of legal unity. See Lon L. Fuller, *Legal Fictions* (Palo Alto, CA: Stanford University Press, 1967), pp. 128–30. The book was originally published as a series of articles in the early 1930s.

[25] See, e.g., Ronald Dworkin, *Law's Empire* (London: Fontana, 1986), e.g. p. 293.

[26] The problem, as a later chapter will suggest, is often that a state will be bound to conflicting treaties (with different partners). This is a different situation from that where a single legislator enacts irreconcilable laws.

is that jurisprudence suggests an intimate relation between rules and the purposes behind them, which in turn suggests that a conflict between rules may fruitfully be analysed (and perhaps resolved) by looking more closely at those underlying purposes. Second, the jurisprudence literature suggests that problems between conflicting rules assume prominence in particular when the rules are cast in absolute fashion or, more plausibly perhaps, are perceived as laying down absolute standards. Third, the distinction between rules and principles, made famous by Dworkin, may have a bearing (albeit in a different guise) also in the context of treaty conflict.

The classic debate between Hart and Fuller concerned, on one level of analysis, the question to what extent rules have meanings of their own (circumscribed by the properties of language) or whether rules depend, in various ways, on justifications. Hart derived from his 'No Vehicles in the Park' the idea that rules have a core of certainty and a penumbra of uncertainty. Clearly, when a functioning automobile enters the park, the rule is violated: this falls within the standard instance of what we mean by vehicle. Things would be less clear-cut with, for example, wheelchairs or airplanes: are these vehicles, or are they not?[27]

To Fuller, in a vitriolic comment[28] which, reportedly, left Hart distinctly unimpressed,[29] this division of rules into a core of certainty and a penumbra of uncertainty ignored the circumstance that when we interpret rules, we rarely interpret individual words devoid of any context; instead, we tend to read the rule as whole, in light of its purpose or, more accurately perhaps, what we hold to be its purpose. Fuller wondered out loud what Hart would make of the plan to erect a statue (a war memorial) in the park which included a fully functioning military car, and seemed to suggest that Hart would have to make an exception here to his standard instance of vehicle and therefore to his rule that no vehicles are allowed. The purpose of Hart's rule, after all, would be something to the effect of guaranteeing peace and quiet in the park; surely, prohibiting a war memorial would disconnect the rule from its purpose.

---

[27] See Hart, 'The Separation', pp. 607–8 (for the airplane example); see Hart, *Concept of Law*, p. 123 (the wheelchair).

[28] See Lon L. Fuller, 'Positivism and Fidelity to Law – A Reply to Professor Hart', *Harvard Law Review*, 71 (1958), 630–72. Fuller apparently felt his debate with Hart constituted something of a showdown. See Robert S. Summers, *Lon L. Fuller* (London: Edward Arnold, 1984), p. 10.

[29] See Nicola Lacey, *A Life of H.L.A. Hart: The Nightmare and the Noble Dream* (Oxford: Oxford University Press, 2004), p. 198.

What makes this discussion interesting for present purposes is that it does not take much to reformulate Fuller's example in terms not of a rule (no vehicles in the park) and an exception to the rule (except when those vehicles form part of a war memorial), but in terms of two different rules, which would serve different purposes: one rule would remain Hart's 'No Vehicles in the Park', while the second could be, for instance, a rule (however silly perhaps) to the effect that war memorials shall not be disturbed. In such a case, the question would not be one of rule and possible exception, but rather of two different (and potentially, but not actually conflicting) rules, each with their own justification.

This becomes clearer still in light of Schauer's reworking of the example: Schauer adds a military parade involving the queen driven in a vehicle, making a stop at the memorial. Surely, this could be rephrased into a rule respecting military and royal parades or even simply in terms of freedom of expression (surely, the military should not be excluded from freedom of expression, though the queen might be deemed to be beyond such mundane matters perhaps), leading to a conflict between, on the one hand, the 'no vehicles' rule, designed to guarantee peace and quiet in the park, and the freedom of expression rule, designed (in one rendition, at least[30]) to guarantee the possibility of democracy.

The point, for present purposes, is to suggest (with Fuller, by and large[31]) that rules can be analysed in terms of their purposes, or perceived purposes; rules which tap into values held in great esteem might then, in cases of conflict, be given preference over rules which do not tap into values but merely serve to solve coordination problems.[32] This, it would seem, is precisely what happens in some, perhaps most, cases of

---

[30] The purpose of human rights or fundamental rights or constitutional rights is itself, of course, highly controversial, but that need not detain us here. For one formulation close to the one utilised here, see John Hart Ely, *Democracy and Distrust: A Theory of Judicial Review* (Cambridge, MA: Harvard University Press, 1980).

[31] But not necessarily against Hart: it has been observed, that Hartian uncertainty about penumbral meanings of rules might actually extend to their core meanings as well, something which would make Hart more receptive to think in terms of purposes than he himself may have realised. The argument is rendered by David Dyzenhaus, *Legality and Legitimacy: Carl Schmitt, Hans Kelsen and Hermann Heller in Weimar* (Oxford: Oxford University Press, 1997), p. 15.

[32] A similar idea is expressed by Alexy: rule conflicts may be solved by leaving one or the other unapplied, and the decision which one to sacrifice may depend on the importance of the rule concerned. See Robert Alexy, *Theorie der Grundrechte* (Frankfurt am Main: Suhrkamp, 1994, first published 1985), p. 78. With respect to conflicts between principles (given their fundamental importance) a different solution would have to be chosen, though.

treaty conflict: intuitively, conflicts between rules embodying values and rules embodying coordination problems are resolved in favour of rules embodying values; the really difficult cases, then, are those cases where both rules tap into values held dear.[33]

And this leads to the second insight from general jurisprudence that is of some use here: Dworkin's example of the trumpet-playing and algebra-studying neighbours, and the escalation of their positions (a desire to study algebra or play the trumpet 24 hours a day), indicate that on occasion things that could be settled with some common sense and some sense for coordination (surely, it must be possible between neighbours to negotiate a window in time for the trumpet-player to practice) harden into more fundamental positions: the facility to practice the trumpet may turn into a perceived absolute right, rendering the position inflexible and tapping into all the values commonly associated with rights.

This is not untypical in international relations. One example is how the process of European integration which, in all likelihood, started out in pursuit of higher purposes (peace between Germany and France, in particular), has for many become a value in its own right, something to cherish, to protect and, if necessary, to give preference to over conflicting values. A more recent manifestation of the same phenomenon is the upgrading of international free trade as a value in its own right: a report such as that produced by a committee chaired by Peter Sutherland and published in 2005,[34] can without problems suggest that trade is not just a means to an end (higher standards of living, that sort of thing), but has become an end in itself: it has become reified, one might say.[35]

The distinction between rules and principles is the third way in which jurisprudence may provide inspiration when it comes to treaty conflict. The most authoritative distinction between rules and principles

---

[33] Tuori suggests, along similar lines, that norm conflicts need to be resolved by reference to substantive principles, and cannot depend on conflict rules alone. See Tuori, *Critical Legal Positivism*, pp. 272–5.

[34] See the Sutherland report, officially known as *The Future of the WTO: Addressing Institutional Challenges in the New Millennium. Report by the Consultative Board to the Director-General Supachai Panitchpakdi.* For commentary, see *International Organizations Law Review*, 2 (2005), 127–225.

[35] It also still serves as a means to various ends which, in turn, helps to upgrade its value as well. Thus, trade is not just a lofty goal in its own right, it is also thought helpful in protecting human rights (traders would abide by markets and democracy, and thus not dream of stepping on human rights) and useful in protecting the environment (trade creates economic growth which then can be use for protecting the environment). I will address such issues more in depth in a later chapter.

is undoubtedly the one formulated by Ronald Dworkin.[36] According to Dworkin: '[r]ules are applicable in an all-or-nothing fashion. If the facts a rule stipulates are given, then either the rule is valid, in which case the answer it supplies must be accepted, or it is not, in which case it contributes nothing to the decision.'[37] Principles, by contrast, do not dictate a particular result, and are not valid in an all-or-nothing fashion. Instead, a principle 'states a reason that argues in one direction, but does not necessitate a particular decision.'[38]

It follows, as Robert Alexy further explains, that whereas rules operate along dimensions of validity (they are either valid or not), principles operate along dimensions of weight: legal principles can be more or less weighty, or relevant, or important, and a conflict between them does not result in invalidating one or the other, but results in a balancing between the various principles at issue.[39]

Much can be said about Dworkin's and Alexy's distinction and its effects. It may be that Dworkin makes too much of the possible invalidity of rules in case of conflict; it may also be that, since only valid rules can conflict, invalidity is too easy an option. Either way, it is clear that the distinction is predominantly useful in domestic settings, as in international law, spheres of validity are limited to the parties to norms, and it is precisely here that conflicts often operate: because parties have diverging commitments to different partners.

Still, what makes the distinction useful in the present context is its suggestion that, with respect to principles, what matters is their relative weight or importance in the context of a dispute. It is this that helps create possibilities for understanding treaty conflicts: often the relative weight of the norms concerned may differ, even if their formal status may be alike. The Vienna Convention, as noted above, is unable to accommodate this type of thought; yet it may be helpful in coming to understand the dynamics of treaty conflict.

---

[36] A similar distinction was drawn by Sir Gerald Fitzmaurice in his Hague lectures. See Sir Gerald Fitzmaurice, 'The General Principles of International Law Considered from the Standpoint of the Rule of Law', *Recueil des Cours*, 92 (1957/II), 1–227.

[37] See Ronald Dworkin, *Taking Rights Seriously* (Cambridge, MA: Harvard University Press, 1977), p. 24.

[38] *Ibid.*, p. 26.

[39] *Ibid.*, pp. 26–8. See also Alexy, *Theorie der Grundrechte*, p. 79: 'Regelkonflikte spielen sich in der Dimension der Geltung ab, Prinzipienkollisionen finden, da nur geltende Prinzipien kollidieren können, jenseits der Dimension der Geltung in der Dimension des Gewichts statt.'

In addition, a useful perspective is offered by Burton.[40] In a work that has remained somewhat unnoticed, Burton posits the idea that it might be helpful to think of law not so much as a system of rules leading inevitably to a single right answer, but rather to think of law as providing reasons to decision-makers to base decisions on. Burton wrote more specifically about judges, but there is no specific reason to exclude other decision-makers: law, so Burton has it, is not about achieving certain specified results, but rather is about providing more or less plausible reasons for decisions. In this light, there is nothing all that abnormal about treaty conflict. Whereas in 'normal cases' a judge or other decision-maker may have four, five or six often competing reasons for a decision, where norms collide it is merely the case that yet a seventh reason is added. This adds, obviously, to the reasons to place in the balance, but this addition is precisely, and merely this: an addition, nothing else.

Burton's main example is a decision from the US Supreme Court involving racial discrimination at work, in light of a statute prohibiting racial discrimination in making or enforcing contracts.[41] The case delivered several legal reasons upon which a judgment could be based: one could argue that discrimination at work is not the same as discrimination in either making or enforcing contracts. One could also argue that concluding contracts usually happens in the expectation that no discrimination shall take place. One could argue that it would be silly to have the law address the making and enforcement of contracts, but not their performance. One could argue that enforcement would by definition have to be related to performance: what else could it meaningfully relate to? One could argue that the law in question was intended to give freed slaves the same contractual possibilities as white citizens; one could also argue that it was intended as being limited to making contracts and enforcing them, since at the time of its drafting those were the problematic points. One could also argue that the law in question should read against the background of general contract law, and so on. Either way, the point of the example is that the law, from whatever angle, comes up with a number of arguments or reasons, and that a judge, when deciding, will have somehow to arrange and weigh those reasons, and only those reasons: in Burton's view, resort to policy arguments would be unacceptable and – we may presume even though Burton does not spell it out – unnecessary as

---

[40] See Steven J. Burton, *Judging in Good Faith* (Cambridge: Cambridge University Press, 1992).
[41] *Ibid.*, pp. 70–89.

well, as most legal arguments tend to encompass a wide variety of policy arguments.

Burton's position has its limits, as a matter of general jurisprudence. To some extent, he aims to sell a virtue ethics (relying on the exercise of good faith by judges) under the heading of an ethics of principle – and that will always be vulnerable to the charge that he is confusing categories.[42] Moreover, as some have pointed out,[43] he would seem to assume that hard cases are not about what the law says, but about something else, and that too is a difficult proposition to maintain. Still, the idea of law as being not so much result-oriented, but oriented towards providing decision-makers with reasons, exercises a strong pull, in particular perhaps with respect to rules on treaty conflict, for these are indeed best regarded as addressed at judicial or quasi-judicial decision-makers. The rules on treaty conflict of the Vienna Convention do not tell states what is right and wrong; instead, they tell courts and other decision-makers how to address instances in which they are confronted with a conflict of norms. As Burton puts it: 'Understanding that rules serve a framework function and provide reasons, not necessarily results, makes it possible to think of the law, if not as a full coherent scheme, at least as a scheme whose inherent conflicts are not so disturbing'.[44]

To summarise then, this brief excursion into jurisprudence suggests that, for present purposes, it might be useful to regard international law as providing decision-makers (judicial or otherwise) with arguments. Those arguments (in the form of applicable norms,[45] be it rules or principles) usually can be traced back to some purpose, and while formally neutral, reference to those purposes will assist the decision-maker in deciding which norms to prefer. Moreover, to think of norms as essentially Dworkinian principles, rather than absolute rules, may assist in coming to reasonable conclusions. This last point can be put differently: a tendency to absolutise norms may render normative conflict all the more

---

[42] It is surely no coincidence that a similar conception (thinking of rules as reasons) is endorsed by one the leading virtue ethicists. See Philippa Foot, *Natural Goodness* (Oxford: Oxford University Press, 2001). On virtue ethics generally, see Roger Crisp and Michael Slote (eds.), *Virtue Ethics* (Oxford: Oxford University Press, 1997).

[43] See William Lucy, review of Steven J. Burton, *Judging in Good Faith*, *Cambridge Law Journal*, 52 (1993), 323–7, esp. p. 325.

[44] See Burton, *Judging*, p. 168.

[45] I use the term 'norms' here in a generic sense, encompassing both rules and principles. International lawyers typically tend to be a bit uncomfortable with talk about 'norms', but that cannot be helped. For an example, see Anthony Aust, *Handbook of International Law* (Cambridge: Cambridge University Press, 2005), pp. 9–10.

intractable and, eventually, un-resolvable. While obviously not all norms can be seen as principles (some are, after all, fairly single-minded: there are only so many ways in which 'Thou shalt not kill' can be applied), nonetheless the notion of principles suggests an openness to debate; on this ground too I will come to defend the so-called principle of political decision when it comes to treaty conflict.

Clashing values

Treaty conflicts may have many practical sources: states might willingly ignore existing commitments; or they might intentionally aim to override existing obligations; or the existence of commitments may be unknown to current negotiators; or current negotiators may interpret existing commitments wrongly – the list is sheer endless. What matters though is that, as Wolfram Karl observed a long time ago, some conflicts can fairly easily be solved, whereas others cannot.[46]

The type of conflict that can usually be easily solved is what one might refer to as coordination conflicts: A has a taxation agreement with B; A concludes a conflicting one with C: what to do? Often enough, the terms of the two treaties, in this sort of case, can be easily reconciled, and if not, neither B nor C will lose a lot of sleep over being confronted with a Janus-faced A. For one thing, the treaty with either B or C can usually be renegotiated without much further ado. These cases then end up being less than spectacular – and less than problematic.

The same reasoning applies typically (at least in the abstract) to all treaties that aspire to deal with the same sorts of issues. Conflicting extradition agreements can often be reconciled; conflicting agreements to cooperate in the field of environmental protection may often be reconciled, and even diverging human rights will often be reconcilable: typically, as in the case of Dworkin's conflicting principles, a balancing or weighing of the rights concerned can take place and will generally be considered as acceptable. One of the underlying reasons is that there is no clash of values involved, as the values at issue tend to be the same, or at least similar enough.

This holds true even, as noted, with human rights treaties, as long as the conflicts remain limited to conflicts between the same categories of rights. Put differently, one might argue that the standards of freedom

---

[46] See Wolfram Karl, 'Treaties, Conflicts between', *Encyclopedia of Public International Law*, IV (2000), 935–941.

of expression under the European Convention on Human Rights and the International Covenant on Civil and Political Rights are divergent: it might be possible to say things which are protected under one of them, but not under the other. This will not normally cause unsolvable problems or, more accurately perhaps, this is ill-classified as a treaty conflict to begin with:[47] the problem here is one of differing standards, not one of conflicting standards. And either way, at least the European Convention contains a provision outlining that the highest degree of protection shall prevail.[48]

For the same general reason, things do not even become problematic when it concerns a right mentioned in one of the instruments but not in the other. Thus, under the first Protocol to the European Convention, the right to property finds protection; under the ICCPR, no such protection is granted. As a result, again, there is no conflict. Things would be different only if the ICCPR would actively deny a right to property and literally prohibit private property. In that case, there might indeed be a treaty conflict for those states that would have signed up to both instruments.

The problem is atypical, however, and not likely to materialise in practice, for two distinct reasons. One of these is that human rights often are cast in the open-textured language of principles, and principles are by definition incapable of clashing with each other in such a manner that resolution would be impossible. Where rules, typically, dictate absolute results (there are only so many ways in which a rule like 'No Dogs Allowed' can faithfully be interpreted), things are different with principles. These are, as Dworkin explains, often open-ended in their wording and, in treaty-form, often explicitly allow for exceptions. The typical solution then in case of conflicting human rights provisions is not to apply one of them and leave the other without application, but instead to balance the two. Typically, a judge confronted with a neo-Nazi arguing freedom of expression as an excuse for inciting racial hatred shall not declare freedom of expression

---

[47] For a thoughtful, if abstract, contribution on the definition of treaty conflict, see Erich Vranes, 'The Definition of "Norm Conflict" in International Legal and Legal Theory', *European Journal of International Law*, 17 (2006), 395–418.

[48] See Article 53 of the European Convention on Human Rights and Fundamental Freedoms. For commentary on its earlier incarnation, see Evert A. Alkema, 'The Enigmatic No-Pretext Clause: Article 60 of the European Convention on Human Rights', in Jan Klabbers and René Lefeber (eds.), *Essays on the Law of Treaties: A Collection of Essays in Honour of Bert Vierdag* (The Hague: Martinus Nijhoff, 1998), pp. 41–56.

inapplicable, not even under *lex posterior* or *lex specialis* rules.[49] Nor shall she declare the right to be free from racial hatred inapplicable; instead, she will weigh the two principles in light of the context of the dispute and influenced by the social conventions typical to the community where the dispute takes place, and will reach a decision somewhere on a continuum while leaving both principles intact and applicable.[50]

More importantly perhaps for present purposes, the general point to make is that where treaty conflicts occur, they find their cause in clashing values. To stick to the earlier hypothetical example of a right to private property versus a prohibition of private property: the right to private property typically attests to a liberal, market-oriented mindset. A hypothetical prohibition of private property, by contrast, taps into a radically different set of values: those where community interests take preference over individual interests.

The red thread running throughout this study will be that conflicts are unsolvable as a matter of law as soon as they emanate from clashes of values and cannot plausibly be re-cast as coordination problems.[51] Hence, provisions in trade agreements may come to clash with provisions in human rights treaties; environmental treaties may contain provisions irreconcilable with provisions in economic agreements – in such cases, international law does not have an answer.

Systems theory?

The distinction between coordination problems and clashing values outlined above would, at first sight, come close to the distinction made by Andreas Fischer-Lescano and Gunther Teubner between policy conflicts and rationality conflicts. Fischer-Lescano and Teubner, in an important

---

[49] The example is borrowed from J. H. H. Weiler, 'Fundamental Rights and Fundamental Boundaries', reproduced in his *The Constitution of Europe* (Cambridge: Cambridge University Press, 1999), pp. 102–29. He uses it to suggest that different courts (or other decision-makers) in different places would likely reach a different balance.

[50] The conclusion to draw from this sort of scenario is that human rights are intensely political, for the judge's balancing cannot be other than a political act. See Martti Koskenniemi, 'The Effect of Rights on Political Culture', in Philip Alston (ed.), *The EU and Human Rights* (Oxford: Oxford University Press, 1999), pp. 99–116.

[51] Likewise, Trachtman suggests that linkage issues (including treaty conflicts) are 'not about turtles or shrimp, labor rights or trade, but about societies and their respective interests'. See Joel P. Trachtman, 'Institutional Linkage: Transcending "Trade and . . ."', *American Journal of International Law*, 96 (2002), 77–93, p. 80.

study,[52] posit the proposition that in society at large, horizontal forms of organization are being displaced by vertical forms: states are, if not disappearing, at least losing some of their relevance, whereas functionally based systems are taking over. Hence, they distinguish the trade system from the environmental system, the security system from the human rights system, etc. The norms applicable within those systems, moreover, do not necessarily spring from recognised, state-controlled sources such as treaties or custom; they may, instead, also evolve through the practices of users and practitioners. Thus, the *lex mercatoria* owes a lot to commercial usage; the *lex constuctionis* owes much to the practices of engineers and architects. And, what is more, it is not just the world of international law that is thus fragmenting, but society at large: science employs its own rationalities, as does technology, as does education, etc. Indeed, to a large extent conflicts between legal systems are but expressions of deeper conflicts between social systems, between 'institutionalised rationalities'.[53]

Obviously then, it would seem that those various systems can find themselves in conflict with one another. However, such conflicts cannot, as Fischer-Lescano and Teubner insist, be solved by traditional lawyerly means: as those systems operate to a large extent on their own, notions of a hierarchy of laws are unavailable. By the same token, there is little point in nominating a central supreme court or some similar entity to settle conflicts between those various systems, and dogmatic ideas about the unity of law are of little help either.[54]

This does not mean, Fischer-Lescano and Teubner continue, that all is hopeless; those systems themselves have a core and a periphery, and typically, to the extent that those systems are legal systems, courts will have a place at the core. Those various courts may then be able to communicate with each other, and dampen conflicts between systems: thus, by way of example, a trade court confronted with a dispute involving environmental considerations may well take those environmental considerations into account; an environmental court confronted with a dispute

---

[52] See Andreas Fischer-Lescano and Gunther Teubner, *Regime-Kollisionen: Zur Fragmentierung des Globalen Rechts* (Frankfurt am Main: Suhrkamp, 2006).
[53] *Ibid.*, p. 24.
[54] *Ibid.*, p. 21: 'Weder mit rechtsdogmatischen Formeln der Einheit des rechts noch mit dem rechtstheoretischen Ideal einer Normenhierarchie noch mit der Institutionalisierung von gerichtshierarchien sei solchen Konflikten beizukommen.'

involving human rights may well take human rights into account; and, it would seem to follow, an environmental court confronted with a trade dispute may well take trade law into account.[55]

At this point, Fischer-Lescano and Teubner introduce a distinction between various systems, in light of their density or, perhaps, their openness towards the general environment. There are, to begin with, substantive fields of law, such as space law, refugee law, or the law of state immunity.[56] These are substantive, separate fields of international law, but do not and cannot exist in splendid isolation. By contrast, other systems or regimes are self-contained, in that they have their own mechanisms for creating law and therefore are not dependent on general law-making mechanisms.[57]

The relevance of the distinction would seem to reside[58] in the relative ease with which disputes can be settled: disputes between legal fields ('*Rechtsgebiete*') can, in all likelihood, be settled with relative ease, those

---

[55] The latter, however, is not self-evident, as elsewhere they suggest that law's classic function is to provide 'compensation for and curb damage to human and natural environments', which would suggest something of a hierarchy of values. See Andreas Fischer-Lescano and Gunther Teubner, 'Regime-Collisions: The Vain Search for Legal Unity in the Fragmentation of Global Law', *Michigan Journal of International Law*, 25 (2004), 999–1046, p. 1046.

[56] See Fischer-Lescano and Teubner, *Regime-Kollisionen*, p. 54. They include the law of treaties in this category, which would seem to neglect the circumstance that the law of treaties adds a horizontal element (validity across legal systems) to their perceived vertical organisation of the world. It is no coincidence that Koskenniemi can fall back on the rules of treaty interpretation as somehow holding international law together. See Martti Koskenniemi, *Fragmentation of International Law: Difficulties Arising from the Diversification and Expansion of International Law. Report of the Study Group of the International Law Commission* (Helsinki: Erik Castrén Institute, 2007).

[57] Thus far, the distinction is reminiscent of Hart's distinction between 'law' and 'legal systems': the former would consist of rules of behaviour ('primary rules') while the latter would also entail rules relating to the making, changing and enforcement of those primary rules, topped by a rule of recognition. See generally Hart, *Concept of Law*. Fischer-Lescano and Teubner add a third category still: the category of 'autoconstitutional regimes', which are characterised by their close connections ('coupling') with non-legal elements. See *Regime-Kollisionen*, p. 55, or 'The Vain Search', pp. 1014–17. For present purposes, I will not address these, but rather treat them as versions of what they refer to as self-contained regimes.

[58] The hesitant nature of my formulation is the result of the highly abstract nature of their writings: they rarely become concrete enough to test properly whether one has actually grasped what it is they intend to convey. As a result, much of my reading of Fischer-Lescano and Teubner remains a bit speculative: I think they might mean X, but can not be sure X is really what they mean.

between self-contained regimes would create more difficulties, precisely because of the self-contained nature of these regimes.[59]

This distinction, then, comes close to the one outlined above between coordination conflicts and value clashes, but there are nonetheless important differences. One of these is that the notion of value clashes, as I employ it, perhaps puts a greater emphasis on human agency. One of the consequences of Fischer-Lescano's and Teubner's systems approach is that the role of individual humans may well be overshadowed, perhaps even completely negated.[60] Those systems operate; they reproduce themselves; they refer to themselves; they have, in a word, their own rationality, and taken to the extreme this could imply that the role of individuals is thought to be irrelevant: it does not matter who is running the WTO, because the WTO directs itself. The notion of value clashes, by contrast, suggests a greater role for human agency, precisely because values may differ from individual to individual, from setting to setting.[61]

It is not clear whether Fischer-Lescano and Teubner would downplay human agency altogether. One of the points they make is that in a world of competing regimes or systems, conflicts cannot be solved by means of thinking in terms of competition, but rather in terms of reciprocity between regimes: it demands mutual recognition, observation, adaptation and cooperation between regimes.[62]

---

[59] Note that Fischer-Lescano and Teubner use a fairly liberal notion of what constitutes a self-contained regime, probably because, to their minds, there is no cost involved in doing so. Others have more narrow definitions, presumably on the realisation that if regimes are truly self-contained, then they might fall outside the scope of international law altogether. For such a stricter reading, see Bruno Simma and Dirk Pulkowkski, 'Of Planets and the Universe: Self-contained Regimes in International Law', *European Journal of International Law*, 17 (2006), 483–529; see also Lindroos and Mehling, 'Dispelling the Chimera'. Both articles suggest that regimes are only self-contained when they are completely closed off.

[60] Similarly, Andreas Paulus criticises the Fischer-Lescano/Teubner approach for paying insufficient attention to the continued role of states and the choices that those states may make which will eventually influence outcomes. See Andreas Paulus, 'Commentary to Andreas Fischer-Lescano & Gunther Teubner: The Legitimacy of International Law and the Role of the State', *Michigan Journal of International Law*, 25 (2004), 1047–58.

[61] They do discuss values, under that designation, as possibly contributing to solving conflicts, only to reject an appeal to values. The one thing they concede is that positive values (such as peace, liberty or equality) would overrule negative values (the negations thereof: war, illiberty, inequality). It remains unclear, however, why this would be so. See Fischer-Lescano and Teubner, *Regime-Kollisionen*, p. 107.

[62] See Fischer-Lescano and Teubner, *Regime-Kollisionen*, pp. 61–2: 'Regimevernetzung' demands 'wechselseitige Anerkennung, Beobachtung, Anpassung und Kooperation der Regime. Im Gegensatz zum kompetitiven Verhalten auf Märkten ist generalisierte Reziprozität der grundlegende Mechanismus spontaner Ordnungsbildung im Netzwerk.'

A second important difference between the approach outlined above and that of Fischer-Lescano and Teubner is that the insistence on systems and their own rationality would seem to suggest that certain topics naturally fall within a certain domain, at the exclusion of other domains. At least, they are somewhat ambivalent on this pont. While actually much of their work can be read as suggesting that a policy choice is involved in classifying a problem as being either a trade problem or an environmental problem, either a human rights problem or a security problem, etc., they themselves assert, in no uncertain terms, that regimes can turn elements of problems into legal questions (they refer to this as the *quaestio juris*) and submit them to dispute settlement. On this construction, it seems to be a given that topic X belongs within system Y, rather than system Z.[63]

Again, though, this may overlook the human factor: human agency may well force a rephrasing of the issue. In much the same way as economic issues such as the free movement of goods in the EU can come to be classified as human rights (see the discussion below), so too it is by no means clear that the marketing of genetically modified organisms should be regarded as a trade issue rather than, say, a health issue, an environmental issue, a security issue, or a human rights issue. How to constitute the proper field (or system) is itself a political question, something the mechanics of a system approach have a hard time accommodating.

Different approaches

This position I outline above, with its distinction between coordination problems and value clashes, is of course vulnerable to criticism. An obvious point is that this ignores the fact that much of the problem is a matter of perspective: is an agreement about allowing emissions trading to be regarded as an environmental agreement, or as a trade agreement? Is the death penalty exception in an extradition treaty to be regarded as itself an emanation of extradition law, or as a manifestation of human rights law? There are no easy answers here, but fortunately this need not detain us, as what matters is the general perception of a problem falling into one box or the other, rather than any objective classification: if most people (lawyers included) view an agreement on emissions trading as an environmental agreement, then for all practical purposes this is what it will be.

---

[63] *Ibid.*, p. 69.

Another and perhaps more relevant point of critique is that it might be well nigh impossible to distinguish between a clash of values and a coordination problem: is it not the case that most things in life can be construed as emanations of values? Surely, so the argument might run, extradition treaties are not merely devices to smooth cooperation between states, but are also expressive of a higher value: the value of law and order or, if nothing else, the value of international cooperation. Hence, how can it be suggested that a conflict between an extradition treaty and a human rights agreement is not, in one way or another, a clash of values?

The answer is twofold. First, it would seem to be a mistake of categories to regard the protection of the law by the law itself as a higher value: an instrument cannot rely upon itself for its own justification – the law is not created to uphold the law, and one does not cooperate merely in order to cooperate. While law and order, and cooperation, may well be values underlying the law – the internal morality of the law, as Fuller would have it[64] – it would be too easy to invoke them, for if it is true that they are part of the law's inner morality, then they are part of every single treaty: every single treaty, after all, promotes law and order simply by being a treaty: even states agreeing by treaty to create mayhem and disorder would expect their treaty to be respected, and thereby contribute to law and order. And even a treaty between A and B to obstruct cooperation is nonetheless itself a cooperative venture. Hence, the law and order and cooperation values are not, so it would seem, the sort of values one could meaningfully invoke in cases of treaty conflict.

Second, there are considerations of practice. Courts tend to have fairly little difficulty in solving conflicts between extradition treaties and human rights treaties,[65] partly because the extradition treaty will often leave some discretion on whom to extradite and in what circumstances, and partly because few people would intuitively place the extradition agreement on the same level as the human rights agreement. Technically, there may not be a hierarchy of norms in international law;[66] intuitively, however, many lawyers (and others) would be decidedly uncomfortable when applying an extradition agreement against (and so as to overrule) a human rights treaty.

[64] See Fuller, *Morality of Law*.   [65] See generally Mus, *Verdragsconflicten*.
[66] See, e.g., Ignaz Seidl-Hohenveldern, 'Hierarchy of Treaties', in Jan Klabbers and René Lefeber (eds.), *Essays on the Law of Treaties: A Collection of Essays in Honour of Bert Vierdag* (The Hague: Martinus Nijhoff, 1998), pp. 7–18.

The more serious problem might well be that what seem to be less than fundamental values become 'fundamentalised'. In other words: instead of accepting a coordination problem for what it is, or accepting a conflict between a 'value-loaded' and a 'value-neutral' treaty for what it is, sometimes attempts are made to turn a coordination problem into a clash of values. Jones provides a first glimpse as to how this may occur. Writing about the WTO and trying to persuade his readership of the wisdom of having a set of rules regulating world trade to begin with, in the context of a discussion on trade versus such things as labour standards or environmental standards, he writes:

> Recall that the very existence of the WTO rests on a simple but compelling consensus on the benefits of trade. In particular, WTO rules allow each member country's exporters and importers to make investments in trade activities without having to fear arbitrary market closures and corresponding losses in their investments. The entire thrust of the WTO is to generate certainty in the conduct of commercial policy; without this certainty, the value of the WTO to its members diminishes precipitously.[67]

The upshot of such a statement (no doubt defensible in its own right) is the elevation of trade from something which might make our lives easier, which might enhance the quality of life, to something of more fundamental importance: a value in its own right. Indeed, a few pages later the same point emerges even more strongly, or rather: competing values are subjected to devaluation.[68] Owing to the law of unintended consequences (the road to hell, after all, being paved with good intentions), it is not just the case that world trading rules embody great values for states. It is also the case, so Jones suggests, that other values offer fewer chances for success:

> A trade ban on goods made with child labor may very well increase child prostitution. Environmental antidumping regulations that prevent poor countries from exporting certain goods would typically reduce economic growth and possibly lead to greater deforestation as alternative fuels are no longer affordable.[69]

In conjunction with each other, then, Jones's two claims end up placing trade as the highest value of all, superior to labour standards, human rights standards, or environmental standards, precisely because, apart

---

[67] See Kent Jones, *Who's Afraid of the WTO?* (Oxford: Oxford University Press, 2004), p. 89.
[68] And elsewhere still, he draws the logical conclusion: '. . . the global trading system not only facilitates exchange but is in itself a global public good.' *Ibid.*, at p. 184.
[69] *Ibid.*, p. 99.

from having become a value in its own right, trade also retains its instrumental characteristics: it is both a useful means to an end, and an end in itself.[70]

One additional element of Jones's approach is the injunction that the WTO sticks to what it does best. To the extent that the world can agree on environmental values, or social values, or human rights, those should be dealt with in separate institutions.[71] While this does mean that different institutions embodying different values may end up in conflict with each other, Jones downplays such problems a bit as 'coordination problems'[72] and, at any rate, their solution should be left to international law.[73]

Jones's approach is fairly typical, and can be recognised in other works on the relationship between WTO law and other branches of international law, complete with international law techniques aimed at mitigating treaty conflicts. Often, it is merely the choice of words that is revealing. Thus, Marceau can write, adopting the trade perspective, that in order to demonstrate the existence of a conflict between human rights law and WTO law, 'one would have to be able to demonstrate that compliance with the WTO *necessitates* violation of a human rights treaty', thus unwittingly turning the WTO into the standard, with human rights – possibly – deviating from that standard:[74] the burden of proof comes to rest on those who invoke human rights. Likewise, Trachtman suggests that if the WTO's member states 'wish to make an arrangement permanently permitting compliance with the Montreal Protocol, even where such compliance may violate the GATT, the most effective way is through a specific reference to, and exception for, compliance with the Montreal Protocol'.[75] The same approach is often also visible in writings on EU law and its relationship to

---

[70] A more minimalist vision on the WTO (but, oddly enough, almost equally reifying) is offered by John O. McGinnis and Mark L. Movsesian, 'The World Trade Constitution', *Harvard Law Review*, 114 (2000), 511–605.

[71] Guzman, by contrast, suggests integration of all sorts of issues into the WTO, and comes close to proposing a world government revolving around the WTO, complete with departments dealing with discrete issues. See Andrew Guzman, 'Global Governance and the WTO', *Harvard International Law Journal*, 45 (2004), 303–51.

[72] Jones, *Who's Afraid*, p. 191 (discussing 'coordination problems' between WTO and the Bretton Woods institutions).

[73] *Ibid.*, p. 190: 'The best way to resolve these conflicts will be found within the framework of international law.'

[74] See Marceau, 'WTO Dispute Settlement', p. 792 (emphasis in original).

[75] Trachtman, 'Institutional Linkage', pp. 88–9. He does recognise, however, that there is no *a priori* reason to have one set of norms prevail over another.

the world around it, and can also be identified in the holdings of the EC courts.[76]

An alternative approach is more subtle and, arguably, more problematic still. At least in the relationship between trade and human rights, it is not uncommon to think of trade itself in human rights terms. The EC Court, for example, has on occasion held that there is a fundamental right to trade[77] as well as a fundamental right to choose one's profession or have free access to employment,[78] and that other economic activities too can be cast in rights terminology.

Amongst authors, such an approach is perhaps most often associated with the writings of Ernst-Ulrich Petersmann.[79] Petersmann consciously aims to merge human rights law and trade law, thereby defining any conflict between the two away: turning vice into virtue. Doing so involves two separate moves on his part. Most of all, it involves elevating trade law notions (or private law notions) into human rights. Thus, he can without blushing refer to the freedom of contract as a human right,[80] and is far more sanguine about the human rights nature of the right to property than many human rights lawyers would be.[81] Economic liberties, moreover, are placed on a par with civil and political freedoms.[82]

The second, related, rhetorical move Petersmann makes is to instrumentalise human rights. Whereas others, such as Marceau, end up turning trade law notions into values, Petersmann walks, in part, down the opposite road: human rights are not seen, as many would have it, as ends in themselves, but as instrumental in the pursuit of economic well-being. As he phrases it:

---

[76] For an overview, see Peter Oliver and Wulf-Henning Roth, 'The Internal Market and the Four Freedoms', *Common Market Law Review*, 41 (2004), 407–41. See also below, Chapters 6 and 7 in particular.

[77] See Case 44/79, *Hauer* v. *Land Rheinland-Pfalz* [1979] ECR 3727.

[78] See Case 222/86, *Union nationale des entraineurs et cadres techniques du football (Unectef)* v. *Georges Heylens and others* [1987] ECR 4097.

[79] See especially Petersmann, 'Integrating Human Rights'. Some of the work of John McGinnis goes in the same direction. See John O. McGinnis, 'A New Agenda for International Human Rights: Economic Freedom', *Catholic University Law Review*, 48 (1998–99) 1029–34; see also McGinnis and Movsesian, 'The World Trade Constitution'.

[80] See Petersmann, 'Integrating Human Rights', p. 626.

[81] Whereas some human rights instruments recognise a right to property (e.g. the European Convention on Human Rights, in its First Protocol), others do not. It is conspicuously absent, e.g., from the International Covenant on Civil and Political Rights.

[82] See Petersmann, 'Integrating Human Rights', p. 629.

> Lack of effective legal and judicial protection of liberty rights and property
> rights inhibits investments and acts as an incentive for welfare-reducing
> private and governmental restrictions of competition and collaboration
> between cartelized industries and authoritarian governments.[83]

Whatever the normative merits of Petersmann's approach (and his normative stance has been severely criticised[84]), what matters for present purposes is that the identification of trade notions and human rights notions tends to define any conflicts away: if human rights are really instrumental in promoting trade, and if trade notions themselves can be considered as human rights, then there can hardly be any systemic conflict.[85] At worst (as Petersmann notes in a follow-up piece[86]), the result would be a conflict between various rights: for example, a right to trade versus freedom of expression. And in such a case, the intra-systemic technique for solving the conflict would simply be one of balancing the two human rights of freedom to trade and freedom of expression.[87]

There is no obvious explanation for what might be labeled the 'fundamentalisation' of cooperative ventures. To some extent, an answer (while somewhat vulgar) might be found in neo-functionalist integration theory, something to the effect that those who work for a regime tend to promote it in order to boost their own careers. It has been noted, for example, that professors of EU law tend to endorse the value of European integration, if

---

[83] *Ibid.*, p. 632.
[84] See in particular Philip Alston, 'Resisting the Merger and Acquisition of Human Rights by Trade Law: A Reply to Petersmann', *European Journal of International Law*, 13 (2002), 815–44. It has also been noted that the decisions of WTO panels and its Appellate Body offer no empirical support for Petersmann's theses – quite the opposite. See Jeffrey L. Dunoff, 'Constitutional Conceits: The WTO's 'Constitution' and the Discipline of International Law', *European Journal of International Law*, 17 (2006), 647–75, esp. p. 659.
[85] It is surely no accident that he downplays the potential for conflict also in other spheres when observing, somewhat overly optimistically, that the WTO's dispute settlement organs usually defer to national public policy considerations (*ibid.*, at 635). In fact, the one case he cites is probably the only available example: see *European Communities – Measures Affecting Asbestos and Asbestos-containing Products*, report of the WTO Appellate Body, 12 March 2001, WT/DS135/AB/R.
[86] See Ernst-Ulrich Petersmann, 'Taking Human Dignity, Poverty and Empowerment of Individuals More Seriously: Rejoinder to Alston', *European Journal of International Law*, 13 (2002), 845–51, at 846.
[87] Such a scenario occurred before the EC Court in Case C-112/00, *Eugen Schmidberger, Internationale Transporte und Planzüge v. Austria*, [2003] ECR I-5659, discussed in Chapter 7 below. Like the EC Court, Petersmann would place market freedoms as hierarchically superior, as Howse has observed. See Robert Howse, 'Human Rights in the WTO: Whose Rights, What Humanity? Comment on Petersmann', *European Journal of International Law*, 13 (2002), 651–9, p. 655.

only because in that way they remain eligible for appointment as judges at the EC courts.[88] If enough people have a stake in the further development and increasing importance of a set of rules, it follows, so the argument would seem to go, that those people will do their best to make those rules seem more important at every opportunity.

Along similar lines, it might be a perfectly logical psychological instinct for people to upgrade the enterprise they work in, if only to feel good about themselves. People identify with their employer, with the regime they work for, or the rules they are supposed to defend day in, day out. Academics too are not free from this tendency, and tend to identify with the topic they are studying.[89] Indeed, it is notable that critical writings about the WTO stem rarely from academics, but instead come predominantly from activists or journalists, and they would have a greater affinity with the values they themselves represent (public participation, perhaps, or journalistic obligations to inform the public and remain critical of public authority) than with the world trading system.[90]

And then there might be the often-observed tendency of bureaucracies to grow and multiply, something which almost automatically implies the blowing up of the relevance of one's own work.[91] All these factors may contribute to the 'fundamentalisation' of instrumentalities, or of modalities of cooperation.

Conclusion

It is a truism to state that values may clash: even within liberalism, traditionally the political doctrine most inclined to perceive universal values,

---

[88] See Anne-Marie Burley and Walter Mattli, 'Europe before the Court: A Political Theory of Legal Integration', *International Organization*, 47 (1993), 41–76.

[89] This is perhaps especially the case in international law. International lawyers, as David Kennedy once famously remarked, have an 'international project'. To be an international lawyer is to be for international law, in ways which do not hold true to quite the same extent in other branches of the law: to be a banking lawyer is not to be for banking *per se*. See David Kennedy, 'A New World Order: Yesterday, Today, and Tomorrow', *Transnational Law and Contemporary Problems*, 4 (1994), 1–47.

[90] Useful examples would include Fatoumata Jawara and Aileen Kwa, *Behind the Scenes at the WTO. The Real World of International Trade Negotiations: The Lessons of Cancun*, updated edn (London: Zed Books, 2004); Lori Wallach and Patrick Woodall, *Whose Trade Organization? A Comprehensive Guide to the WTO* (New York: New Press, 2004).

[91] Possibly the leading study on international bureaucracy is Michael Barnett and Martha Finnemore, *Rules for the World: International Organizations in Global Politics* (Ithaca, NY: Cornell University Press, 2004).

the thought has gained a foothold (in particular through the work of Isaiah Berlin[92]) that different people may have different ideas as to what constitutes the good life. This may find its cause in different ideologies; it may also find its cause, as some have suggested, in the fact that values follow interests, and it is simply the case that different people have different interests.[93]

If it is the case that values can be incommensurable yet of equal weight or relevance, then it would seem to follow that there can be no general rule for solving conflicts between them; and it is no fluke that this is precisely the situation in which international law finds itself. The legal order can of course try to accommodate diverging values; it can create methods for conciliation, discussion and debate;[94] it can try to point out, by reference to a principle of systemic integration, that values ought not to be reified,[95] but it cannot place one value systematically over another one without becoming incoherent, at least not in the absence of common agreement that the one is superior to the other.

It is no surprise then that international law finally had to settle for the so-called 'principle of political decision': anything more definite simply proved to be out of reach. It took the discipline a while to reach that conclusion, however, and the function of the next three chapters is to tell the story of how it got there. The third part of the book, moreover, will suggest that while the ECJ favours application of a general rule (the rule, simply put, that in case of conflict EC law prevails), such application is not always without its problems and may, at times, result in unfairness or at least politically controversial findings.

---

[92] See, in particular perhaps, Isaiah Berlin, *Four Essays on Liberty* (Oxford: Oxford University Press, 1969). A useful discussion of aspects of Berlin's thought can be found in Mark Lilla, Ronald Dworkin and Robert B. Silvers (eds.), *The Legacy of Isaiah Berlin* (New York: New York Review of Books, 2001), as well as in the fine biography by Michael Ignatieff, *Isaiah Berlin: A Life* (London: Verso, 2000, first published 1998).

[93] See, e.g., John Gray, *Two Faces of Liberalism* (New York: New Press, 2000).

[94] Gray notes that this is precisely the function of democracy within domestic societies: *Ibid.*, ch. 4.

[95] See generally Koskenniemi, *Fragmentation of International Law.*

PART II

International law

3

The pre-Vienna Convention regime

Introduction

Deceit is timeless. Machiavelli, in 1513, instructed his prince to tell little
white lies whenever this would serve the national (or princely) interest.[1]
Over a century later, Grotius, often heralded as the founding father of
international law, was well aware of the possibility of concluding conflicting alliances,[2] as was his heir apparent, Emeric de Vattel.[3] Earlier medieval
lawyers had to come to terms with the validity of a local custom when
set against the imperial rules of the *Corpus iuris*.[4] The newly independent
United States of America, in the 1770s, made a separate peace with Britain
despite having solemnly pledged to France not to do so.[5] And Hitler,
never a good advertisement for decency of course, saw fit to accuse France
and the Soviet Union of concluding a bilateral assistance agreement in
1935 which would be incompatible with their obligations under the 1925
Locarno Treaty[6] – and that was after Nazi Germany and the UK had concluded a naval agreement which conflicted with their obligations under
the Versailles Treaty.[7]

While deceit may be timeless, this is not to say that all treaty conflicts
are necessarily the result of deceitful intentions; indeed, sometimes negotiators do their utmost to prevent any conflict from occurring. Thus, one

---

[1] See Niccolò Machiavelli, *De vorst* (Amsterdam: De Bussy, 1983, Otten trans.), ch. XVIII.
[2] See Hugo Grotius, *On the Law of War and Peace* (Oxford: Clarendon Press, 1925, Kelsey
     trans., first published 1625), book II, ch. XV.
[3] See Emeric de Vattel, *The Law of Nations* (New York: AMS Press, reprint of 1863 edn, Chitty
     trans., first published 1758), Book II, ch. XII.
[4] See Peter Stein, *Roman Law in European History* (Cambridge: Cambridge University Press,
     1999) p. 62.
[5] See Gordon S. Wood, *The American Revolution: A History* (New York: Modern Library
     Chronicles, 2002), pp. 87–8.
[6] See Ian Kershaw, *Hitler 1889–1936: Hubris* (London: Penguin, 1998), p. 587.
[7] *Ibid.*, pp. 556–8. Further examples are provided by Jean Salmon, 'Les antinomies en droit
     international public', in Chaim Perelman (ed.), *Les antinomies en droit* (Brussels: Bruylant,
     1964), pp. 285–319.

of the more difficult points in the negotiations of the Atlantic Charter, the war-time agreement between US president Roosevelt and UK prime minister Churchill which set the scene for the post-war world order,[8] was the trade paragraph: trying to reconcile the general idea of free trade with Britain's commitments of trade preferences for its empire.[9]

Perhaps the most obvious cause for a state's entering into conflicting obligations is inherent in modern bureaucracy: the left hand not knowing what the right hand does. Thus, it may well be the case that environmental ministries conclude an agreement between them which is incompatible with an agreement concluded between the trade ministries of the same states, without them even being aware of each other's existence. In particular with the widespread use of so-called memoranda of understanding or administrative agreements, concluded between departments and ostensibly not intended to have legal effects, such conflicts are well-nigh inevitable.[10]

It is also possible (though not terribly likely, perhaps) that states may be convinced that the earlier treaty has ceased to be in force, for instance due to *desuetudo*.[11] In such a case, should it transpire that the earlier treaty has not been terminated after all, surely the resulting conflict is not caused by bad intentions. And finally, it is also possible that the terms of the earlier treaty receive a different interpretation (e.g., by a court) than the parties thought when drafting the subsequent treaty, so that what looked like a compatibility may turn out to be an incompatibility after all. While these scenarios are rare – so rare as to come close to being hypothetical – it is nonetheless important to underline that treaty conflict need not necessarily result from perfidy.

[8] Note that, for many commentators, the Atlantic Charter was not even meant to be legally binding. If so, there would be little legal reason to insist on preventing conflict with other, binding, norms. For a critical review of the thesis that non-legally binding agreements can be concluded, see Klabbers, *The Concept of Treaty*.

[9] See generally Richard N. Gardner, *Sterling-Dollar Diplomacy in Current Perspective: The Origins and Prospects of Our International Economic Order*, 2nd edn (New York: Columbia University Press, 1980, first published 1956).

[10] As Anthony Aust, writing in defense of concluding informal agreements, warns, often there may be "retrieval problems." See Anthony Aust, 'The Theory and Practice of Informal International Instruments', *International and Comparative Law Quarterly*, 35 (1986), 787–812, p. 792.

[11] See E. W. Vierdag, *Oorlogsverklaring* (inaugural address, University of Amsterdam, 1992). Aufricht suggests that the Covenant of the League of Nations has been revoked by means of *desuetudo*: the League Assembly had formally terminated the League's activities in 1946, but never formally terminated the underlying Covenant. See Hans Aufricht, 'Supersession of Treaties in International Law', *Cornell Law Quarterly*, 37 (1951–52), 655–700, p. 697.

In international law, treaty conflicts may lead to awkward, politically difficult situations. This stands in marked contract with contract law. In business life, it would seem that conflicting obligations arising out of contracts with several parties are not considered to be much of a problem: a commitment to deliver a party of goods to A as well as to B may often be met by producing more of the goods or, if all else fails, by compensating the losing side. More embarrassing (but not necessarily more legally problematic) might be the situation where the contract is not a business contract strictly speaking, but deals with personal matters:[12] A, having sold her house simultaneously to B and to C, will have a problem – one that she cannot solve simply by producing more houses.

If this is indeed the case, then international law too has little to expect from importing notions from contract law, as Jenks, for one, has suggested,[13] for contract law is not geared to solving problems arising out of such 'personal' compacts. Yet, typically, international transactions would be of such a nature: the cession of territory; the sale of military installations. Moreover, as also Jenks realised, the bigger problem in international law relates to treaties which are not contractual in nature to begin with.

Still, as with much in the law of treaties, the contractual prism has exercised a strong hold on the imaginations of international lawyers, also when it comes to solving conflicts between treaties. Partly this finds its cause, no doubt, in the fact that even if it would be stretching things to apply contractual notions, it would be even less plausible to apply anything else: in many cases, contractual notions, or principles derived from contract law, might be all that can be applied with some cogency, as borrowing from legislative principles would be even more awkward.

It should come as no surprise, then, that international law has traditionally been highly ambivalent about conflicting treaties. With contractual undertakings, typically solutions derived from contractual notions have been advocated (and are still being advocated, as will be shown below), despite the circumstance that most 'contractual' undertakings in international law would tend to be personal rather than commercial, and thus may only awkwardly be encompassed by notions developed for commercial transactions.

---

[12] For the distinction between commercial and personal contracts and its relevance, see John Wightman, *Contract: A Critical Commentary* (London: Pluto, 1996), pp. 96–8.

[13] So, e.g., C. Wifred Jenks, 'The Conflict of Law-making Treaties', *British Yearbook of International Law*, 30 (1953), 401–53, p. 404 (stating that conflicts between bilateral treaties involving different parties can be 'resolved by the application of established principles derived from the law of contract').

With legislative treaties, there has always been a tendency, natural enough, to hold that later conflicting treaties be void, or at least left inapplicable, but this always stumbles over a number of hurdles. One of these is that the later treaty is bound to reflect more accurately the political configurations of the day; there is fairly little point in insisting on keeping a treaty alive if that treaty is no longer, in one way or another, supported by a majority of its parties.

The alternative, however, would be to sanction a breach of the earlier treaty, something that can only with some reluctance be advocated, especially where legislative undertakings are concerned. It is no coincidence, then, that general multilateral treaties are often re-conceptualised as bundles of bilateral commitments; this, while sometimes far-fetched, would somehow make it seem more natural to apply a contractual principle.[14]

The classics

While a political theorist like Machiavelli could hold that problems of conflicting commitments would often be circumvented by means of the virtues of statecraft,[15] some of the classic writers on international law already struggled with the question of what to do with conflicting treaty commitments, and in doing so reflect the underlying ambivalence. Grotius, for example, when discussing which ally to support in case of armed conflict between allies, invoked the support of an external criterion to decide most cases: since an unjust war was intolerable, one would have to help the ally whose cause was just, and refrain from helping the ally whose cause was unjust. That, however, would not solve all potential problems, as Grotius readily recognised: 'Now if allies are engaged in war with each other for unjust causes on both sides – and this can happen – it will be necessary to refrain from aiding either party.' Conversely, and note the contractual overtones already, if 'two allies are waging war against others, and each for a just cause, aid in men and money will have to be sent to both, just as happens in the case of personal creditors'.[16]

---

[14] I have argued elsewhere that when it comes to reservations to multilateral treaties, a contractual perspective might still serve useful purposes. See Klabbers, 'On Human Rights Treaties'.

[15] He strongly suggests that Ferdinand of Aragon was an enemy of both peace and good faith: had he kept his promises, he would have lost his country or his fame. See Machiavelli, *De vorst*, p. 158.

[16] See Grotius, *War and Peace*, book II, ch. XV, para. XIII. Kelsey's translation here might suggest that the two allies are both allied against another; the context, however, suggests that

Interestingly, then, even alliances are reduced to undertakings of a contractual nature, as the analogy with personal creditors suggest.[17] And since personal creditors can be pleased simultaneously, so too can allies: hence, the sting is taken out of the problem. No longer is treaty conflict an intractable conflict over principles; instead, it is merely a matter of accommodating both sides. Elsewhere, Grotius devoted some attention to conflicting treaties under the heading of interpretation, therewith also suggesting (without putting it in so many words) that on the correct interpretation and with the help of some interpretative maxims, conflicts will simply disappear.[18]

Thus, for instance, one of Grotius's maxims of interpretation (in fairness, not his main maxim) was that 'that provision should prevail which has either the more honourable or the more expedient reason'.[19] Needless to say, this did little to solve the problem: instead of trying to figure out which commitment to honour, authorities would now have to figure out whether to favour honour or expediency, and which of their commitments would either be more honourable or more expedient.

Vattel, by contrast, took a hard line. States were, to his mind, not entitled to enter into conflicting treaties, and if they were to do so, the later in time would be null and void, at least insofar as it conflicted with the earlier treaty. For his argumentation, Vattel invoked an underlying contractual notion by suggesting that the balance of concessions had been upset due to the conclusion of a conflicting treaty: 'The things respecting which he has entered into engagements are no longer at his disposal'.[20]

---

they are in conflict with each other, an option also recognised in a later Dutch translation, which speaks of 'onderling oorlog voeren.' This is contained in A. C. Eyffinger and B. P. Vermeulen (eds. and trans.), *Hugo de Groot: Denken over oorlog en vrede* (Baarn: Ambo, 1991).

[17] This is perhaps no cause for surprise, as the relevant parts of the work are structured so as to make the contractual analogy well-nigh inevitable. Grotius starts by addressing promises (ch. XI of Book II), moves from this moral background to the typical legal embodiment: contracts (ch. XII), subsequently discusses a way of strengthening the obligation (the oath; book XIII), discusses all three with special reference to sovereigns (ch. XIV) and only then ends up writing on treaties and sponsios (ch. XVI) and interpretation (Ch. XVI). As Lesaffer observes, Grotius 'clearly considered treaties as an integral part of the broad category of contracts'. See Randall Lesaffer, 'The Medieval Canon Law of Contract and Early Modern Treaty Law', *Journal of the History of International Law*, 2 (2000), 178–98, p. 186.

[18] See Grotius, *War and Peace*, Book II, ch. XVI, para. XXIX. [19] *Ibid.*

[20] See Vattel, Law of Nations, p. 196.

Vattel clung to his approach with great tenacity, arguing that the deceived party (the one with whom the later in time was concluded[21]) would be at liberty to denounce the treaty. But, should the aggrieved party stick to it, 'it will hold good with respect to all the articles that do not clash with the prior treaty'.[22]

When addressing Grotius's hypothesis of two allies going to war with each other, Vattel felt that the more ancient ally was entitled to preferential treatment. This followed, dixit Vattel, from justice, as the 'engagement was pure and absolute' with respect to the more ancient ally.[23] Nonetheless, here his thoroughly formal approach started to show cracks and, perhaps in response to Grotius, he felt the need to add that the justness of war could be another reason for preferring one ally over another. For, to assist an ally in an unjust war would be 'the same thing' as contracting for unjust purposes, and this now was in itself not allowed.[24]

Like Grotius, Vattel too devoted some words (quite a few, actually) to interpretation as a means to solve or settle treaty conflicts. He devised no fewer than ten rules[25] to be applied where appropriate, ranging from familiar notions such as the *lex specialis* maxim and the *lex posterior* maxim to such common sense rules as '[w]hat will not admit of delay, is to be preferred to what may be done at another time'.[26] Here too, however, formal rules and substantive rules became intertwined. While the *lex posterior* maxim may be seen as a formal device, a rule that 'preference is undoubtedly to be given to the more important and necessary'[27] obligations is more substantive in nature.

In the end, then, Vattel's position was ambivalent. Whereas Grotius combined a substantive yardstick with a flight into interpretation, Vattel, while starting out with a formal yardstick, ended up with a substantive one as well. Like Grotius, he sought refuge in interpretation and, again like Grotius, his interpretative devices combine formal with substantive rules.

Yet substantive yardsticks are awkward. They presuppose underlying agreement on the values with which to tackle treaty conflicts, yet the problem is precisely that such underlying agreement is lacking. It is one thing to take sides with the just war; it is quite another to figure out which ally actually has justice on its side. In other words, as long as it remains

---

[21] The deception could arise from the first treaty being kept secret.
[22] See Vattel, *Law of Nations*, p. 196.   [23] *Ibid.*, p. 197.   [24] *Ibid.*, p. 197.
[25] *Ibid.*, pp. 270–4.   [26] *Ibid.*, p. 272.   [27] *Ibid.*, p. 273.

debatable when exactly a war is just,[28] using the justness of war as the criterion to separate legal actions from illegal actions is bound to remain self-defeating.

But formal rules cannot do the trick either. A rule that the later in time should always prevail would be difficult to maintain if the general sentiment is that the earlier one is by far the more relevant. Thus, few would accept the position that a later extradition treaty should prevail over an earlier human rights treaty. But simply to posit the opposite rule (holding that the earlier one should always prevail) would run the risk of making a mockery of later developments and, indeed, preclude normative progress (itself an awkward notion). The ambivalence characterising both Grotius and Vattel, so often regarded as each other's counterparts,[29] should not therefore come as a surprise.

The classic cases

Like the classic writers, so too courts and tribunals have always shown a certain ambivalence on successive treaties, or a reluctance to meet the issue head-on (or, understandably, a combination of the two).[30] This was already apparent in 1925, when the PCIJ had to address the question of possibly competing concessions relating to the establishment of water works in Jerusalem.[31] While Mr Mavrommatis had obtained a concession from the Ottoman Government which, after the First World War, subrogated to the Mandatory for Palestine, this Mandatory (the UK, in fact) had itself granted a similar concession to a different person, a Mr Rutenberg. The Court concluded that there was a certain incompatibility, but that this had mostly led a paper existence, as Mr Rutenberg had never utilised his possible right to get Mr Mavrommatis's concession annulled. Hence, Mr Mavrommatis could not prove any losses suffered as a result

---

[28] The leading study suggests that it might be easier to recognise an unjust war than to develop abstract criteria for recognising just wars. See Michael Walzer, *Just and Unjust Wars*, 3rd edn (New York: Basic Books, 2000, first published 1977).

[29] Van Vollenhoven, possibly Grotius's biggest fan, once characterised the difference between the two as being symbolised in their first names: whereas Hugo (Huig, in colloquial Dutch) would be solid, Vattel's first name, Emer or Emeric, was that of a 'ballet dancer'. See C. van Vollenhoven, *De drie treden van het volkenrecht* (The Hague: Martinus Nijhoff, 1918), p. 24.

[30] The seminal study, outlining and tracing this ambivalence with great care and persuasion, is Binder, *Treaty Conflict and Political Contradiction*.

[31] See *The Mavrommatis Jerusalem Concessions* [1925] Publ. PCIJ, Series A, no. 5.

of the incompatibility, and the Court could, by and large, circumvent the thorny issue of conflicting obligations.[32]

Not many general conclusions can be based on this case. At first sight, the Court seemed to have implicitly upheld the *lex prior* notion: it worked on the basis of there being a possible conflict between the earlier concession granted to Mr Mavrommatis and the later one granted to Mr Rutenberg, and that the latter one would be in violation of the earlier one. Still, the specific legal regime at issue allowed for expropriation of the earlier concession, if accompanied by compensation, and clearly the Court clung to the specific legal regime, rather than any general rule or principle.

Likewise, in the *Austro-German Customs Régime* opinion,[33] the PCIJ had limited itself (perhaps inspired by the questions put to it) to providing an abstract answer, without addressing any possible legal consequences. The Council of the League of Nations had asked the Court whether a scheduled Austro-German customs régime was compatible with Austria's obligations under the 1919 Convention of Saint-Germain-en-Laye and a Protocol, concluded in 1922, on the reconstruction of Austria. Both instruments were to the effect that Austria's independence established in 1919 was 'inalienable'; Austria would, as the 1922 Protocol provided, 'abstain from any negotiations or from any economic or financial engagement calculated directly or indirectly to compromise this independence'.

The scheduled customs regime now was regarded, by a narrow majority, as incompatible with this general obligation. Given the terms of the proposed régime, the Court found that 'it is difficult to maintain that this régime is not calculated to threaten the economic independence of Austria'. Consequently, the Court found that the régime 'would not be compatible' with the 1922 Protocol.[34] While the reasoning of the Court has been

---

[32] *Ibid.*, esp. p. 45: 'even if the clause in Article 29 of the conditions of M. Rutenberg's concession is to be regarded as contrary to the Mandatory's international obligations, insofar as it gave M. Rutenberg the right to require the expropriation of concessions conflicting with his own, this clause has not in fact either led to the expropriation of M. Mavrommatis' concessions, or caused him any loss which might justify a claim on his behalf for compensation in the present proceedings.'

[33] See *Customs Régime between Germany and Austria*, advisory opinion, [1931] Publ. PCIJ, Series A/B, no. 41.

[34] *Ibid.*, p. 52. The Court did not render final judgment on the compatibility with the 1919 Convention; it merely held that the regime was incompatible with the 1922 Protocol. Six of the eight majority judges though declared that to their minds, the regime was also incompatible with the 1919 Convention.

subject to much criticism,[35] the relevant point for present purposes is that the Court did not suggest anything about the legal consequences of its finding: there is not a word on whether the German-Austrian treaty must be regarded as null and void, or whether it ought to be left unapplied, or even whether it would nonetheless remain a viable and valid agreement which merely happened to be incompatible with an earlier one.

The complicated nature of treaty conflict (and consequently the prevailing ambivalence among international lawyers) came most prominently to the fore in 1934, when the PCIJ decided the *Oscar Chinn* case: in this case, arguably still the leading case on the topic, the majority decided to treat the later Treaty of St Germain, without spelling it out, as an agreement *inter se* between some of the parties to the Berlin Act of 1885 (as amended in 1890).[36] The case involved the complaint of the UK, on behalf of Mr Chinn, concerning Belgium's commercial policy in Congo, its colony.[37] In essence, Mr Chinn complained about having been driven out of business when the Belgian government decided that Belgian river transport companies (partly owned by the state) operating in Congo could lower their fees and be compensated by the Belgian government. This constituted unfair competition, and would be 'in conflict with the international obligations of that Government towards the Government of the United Kingdom'.[38]

Those obligations, so the parties agreed, were obligations arising from the international Congo Basin régime under the 1919 Convention of Saint-Germain-en-Laye, and obligations stemming from general principles of international law. Given the circumstance that both parties stipulated that these were the direct sources of their obligations, the Court seemed

---

[35] Even from its own (past) ranks. Former Judge Loder wrote in private correspondence about the Court having become 'a political club. The German-Austrian case has done much harm to the Court, with its merely ridiculous argumentation'. As quoted in Ole Spiermann, *International Legal Argument in the Permanent Court of International Justice: The Rise of the International Judiciary* (Cambridge: Cambridge University Press, 2005), p. 314.

[36] They did so, most likely, because the parties to the dispute had suggested this was the applicable law, thus arguably rendering further discussion unnecessary, at least from the parties' point of view.

[37] A useful overview of the case is provided by Manley O. Hudson, 'The Thirteenth Year of the Permanent Court of International Justice', *American Journal of International Law*, 29 (1935), 1–24.

[38] See *The Oscar Chinn Case* (United Kingdom v. Belgium) [1934] Publ. PCIJ, Series A/B, no. 63, p. 77.

to think it had no choice but to apply them, to the exclusion of other instruments.[39] Interpreting the 1919 Convention, the Court would eventually hold that Belgium had acted in conformity with its commitments.

The 1919 Convention had provided, in so many words, that it abolished (in part) the terms of the 1885 General Act of Berlin and the 1890 Brussels Declaration between the parties to the 1919 Convention *inter se*. This was a reason for the Dutch judge on the bench, Van Eysinga, supported by his German colleague Schücking, to dissent.[40] For them, the Berlin Act (and Brussels Declaration) constituted a 'highly internationalized regime',[41] indeed 'rather a constitution established by treaty':[42] the régime thus created 'does not constitute a *jus dispositivum*, but it provides the Congo Basin with a régime, a statute, a constitution'.[43] While it would be possible to revise such a régime, doing so would require the consent of all parties, and could not be done by a number of them *inter se*.[44] This conclusion followed both from general international law and from the Berlin Act itself, as Van Eysinga argued.[45]

The Court, Van Eysinga continued, should have addressed the legality of the 1919 Convention *ex officio*; by so doing, it would have ended up applying only the Berlin Act. For he made the principled point that whether or not the parties to the dispute would accept the 1919 Convention was immaterial; its validity could not, as a matter of law, depend on the wishes of the parties to the dispute.[46]

---

[39] The formulation suggests as much: 'No matter what interest may in other respects attach to . . . the Berlin Act and the Act and Declaration of Brussels – in the present case the Convention of Saint-Germain of 1919, which both Parties have relied on as the immediate source of their respective contractual rights and obligations, must be regarded by the Court as the Act which it is asked to apply; the validity of this Act has not so far, to the knowledge of the Court, been challenged by any government.' *Ibid.*, p. 80.

[40] The British Judge, Sir Cecil Hurst, merely ducked the issue. Reading between the lines, one might conclude that he too was inclined to consider the 1919 Convention a nullity, but refrained from stating this overtly because this would have torpedoed the entire British claim, which was precisely that Belgium had violated the 1919 Convention. See *Oscar Chinn*, Hurst J. dissenting, pp. 122–3.

[41] *Ibid.*, Van Eysinga J., dissenting, p. 132.   [42] *Ibid.*, p. 133.   [43] *Ibid.*, p. 134.

[44] *Ibid.*

[45] Judge Schücking's brief dissent did not add much except semantics, calling the 1919 Convention 'an absolute nullity.' See *Oscar Chinn*, Schücking J. dissenting, p. 149. In a letter to his friend Hans Wehberg, Schücking hypothesised that the majority did not address the issue of the legality of the 1919 Convention because a finding of illegality would have insulted quite a few Great Powers. The letter is reproduced in Spiermann, *International Legal Argument*, pp. 362–3.

[46] *Ibid.*, Van Eysinga J., dissenting, p. 135.

The point on treaty conflict and its consequences then remained unsettled: the majority did not address it, and Van Eysinga, supported by Schücking, dissented strongly, focusing on the validity of the 1919 Convention. This, however, evokes another, related, issue, as Van Eysinga's remark concerning the wishes of the disputants makes clear. Even if it were possible to hold that invalidity might result from conflict with an earlier treaty, would this invalidity be automatic, or would it merely be a possibility? Van Eysinga and Schücking clearly thought that the first option (absolute nullity) was the proper one; this opinion is shared by an influential commentator such as Verzijl, for whom the Berlin Act, or at least parts thereof, constituted *jus cogens*. In this light, the Court ought to have left the 1919 Convention unapplied, 'comme étant absolument nul'.[47] The nullity would follow from the law, regardless of the parties' wishes.

Other commentators begged to differ, not so much on the point whether a recent treaty can depart from an older one,[48] but on how invalidity should come about. Thus, Vitta recalls that not a single government (including the parties to the Berlin Act) contested the validity of the 1919 Convention. This suggests, so Vitta notes with enthusiastic approval, that the Court opted implicitly for a 'relative nullity' thesis: nullity would depend on the desires of the parties concerned (parties to the dispute, but also those to the earlier treaty).[49]

This sketches quite nicely the dilemma pervading much of international law, and dominating conflict of treaties: are matters governed by a more or less objective notion of law (as Van Eysinga, Schücking and Verzijl held), or is everything relative, dependent on the parties, as the majority implicitly held, and as was later supported by Vitta? The first approach would naturally conclude that the law prohibits certain treaties, and that their conclusion would create an absolute nullity; it would, however, as Van Eysinga's opinion makes clear, also invoke the intentions of the parties: later treaties involving some of the parties only were to be considered as null and void precisely because the drafters of the Berlin Act allowed only modification by common consent, not modification between parties *inter se*.

---

[47] See J. H. W. Verzijl, 'La validité et la nullité des actes juridiques internationaux', *Revue de Droit International* (1935), 3–58, p. 40.

[48] For such a comment, see 'O' (a pseudonym), 'The Chinn Case', *British Yearbook of International Law*, 16 (1935), 162–4 (analysing the Berlin Act as a contractual arrangement which can be modified by some of its parties *inter se*).

[49] See Edoardo Vitta, *La validité des traités internationaux* (Leiden: Brill, 1940), p. 208.

The other approach would equally naturally hold that later treaties must be acceptable unless someone objects, and that any nullity too would depend on intentions. But, importantly, these rules would not themselves follow from intentions; these rules would be set by the law; it is the law that refers back to intent and makes it decisive. In turn, this oscillation hovers around sentiments about treaties as contractual arrangements and treaties as instruments of legislation. As Lauterpacht sketched the opposition with characteristic clarity:

> States conclude multilateral treaties not only to secure for themselves con-
> crete mutual advantages in the form of a tangible give and take, but also in
> order to protect general interests of an economic, political or humanitarian
> nature, by means of obligations the uniformity and general observance of
> which are of the essence of the agreement.[50]

This distinction then, in its turn, taps into almost primordial sentiments about the nature of international law, as either a legal system with a source outside the will of states, or a legal order firmly based on the will of states.[51]

Not surprisingly, other courts or tribunals addressing a conflict of treaties tend to get caught in the same dilemmas.[52] In 1916, the Central American Court of Justice was confronted with a dispute between Costa Rica and Nicaragua concerning the Bryan-Chamorro Treaty concluded between Nicaragua and the US. In this treaty, Nicaragua granted the US a perpetual right to construct, operate and maintain an inter-oceanic canal on Nicaragua's territory, something Costa Rica claimed was done in conflict with the earlier boundary treaty (the 1858 Cañas-Jerez Treaty) between Costa Rica and Nicaragua.[53] The Cañas-Jerez Treaty, confirmed

---

[50] See Hersch Lauterpacht, 'The Chinn Case', *British Yearbook of International Law*, 16 (1935), 164–6.

[51] This analysis owes something to David Kennedy, *International Legal Structures* (Baden-Baden: Nomos, 1987) and especially to Martti Koskenniemi, *From Apology to Utopia: The Structure of International Legal Argument* (Helsinki: Finnish Lawyers' Publishing Co., 1989).

[52] The Paris Court of Appeals decided a dispute in 1934 by accepting a modification of a multilateral treaty between some of the parties *inter se*, devoting much time to the powers of the government minister concerned to effectuate such modifications under French law. See *P. L. M. Railway Co.* v. *Société Coopérative Agricole dite "L'Union Maraîchère de Saint-Marcel et Saint Jean des Vignes"* Paris Court of Appeals, 19 July 1934, reported in 7 *International Law Reports* 420.

[53] For the text of the judgment, dated 13 September 1916, see *American Journal of International Law*, 11 (1917), 181–229. The case is usefully discussed in Christine Chinkin, *Third Parties in International Law* (Oxford: Oxford University Press, 1993), pp. 73–80. Salmon, 'Les antinomies', also mentions and briefly discusses (but without reference) a decision by the same Court in *El Salvador* v. *Nicaragua*, decided in 1917.

and validated by an arbitral award rendered by then US president Grover Cleveland in 1888, stipulated that Nicaragua should consult Costa Rica before entering into any agreements affecting the San Juan River, as the Bryan-Chamorro Treaty was bound to do. This consultation now had not taken place, urging Costa Rica to demand that the Bryan-Chamorro Treaty be declared null and void, for two reasons. One was rather straightforward: Costa Rica's rights under the Cañas-Jerez Treaty had been violated. The other argument however tapped into a slightly different reasoning: both Nicaragua and the US had been aware of the existence of the Cañas-Jerez Treaty and of Nicaragua's incapacity to sign anything without consulting Costa Rica first.[54] The first argument, then, was a straightforward conflict argument; the second came rather closer to a bad faith argument.

The Court, however, could circumvent this second claim by pointing to the limits of its jurisdiction: as the US was not a party to the dispute, the Court had no jurisdiction over US acts. This also meant that the Court could not declare the Bryan-Chamorro Treaty invalid; all it could do was to declare (as it did) that Nicaragua had violated its obligations towards Costa Rica under the Cañas-Jerez Treaty, but without stipulating what consequences, if any, should follow.[55]

The general conclusion to draw from the classic cases, then, is that international tribunals generally have accepted the co-existence of conflicting treaties as valid instruments within their own sphere. No treaty has ever been declared invalid due to conflict with either an earlier or later treaty; instead, the judicial approach has been to accept them side by side, and look for ways to reconcile or prioritise them.[56]

Doctrine

Doctrine started (with one important exception) to devote systematic attention to the possibility of treaty conflicts only in the 1950s,[57] coinciding with the rise of multilateral, more or less legislative, treaties. In earlier

---

[54] Costa Rica v. Nicaragua, pp. 227–8.

[55] For a brief discussion, see Quincy Wright, 'Conflicts between International Law and Treaties', *American Journal of International Law*, 11 (1917), 566–79, esp. p. 578.

[56] See also Felipe Paolillo, 'Convention de Vienne de 1969: Article 30: Application des traités successifs portant sur la meme matière', in Olivier Corten and Pierre Klein (eds.), *Les Conventions de Vienne sur le Droit des Traités: Commentaire Article par Article* (Brussels: Bruylant, 2006), pp. 1247–83, esp. pp. 1255–6.

[57] Lauterpacht's often-cited 1936 article was, in fact, concerned almost exclusively with English law, although it does have an illuminating, if brief, section on international law. See Hersch Lauterpacht, 'Contracts to Break a Contract', as reproduced in Hersch Lauterpacht, *International Law: Collected Papers. Vol IV: The Law of Peace* (Cambridge: Cambridge

days, conflicts between treaties would have been most likely to occur with respect to military alliances and with respect to trade agreements, but in both cases mechanisms were developed which could defuse the explosive potential of such treaties.

With military alliances, it is probably no exaggeration to suggest that international law has always carved out an exception to the *pacta sunt servanda* rule: military alliances would appear to be subject to the thought that they are only good as long as political circumstances remain constant. The precise legal mechanism to express this may be less than fully clear: some have held (and the Vienna Convention on the Law of Treaties retains a hint to this effect) that the very nature of military alliances implies a unilateral right to denounce or withdraw.[58] It has also been claimed, in related manner, that treaties of guarantee would be subject to the 'implied condition' that the beneficiary would behave properly; if not, the guarantor would be allowed a right to non-performance.[59] And from there it is but a short step to termination or to concluding a conflicting treaty.

With trade agreements, conflicts would tend to get defused by the operation of the most-favoured-nation clause, which in its most general formulation suggests that advantages to traders of any treaty partner shall be no less than those granted to the treaty partner that is subject to the most favourable treatment. If taken seriously, treaty conflict is highly unlikely to occur, as any potential conflict will immediately dissipate. After all, the treatment given to the most favoured partner should be applied to all; and it is no accident that the ILC became inspired to study the topic precisely in connection with discussions of the rights and obligations of third parties to treaties.[60]

Before the advent of the multilateral normative instrument, such attention as had been devoted to the topic of treaty conflict had invariably been

University Press, 1978, E. Lauterpacht ed.), 340–75. The paper was first published in the 52nd volume of the *Law Quarterly Review*, in 1936.

[58] Article 56, para. 1 (b) VCLT holds that treaties without a withdrawal or denunciation clause cannot be unilaterally set aside unless a right to do so 'may be implied by the nature of the treaty'. The ILC Commentary to this article (draft article 53 at the time) makes clear that the Commission was thinking specifically about treaties of alliance. See *Yearbook of the International Law Commission* (1966/II), p. 251.

[59] In this vein Sir Gerald Fitzmaurice, 'Fourth Report on the Law of Treaties', in *Yearbook of the International Law Commission* (1959/II), p. 47.

[60] See Endre Ustor, 'Working Paper on the Most-Favoured-Nation Clause in the Law of Treaties', *Yearbook of the International Law Commission* (1968/II), p. 165.

sporadic, in the form of commentaries on recent judicial decisions.[61] In addition, some attention had been devoted to specific treaty relations, most of all perhaps the relations of treaties to the League of Nations Covenant[62] and, later, the UN Charter.[63] There was one exception though: a brilliant article by Rousseau, published in 1932.[64]

Rousseau, positivist *pur sang*, already recognised that in cases where the parties to treaties would not be identical, international law could not offer any solution. Indeed, even in cases where the parties were identical, a general, one-size-fits-all solution would be difficult to defend, although he was inclined in such a scenario to place a lot of faith in the *lex posterior* principle.[65] After all, the *lex posterior* principle would give effect to the most accurate and up-to-date reflection of the will of the parties, and this, needless to say, was the only proper basis of international law.[66]

Given that the law would not be able to present a general solution, it would be up to the treaty parties themselves to regulate the relation of their treaty to other rules; consequently, Rousseau devoted much of his article to an enumeration of clauses found in treaties. And with respect to treaties involving third parties, he already anticipated that perhaps the best way out would be to insist on state responsibility, but with a twist:

> Peut-être la solution la plus rationelle ici serait-elle de développer le contentieux de l'indemnité, qui aboutirait au maintien du traité incompatible (à l'égard de l'État tiers et dans la mesure où celui-ci était de bonne foi lors de la conclusion dudit traité), avec mise en cause de la responsabilité internationale de l'État signataire de deux traités inconciliables.[67]

The twist then was that Rousseau would still insist that the earlier treaty would have to be given preference over the later in time; the party to the later treaty would need to be compensated while the earlier treaty would be left intact.

---

[61] See, e.g., O, 'The Chinn Case'; Lauterpacht, 'The Chinn Case'; and even Wright, *Conflicts*, despite its more general title.

[62] See Hersch Lauterpacht, 'The Covenant as the "Higher Law"', *British Yearbook of International Law*, 17 (1936), 54–65. While this piece did contain some insightful general considerations (which will be more conveniently discussed below), it does not quite qualify as a general, systematic treatment of the topic of conflicting treaty obligations.

[63] See, e.g., Kelsen, 'Conflicts between Obligations under the Charter of the United Nations and Obligations under Other International Agreements: An Analysis of Article 103 of the Charter', *University of Pittsburgh Law Review*, 10 (1948–49), 284–94.

[64] See Charles Rousseau, 'De la compatibilité des normes juridiques contradictoires dans l'ordre international', *Revue Générale de Droit International Public*, 39 (1932), 133–92.

[65] *Ibid.*, p. 151.   [66] *Ibid.*, p. 144.   [67] *Ibid.*, p. 191.

Rousseau's analysis was followed, a year later, by the Harvard Draft Convention on the Law of Treaties, article 22 of which dealt with con-flict.[68] Without having seen (or so it seems) Rousseau's work, the Harvard group nonetheless came up with similar propositions. When the par-ties are the same, the later in time will generally prevail; derogations from earlier treaties between parties *inter se* are permitted if not pro-hibited and if they do not jeopardise the purpose of the earlier treaty; and where the parties are different, the earlier treaty will prevail. And again, not unlike Rousseau, the Harvard group did not advocate hold-ing the later treaty a nullity without, however, providing much (or any) argument.[69]

Rousseau apart, systematic doctrinal analysis of treaty conflicts only started in the early 1950s, with the publication, almost simultaneously, of two seminal papers, both of them, incidentally, written by practitioners:[70] Aufricht's 'Supersession of Treaties in International Law',[71] and Jenks's 'The Conflict of Law-making Treaties'.[72]

Aufricht, in a wide-ranging paper, forcefully argued in favour of the principle *lex posterior derogat priori* which, for him, served as the starting point of analysis in all (it seems) cases of conflict between treaties.[73] In cases involving the same parties and the same subject matter, the principle would serve to justify implied or tacit supersession of the earlier treaty by the later one.[74] Therewith, Aufricht firmly anchored the *lex posterior* principle in the will of the parties, for in effect he argues that treaties generally contain an implied clause that they may be abrogated by later agreement between the same parties.

Indeed, strictly speaking, he suggests, the very existence of the *lex pos-terior* maxim makes that clauses expressly abrogating earlier treaties are redundant, although such clauses might be helpful in cases of doubt.[75]

---

[68] See Harvard draft, reproduced in *American Journal of International Law*, 27 (1933, supple-ment), 1009–29.

[69] *Ibid.*, esp. pp. 1025–6 (asserting that many hold conflicting treaties to be void and dis-agreeing with that position, but without indicating why).

[70] Rousseau, by contrast, was a lecturer at the law faculty of Bordeaux at the time his seminal paper was published.

[71] See Aufricht, 'Supersession'. Aufricht was affiliated with the Legal Department of the International Monetary Fund.

[72] See Jenks, 'Law-making Treaties'. Jenks was affiliated with the International Labour Orga-nization.

[73] Aufricht, 'Supersession', p. 655 (suggesting that the *lex posterior* principle qualifies as a general principle of law).

[74] *Ibid.*, p. 657.   [75] *Ibid.*, p. 661.

Doubts may occur because the *lex posterior* principle is offset by a competing one, or at least a qualifying one, to wit, the principle that 'tacit or implied abrogation is not favored'.[76] The absence of an express abrogation clause then may be taken 'as an intent to uphold the continued validity'[77] of the earlier treaty.

Whereas Aufricht starts his argument endorsing the application of the *lex posterior* principle with great certainty, already in its simplest application (concerning treaties between the same parties) he is confronted with problems, recognising as he does that the automatic application of the *lex posterior* principle might end up running counter to the intentions of the drafters, if not in practice, then at least as a theoretical matter, for it cannot *a priori* be excluded that the drafters do not intend to abrogate the earlier treaty.

Matters get more complicated still when subsequent treaties partly involving different parties are what is at issue. Here, too, Aufricht argues in favour of the *lex posterior* maxim, but again with a few caveats. Thus, recalling Judge Van Eysinga's dissent in the *Oscar Chinn* case, Aufricht recognises that, on occasion, the *lex posterior* may conflict with the norm *pacta sunt servanda*, as well as with the earlier treaty.[78] He also acknowledges that sometimes multilateral treaties may expressly provide that subsequent agreements between some of the parties *inter se* shall only bind those parties *inter se*, thus not affecting the other parties to the earlier treaty.

Yet, to the extent that this would suggest that the *lex posterior* principle is of limited application in cases involving subsequent treaties without full identity of the parties, he nonetheless also observes that in practice, during 'the nineteenth and twentieth centuries numerous *inter se* arrangements have been concluded between the Great Powers which in effect superseded preceding treaties on the same subject'.[79] Here, then, the *lex posterior* principle works by the grace of the circumstance that the Great Powers are concerned.[80] Aufricht explicitly recognises that this constitutes an exception to the principle of equality of states, and provides, rather provocatively perhaps, the example of the 1938 Munich Agreement, by which Nazi Germany agreed with France, Italy and the United Kingdom to modify the Versailles Treaty as far as the boundary between

---

[76] *Ibid.*, p. 657.   [77] *Ibid.*, p. 659.   [78] *Ibid.*, p. 672.   [79] *Ibid.*, p. 673.

[80] Echoes of this approach (suggesting a legally recognised privileged position for the great powers) can be discerned in Gerry Simpson, *Great Powers and Outlaw States: Unequal Sovereigns in the International Legal Order* (Cambridge: Cambridge University Press, 2004).

Germany and Czechoslovakia was concerned, without obtaining the consent of Czechoslovakia.[81]

More generally, he also puts forward the idea, endorsed in the Harvard Draft Convention, that where the parties to both treaties are not identical the *lex posterior* applies only to the extent that the subsequent treaty is not prohibited by the earlier one, and does not negatively affect its purpose. This rule, he says, 'reflects positive international law'.[82]

Finally, Aufricht devotes attention to what he deems the hierarchical structure of international law, suggesting that the *lex posterior* rule applies to the extent that the treaties concerned are at the same level. If one of them is higher (for instance, the UN Charter), then the formal status in the hierarchy will decide the issue.[83]

In short, while favouring generally the *lex posterior* rule, Aufricht's argument is not without ambiguity. He is forced to concede that it may not always work when the parties are identical, and is forced to concede in even stronger manner that the *lex posterior* principle has no automatic application where the parties are different. In fact, here the issue may be clinched not so much by law, but rather by power politics: the interests of the Great Powers may be the main reason for applying the *lex posterior* principle. In other words, and without stating it overtly, Aufricht suggests that, at the end of the day, international law does not regulate conflict between treaties, or, if it does, only to a limited extent (the extent to which cases involve the same parties, and thus are fairly unproblematic). Instead, it redirects matters back to politics, or seeks refuge in a notion of hierarchy which is posited rather than argued, and which is of fairly limited application (covering at most the League Covenant and the UN Charter, and then only by virtue of those instruments themselves rather than any general international legal rule) at any rate.

Jenks, by contrast, starts from the proposition that international law is still a primitive system, but one undergoing rapid growth. As a result, many treaties are concluded without sufficient coordination; this then leads to conflicts. While conflicts between bilateral treaties, even involving different parties, 'can still be resolved by the application of established principles derived from the law of contract',[84] the really problematic cases

---

[81] *Ibid.*, pp. 673–4. Often, the Munich Agreement is treated as invalid, due for instance to Germany's fraud or coercion. See, respectively, Paul Reuter, *Introduction to the Law of Treaties* (London: Pinter, 1989, Mico and Haggenmacher trans.), p. 138. Anthony Aust, *Modern Treaty Law and Practice* (Cambridge: Cambridge University Press, 2000), p. 256.

[82] Aufricht, 'Supersession', p. 677.   [83] *Ibid.*, pp. 682–3.

[84] Jenks, 'Law-making Treaties', p. 404.

would be conflicts between law-making treaties, and for those, '[n]o particular principle or rule can be regarded as of absolute validity'.[85]

In furtherance of this relativity, Jenks sketched a number of procedural
devices for settling conflicts, and ended up suggesting a number of principles to be applied as appropriate. These included Aufricht's *lex posterior*
principle, but also the contrasting *lex prior* principle, as well as notions
such as *lex specialis* and, like Aufricht, a hierarchical principle of fairly
limited scope.[86]

Importantly, though, Jenks felt he was not in a position to specify
when exactly which principle ought to be applied. Instead, the principles he mentioned 'must be weighed and reconciled in the light of the
circumstances of the particular case'.[87] This, however, would be only a
temporary affliction: experience would lead to the law reaching 'a more
developed stage of maturity',[88] and would sooner or later, so the message
went, crystallise into a more solid rule.

Conclusion

Either way, the two seminal papers produced in the early 1950s, both
in their own way, fall prey to ambivalence. Aufricht proposes a solution
(*lex posterior*), but qualifies it to such an extent that fairly little is left
of it, and Jenks, wisely, does not even try to formulate a general rule,
knowing that such a rule would be, at least for the time being, out of
reach. Importantly, though, both depart from Rousseau's traditionalist
insistence on maintaining the earlier treaty while compensating for the
latter. Both seem to realise that there may be circumstances where states
might wish to do it the other way around, and apply the later in time while
compensating the partner in the earlier venture.

These different positions of Rousseau, Aufricht and Jenks together
nicely sketch the main dilemma: whether to protect an initial undertaking
and label everything later and in conflict with it as invalid (or at least cast
it aside), or whether to put a premium on later expressions of consent as
merely more accurately reflective of present-day political configurations.
The problem, of course, may be that the latter will be more desirable

---

[85] *Ibid.*, p. 407.
[86] He further found a principle of autonomy (holding that regimes might tend to prefer rules
emanating from that particular regime over other rules), a gravity test, and a notion of
legislative intention.
[87] *Ibid.*, p. 436. [88] *Ibid.*, p. 453.

from the perspective of the parties to it, but may be less desirable from a perspective other than that of the parties concerned. In short: it is largely a battle of whose perspective to adopt, and that decision will have to be a political decision. As the next chapter will seek to demonstrate, the International Law Commission, which was already engaged with drafting the Vienna Convention on the Law of Treaties when Aufricht and Jenks wrote, also could not present a single, one-size-fits-all, solution.

4

Drafting the Vienna Convention

Introduction

As Grotius and Vattel already foreshadowed, by treating conflicting commitments partly under the heading of interpretation, there are various possible ways of classifying, categorising, addressing or ignoring problems related to conflicting treaty norms.[1] The 1969 Vienna Convention on the Law of Treaties devotes four or five articles to the topic (depending on how one counts) and, as if to underline the topic's messiness, those articles are scattered across the Convention. The main article is article 30, contained in the section on Application of Treaties. Article 41, included in the section on amendment and modification, deals with a modification of an existing treaty between some of the parties to that treaty and, needless to say, such a modification may come to affect the legal position of the remaining original parties (those who do not participate in the modification). Those two are, arguably, the most relevant provisions for present purposes, and will be central to the rest of this chapter.

Additionally, article 58 opens the possibility that parties suspend the operation of a treaty between some of them; again, the legal position of the original parties may be affected. Article 59, like article 58 included in the section on Invalidity, Termination and Suspension, recognises the possibility of concluding a treaty to abrogate an earlier one. And then there is article 31, paragraph 3(c), in the section on Interpretation, which holds that interpretation shall take into account 'any relevant rules of international law applicable in the relations between the parties'. And

---

[1] It was for this very reason that ILC member Roberto Ago saw little need for a specific rule on treaty conflict: most of the possible situations could be captured under another rule. See Ago, at the ILC's 687th meeting, *Yearbook of the International Law Commission* (1963/I), p. 91. His colleague Gilberto Amado also questioned the wisdom of having rules on treaty conflict, but for a more charming reason: to him, it would be 'inconceivable that States would behave in such a manner that would make such rules necessary'. *Ibid.*, p. 92.

those relevant rules, of course, may well be earlier treaty rules, or perhaps rules included in treaties with different parties.[2]

At the very least then, the topic of conflicting treaties is, dogmatically, a complicated topic. The complications are aggravated by the circumstance that the rules do not really have all that much to say; this applies in particular to the article which was meant to be central to the question: article 30. Perhaps this finds its cause in the circumstance, as Rosenne classically observed, that the Convention deals with treaties *qua* instruments, rather than with treaties *qua* obligations.[3] As a result, a treaty between A and B remains *res inter alios acta*, a thing among the parties. A conflicting treaty with different parties will also be *res inter alios acta*, with the final result being that there are two such documents, and there is no *a priori* way to figure out which should be recognised, and which should not;[4] this, in turn, has led to the circumstance that article 30 is typically a methodological device, specifying not so much what the legal consequences are in case of conflicting treaties, but rather outlining what a law-applying agency (be it a court or a State Department) should do. Those conflicting treaties are, to use a tired old cliché, like ships in the night: they pass each other without even knowing it. Until, that is, a collision occurs.

Lauterpacht's ambivalence

The same ambivalence that characterised early doctrinal writings on the topic would also influence the work of the International Law Commission.[5] The Commission's first Special rapporteur on the law of treaties, J. L. Brierly, never too keen on codification at any rate,[6] did not get around

---

[2] Panayi goes further still (too far, arguably) and suggests that treaty conflicts may also come within the scope of articles 61 and 62 VCLT, addressing supervening impossibility of performance and fundamental change of circumstances, respectively. See Christiana Panayi, 'Exploring the *Open Skies*: EC-incompatible Treaties between Member States and Third Countries', *Yearbook of European Law*, 25 (2006), 315–62, esp. pp. 355–60.

[3] As discussed more thoroughly above, Chapter 2. See in particular Rosenne, 'Bilateralism and Community Interest', p. 205. I am indebted to Andrius Mamontovas for intelligent discussion on this point.

[4] See, likewise, McNair, *The Law of Treaties*, p. 220.

[5] As Karl writes with keen sense of understatement, '[t]he development which led to the rules of the Vienna Convention on the Law of Treaties was anything but rectilinear'. See Karl, 'Treaties, Conflicts between', p. 937.

[6] Just prior to his election to the ILC, he wrote a brief article cautioning against codification conventions, strongly suggesting that codification could not serve as a "cheap method of establishing international order." See James L. Brierly, 'The Codification of International Law', *Michigan Law Review*, 47 (1948), 2–10, p. 4.

to treaty conflict in his reports. However, the work of his successor as Special rapporteur, Sir Hersch Lauterpacht, makes the general ambivalence surrounding the topic eminently visible. Lauterpacht felt keenly that, indeed, a later treaty incompatible with an earlier treaty, would be invalid, or at least subservient to the earlier one. Yet, the same Lauterpacht also observed that this could not always apply.

The first article Lauterpacht drafted on the topic is instructive.[7] It started, in its first paragraph, with a serious, almost peremptory rule: 'A treaty is void if its performance involves a breach of a treaty obligation previously undertaken by one or more of the contracting parties.'

Yet, in paragraph 3, Lauterpacht already had to retreat from this absolute position: it would apply 'only if the departure from the terms of the prior treaty is such as to interfere seriously with the interests of the other parties of that treaty or seriously impair the original purpose of the treaty,' and paragraph 4 carved out yet a bigger exception: the rule of paragraph 1 would not apply to subsequent treaties 'partaking of a degree of generality which imparts to them the character of legislative enactments properly affecting all members of the international community or which must be deemed to have been concluded in the international interest'.

For Lauterpacht, writing in his academic capacity, the starting point of the analysis was the somewhat fragile nature of the international legal order. Where treaties are relatively few, yet highly visible, the international legal order had fairly little choice but to sanctify the earlier agreement: 'Governments cannot be permitted to discredit international law and to render it unreal by filling it with mutually exclusive obligations and by reducing treaties to conflicting makeshifts of political expedience.'[8] Indeed, since *pacta sunt servanda*, and treaties thus constitute binding law, it 'follows that so long as they are in force they govern not only the conduct but also the contractual capacity of the parties; they prevent, in law, the effective rise of obligations inconsistent with their provisions'.[9]

Still, Lauterpacht felt himself compelled to make an exception, 'essentially *de lege ferenda*', with respect to the UN Charter (not surprisingly, given article 103 of the Charter) and other treaties concluded in the general interest, for 'situations may arise in which a treaty concluded by a considerable number of States, though not so numerous as to approach

---

[7] Draft article 16, contained in Lauterpacht, 'Report on the Law of Treaties', p. 93.
[8] See Lauterpacht, 'The Covenant as the "Higher Law"'. The quoted words also appear in part in Lauterpacht, 'Contracts to Break a Contract', p. 375.
[9] *Ibid.*, p. 54.

universality,[10] coincides so patently with general international interest that it may properly be entitled to claim to override previous treaty obligations'.[11]

With admirable clarity, Lauterpacht sketched the horns of the dilemma:

> The safeguarding of the authority of treaties must be reconciled with the equally important international interest involved in preventing the development of international law from being hampered by the obligations of existing treaties.[12]

Lauterpacht's draft did not contain a separate article dealing with modification of a treaty between some of its parties *inter se*. Instead, he encompassed a rule on modification as a qualification to the rule that the prior in time should prevail, to the effect that revision of a treaty could not be held hostage by a single party unwilling to revise. Generally, the prior treaty should prevail, but 'only if the departure from the terms of the prior treaty is such as to interfere seriously with the interests of the other parties to that treaty or seriously impair the original purpose of the treaty'.[13]

On this point too, the argument invoked in justification was an attempt to reconcile special interests with the general interest: insisting on the sanctity of the earlier treaty, however proper in itself, 'cannot legitimately provide a reason for preventing developments which are desirable and generally beneficial'.[14]

Lauterpacht shared with Rousseau a preference for upholding the earlier treaty, something Jenks and, in particular, Aufricht were less sanguine about.[15] Where Lauterpacht possibly parted ways with Rousseau, though, was on the consequences of having concluded an incompatible treaty. Where Rousseau seemed to be in favour of a general obligation to compensate the party to the later treaty, Lauterpacht was unequivocal: an incompatible treaty was void. This followed 'cogently from general principles of law governing the subject, from requirements of international public policy and the principle of good faith which must be presumed to govern international relations'.[16]

The difference between the two stemmed, in all likelihood, from a different outlook on human nature. Lauterpacht held that states must be

---

[10] He would not exclude a treaty in the general interest being concluded between two states only; an example could be a treaty securing an international waterway. Lauterpacht, 'Report on the Law of Treaties', p. 157.

[11] *Ibid.*, p. 157.   [12] *Ibid.*, p. 157.   [13] *Ibid.*, Draft article 16, paragraph 3.

[14] *Ibid.*, p. 158.   [15] As discussed in Chapter 3 above.

[16] 'Report on the Law of Treaties', p. 156.

presumed to be aware of the existence of possible incompatible treaties; only in rare cases (he spoke of a 'remote' possibility[17]) where the parties would both be unaware of the existence of an incompatible treaty should compensation be forthcoming. Rousseau, blessed with a sunnier disposition perhaps, was willing to presume the innocence of both parties and compensate, while insisting that the party concluding the conflicting treaty act in good faith.[18]

Writing in 1932, Rousseau had already pointed out that the problem of conflicting treaties is somehow related to questions of interpretation.[19] Lauterpacht, in his second report, took note, and somewhat softened his earlier stance on the nullity of a later treaty conflicting with an earlier one in two ways. One was that he was more willing to regard the treaty conflict as a problem of interpretation or termination; the other was that he was willing to concede that invalidity would not necessarily affect the entire subsequent treaty. In sum, 'the issue of invalidity of the subsequent treaty or of its individual provisions is not of primary significance'.[20]

Lauterpacht's main rule remained standing: the prior treaty prevails (always assuming, of course, that the parties are not identical), unless the general interest in the subsequent treaty outweighs the sanctity of the prior treaty. Nonetheless, he did generally soften his position, and seemed more understanding of the need, with multilateral treaties, to conclude agreements departing from them between some of the parties *inter se*: such treaties were 'a frequent and necessary occurrence'.[21]

Indeed, he even seemed to have traded in his all-or-nothing approach for a more subtle, pragmatic approach, although this was not yet overtly reflected in the text of the new draft article 16.[22] Invalidity, he suggested with respect to multilateral treaties, need not be an automatic consequence:

---

[17] *Ibid.*, p. 156.
[18] See Rousseau, 'De la compatibilité', p. 191 ('dans la mesure où celle-ci était de bonne foi lors de la conclusion dudit traité').
[19] *Ibid.*, p. 134 ('Le problème qui se pose est un problème de désaccord, d'antinomie – on serait tenté de dire un problème contentieux – connexe à celui de l'interprétation et de la validité des traités.').
[20] See Hersch Lauterpacht, 'Second Report on the Law of Treaties', in *Yearbook of the International Law Commission*, (1954/II), p. 134.
[21] *Ibid.*, p. 136.
[22] The text of the 1954 draft article did not depart much from the 1953 version. Lauterpacht, while acknowledging some alterations of substance, explained that the changes were 'intended mainly to clarify and to supplement the original object of that Article'. *Ibid.*, p. 133.

> there is little substance in the suggestion that, in pure logic, if a provision is made to yield to a provision of another treaty it is, *pro tanto*, invalid. For that provision may be otherwise – i.e., in relation to other treaties and generally – fully valid and operative.[23]

And in line with his newly found mildness and sense of the relevance of interpretation, he was less keen than before to see conflicting obligations: 'On occasion, the apparent conflict resolves itself, upon analysis, into no more than an assumption of additional obligations.'[24] This, then, narrowed the scope of the problem considerably, for if conflicts can be recast as problems of interpretation, they can be defined away; all that is needed, on such a construction, is something of a rule to deal with the (probably few) remaining cases. This then could be found in allowing for severability of conflicting treaty provisions (invalidating these individual provisions, but not the entire subsequent treaty), and hoping, in Jenks's footsteps, that the problem would somehow largely fade out: some conflict was 'probably unavoidable in a progressive and developing society'; some subsequent treaties might amount to 'a pronounced measure of international legislation'.[25] In a fully developed legal order, in other words, the problem of conflicting treaties would be minimised.[26]

Fitzmaurice's analysis

Lauterpacht's reports never were discussed within the International Law Commission, as the Commission found itself preoccupied with other assignments. Having produced two reports, he was called to sit on the International Court of Justice, and duly resigned from his position in the ILC. He was succeeded, both as the UK member and as special rapporteur, by Sir Gerald Fitzmaurice, whose detailed and highly analytical reports have memorably been described as 'a kind of Baedeker's guide to what would otherwise be unanticipated situations and differences that might be thrown up in the application of the law'.[27]

---

[23] *Ibid.*, p. 136.   [24] *Ibid.*, p. 137.   [25] *Ibid.*, p. 139.
[26] On Lauterpacht's thought more generally, see Martti Koskenniemi, 'Hersch Lauterpacht (1897–1960)', in Jack Beatson and Reinhard Zimmermann (eds.), *Jurists Uprooted: German-speaking Émigré Lawyers in Twentieth-century Britain* (Oxford: Oxford University Press, 2004), pp. 601–61.
[27] See Robert Y. Jennings, 'Gerald Gray Fitzmaurice', *British Yearbook of International Law*, 55 (1984), 1–64, at 57.

Sir Gerald departed from Lauterpacht's proposals, and instead was more inclined to follow the work of Rousseau and the Harvard Draft. In his usual analytical mode,[28] and firmly basing himself on the thought that a treaty constitutes a *res inter alios acta*, he proposed that where the parties are identical, the later treaty will prevail.[29] Where the parties are different, the earlier in time should be prioritised, but without this invalidating the later treaty. Instead, a treaty conflict would give rise to a liability to pay damages.[30] And where the parties to an earlier multilateral treaty would wish to depart *inter se*, the earlier treaty would apply between them and the remaining parties to it, while they would be free to apply the later modification between themselves, unless such modification would be prohibited by the earlier treaty or its application would necessarily involve breach of the earlier one. This, however, would only be the case if the earlier treaty would be 'of the reciprocating kind',[31] i.e. if its provisions could be captured in sets of bilateral rights and obligations.[32] With interdependent or integral treaties, any material conflict between such a treaty and a later one would render the later treaty void.[33]

Perhaps the main point to arise from Fitzmaurice's third report, apart from his analytical distinction between reciprocating, interdependent and integral treaties, is his reassessment of the case of a conflicting commitments to different parties. Like Rousseau, and very unlike Lauterpacht (despite his general admiration for the latter, whom he has been said to have regarded as his 'master in the law'[34]), he started from the assumption that the number of treaties concluded is very large, and that often treaties are difficult to retrieve. Hence, the normal situation would be that the treaty partner would be unaware of pre-existing commitments engaged in by its partner. This being the case, and explicitly borrowing from the private Anglo-American law of contract,[35] he opined that generally the prior treaty ought to be prioritised, while the party to the later treaty

---

[28] For a discussion of his judicial legacy, highlighting his analytical rigor, see John G. Merrills, *Judge Sir Gerald Fitzmaurice and the Discipline of international Law* (The Hague: Kluwer, 1998).

[29] See Sir Gerald Fitzmaurice, 'Third Report on the Law of Treaties', in *Yearbook of the International Law Commission* (1958/II), draft article 18, para. 5.

[30] *Ibid.*, draft article 18, para. 6

[31] *Ibid.*, article 18, para. 8. For the limitation to reciprocating treaties, see article 18(2).

[32] Bleckmann would, much later, use the term 'bipolar' to describe such arrangements. See Albert Bleckmann, 'Zur Wandlung der Strukturen der Völkerrechtsverträge – Theorie des multipolaren Vertrages', *Archiv des Völkerrechts*, 34 (1996), 218–36.

[33] Fitzmaurice, 'Third Report', draft article 19.

[34] See Jennings, 'Gerald Gray Fitzmaurice', p. 6.   [35] Fitzmaurice, 'Third Report', p. 41.

would be entitled to damages: 'No doubt . . . a court faced simultaneously with both contracts would give effect to the earlier in date.'[36]

However (and this would prove to be influential):

> there may be no way of preventing the State concerned from electing to honour the later rather than the earlier obligation . . . This does not mean that international law confers a 'right of election,' but only that, in the existing State [sic] of international organization, it may not be possible to prevent a *power* of election from being in fact exercised.[37]

As for modification between parties to multilateral treaties *inter se*, Fitzmaurice did his best to minimise the possible scope of conflict. With reciprocating treaties, it would be possible (and would indeed happen often enough) that treaties may be in conflict, but that this conflict does not result in conflicting obligations: perhaps at the cost of some inconvenience, it would nonetheless often enough be possible to accommodate both treaties. This allowed him to sail a middle course between the 'very unwise'[38] option of holding conflicting treaties void, and the awkward situation of prohibiting any change to a regime unless accepted by unanimous consent, for this would give all original parties an effective right of veto.[39]

The same reasoning could, however, not apply to interdependent or integral treaties. With respect to such treaties, the 'nature of the obligation is such that a directly conflicting treaty, if carried out, must it would seem necessarily invoke a breach of the earlier'.[40] As a result, invalidity would be a reasonable suggestion.

Still, here too Fitzmaurice tried to temper things and chart a middle course. The mere possibility of a conflict would not render the later treaty invalid: 'Only material conflict should rank for present purposes, and only a direct one.'[41] It would, for example, be perfectly possible for parties to an environmental treaty not to insist on performance by one of them; this would simply mean that those parties would renounce their rights.

The construction chosen underlines, once again, a certain ambivalence: even with interdependent or integral treaties, nonetheless Fitzmaurice could not avoid analysing treaty relations in terms of individual rights

---

[36] *Ibid.*   [37] *Ibid.*, p. 42 (emphasis in original).   [38] *Ibid.*, p. 44.   [39] *Ibid.*, pp. 43–4.

[40] *Ibid.*, at 44. Fitzmaurice provided a lengthier explanation of the distinction between the various kinds of treaties at the 482nd meeting of the ILC, on 23 April 1959, as reported in *Yearbook of the International Law Commission* (1959/I), p. 14.

[41] Fitzmaurice, 'Third Report', p. 44.

of individual parties. The whole point of distinguishing between various sorts of treaties was precisely that with integral and interdependent treaties the obligations could not be bilateralised; yet the insistence on the other parties denouncing their own rights under the treaty suggests that this bilateralisation creeps into the analysis once again.

While reorganising his materials in his fourth report, Fitzmaurice's opinion on conflicting treaties remained unchanged.[42] He emphasised once more that treaties are *res inter alios acta*, and thus cannot come to affect non-parties. As a result, both treaties would 'have equal force and effect';[43] non-performance of one of them would result in a liability to pay damages. As for modification, he simply referred to his earlier third report.[44]

Waldock's approach

After the untimely death of Lauterpacht, Sir Gerald was elected to the International Court of Justice. His place, both in the Commission and as Special rapporteur, was taken by Sir Humphrey Waldock. Practical as ever,[45] Sir Humphrey started his analysis by immediately disposing of the most problematic possible consequence of a treaty conflict. Draft article 14, contained in his second report on the law of treaties,[46] made clear in its opening sentence that a later treaty 'is not invalidated'[47] by being in conflict with an earlier treaty. And practical as ever, he advocated generally that treaty conflicts be resolved 'on the basis of the general principles governing the interpretation and application of treaties, their amendment or termination'.[48] There would have to be only one exception (beyond the possibility that international organisations would have their own rules, and beyond article 103 UN or *jus cogens*), and that pertained to the situation where a party to the earlier treaty would contest the 'effectiveness' of the later treaty: here the earlier treaty would prevail.

---

[42] See Fitzmaurice, 'Fourth Report', draft article 8, and at p. 61.   [43] *Ibid.*, draft article 8.
[44] *Ibid.*, p. 43.
[45] See generally Brownlie, 'The Calling of the International Lawyer'. Brownlie pointedly observes (p. 41) that Waldock 'was able to produce drafts which had a markedly more practical aspect than the impressive but highly involved work of his predecessor'.
[46] See Sir Humphrey Waldock, 'Second Report on the Law of Treaties', *Yearbook of the International Law Commission* (1963/II).
[47] *Ibid.*, p. 53.   [48] *Ibid.*, p. 53 (draft article 14 (1) (a)); and p. 54 (draft article 14(1)(b)(ii)).

Waldock's exception was of limited scope though, it may be presumed.[49] For one thing, there is the somewhat unexpected use of the term 'effectiveness', chosen no doubt to avoid the connotations usually associated with more technical legal terms such as 'validity' or 'applicability'. This in turn suggests (in line with Waldock's general thought on the matter) that he would shy away from declaring the later treaty invalid.

This also follows from the equally unexpected condition that effectiveness of the later treaty can only be established after the party to the earlier treaty has contested this effectiveness. The article and its commentary remain silent on what 'contested' can possibly mean; whether, for instance, it would be a strict condition that a party would have to go to court to get its rights under the earlier treaty vindicated, or whether a diplomatic protest would suffice. Either way, Waldock hesitated to lay down anything as resulting from the automatic operation of a rule of law; contesting the effectiveness of a treaty clearly requires some further action on the part of the aggrieved state, and this in turn would it make it possible to argue (in the absence of such action) that the aggrieved state had acquiesced in the later treaty, or would be estopped from contesting its effectiveness.[50]

Finally, it is far from clear what it means to say that in a concrete dispute, the earlier treaty prevails. Does this mean that it prevails only with respect to the state initiating the dispute? Or does the earlier treaty prevail also with respect to other treaty partners? And does it only prevail with respect to this particular dispute, or does it prevail across the board, until such time as either the earlier or the later treaty have been formally terminated or, perhaps, the reluctant state signs up to the later treaty after all?

Some light is shed by a different draft article, draft article 19, dealing with implied termination of a treaty by concluding a conflicting one. Here, Waldock held, where some, but not all, parties to a treaty conclude a later treaty, the earlier can, between them, be considered as terminated, but will remain in force to govern relations between those who do not join the later treaty, and between states parties to the older with states parties to the newer treaty.[51] This then firmly embraces the *res inter alios acta* idea: a treaty is a thing between the parties to it, and can by definition not

---

[49] Curiously perhaps, the commentary to draft article 14, while fairly lengthy, does little to elucidate the intended meaning of the draft article.

[50] As much was suggested, within the ILC, by André Gros. See 687th meeting, *Yearbook of the International Law Commission* (1963/I), at 92.

[51] See Waldock, 'Second Report', p. 72.

have any radiating effects. A conflicting treaty is a different thing between its parties, and cannot have such radiating effect either. Consequently, treaty conflicts cannot really be solved; at best, their practical effects can be mitigated, and this is precisely what Waldock aimed to do by pointing to the principles governing interpretation and application and relating to amendment or termination, and by keeping open the possibility that the parties to the earlier treaty could nonetheless come, over time, to embrace, or at least acquiesce in, the newer treaty.

Waldock built on this flexible, pragmatic approach in his third report, which contained a draft article (article 65) with the telling title 'Priority of conflicting treaty provisions', and indeed throughout the commentary he stressed that one should think in relative terms of priority rather than absolute terms of nullity: 'under the existing law and practice conflicts between treaties of whatever type are regarded as raising questions of the priority rather than of the validity of treaties.'[52] And where such would be to the detriment of a state, the answer would have to be sought in the law of state responsibility: 'If a state in concluding a treaty sets aside its obligations to another State under an earlier treaty without the latter's consent, it engages its international responsibility for the breach of the earlier treaty.'[53]

The ILC's apprehensions

Whereas Lauterpacht's reports were never discussed in the ILC, Fitzmaurice's first report, produced in 1956, was only to be discussed three years later, starting with the Commission's 480th meeting in 1959. It was not until Waldock had been appointed that the ILC would start to discuss treaty conflicts, and as Waldock's first report did not address treaty conflict, the topic only came to be addressed in 1963, on the basis of Waldock's second report.

In introducing the topic, Waldock once again emphasised that his approach differed from those of Lauterpacht and Fitzmaurice in that he advocated not a rule of absolute nullity, but merely a rule of priority.[54] By and large the Commission agreed with this approach, although some

---

[52] See Sir Humphrey Waldock, 'Third Report on the Law of Treaties', in *Yearbook of the International Law Commission* (1964/II), p. 42.

[53] *Ibid.*, p. 44. Note that Waldock leaves open the possibility that the aggrieved state actually consents.

[54] Waldock, ILC 685th meeting, *Yearbook of the International Law Commission* (1963/I), p. 78.

added the observation that rules of *jus cogens* might result in absolute nullity after all – as Waldock's draft article had also recognised.[55]

The virtues of Waldock's approach were neatly summarised by Yasseen, for whom Waldock's approach was:

> both moderate and justifiable; it did not impair the rights of the States parties to an earlier treaty, since that treaty was held to prevail. At the same time there was no bar to the treaty's amendment. The later treaty was not invalidated, but could be carried into effect provided that the States signatories to the later treaty fulfilled their obligations to the States parties to the earlier treaty.[56]

This may, incidentally, have been too rosy a description, in that there might be circumstances where obligations owed under the earlier treaty are not owed so much to other states, but rather to individuals, natural or legal persons,[57] or there might be situations where simultaneously living up to commitments to different parties is either politically or practically unfeasible, or both. Nonetheless, rosy as it may have been, this was the picture embraced by the ILC: a pragmatic solution to cover what was considered as, really, a practical problem.[58]

Not for the first time, the only ones who begged to differ were Rosenne and Tunkin.[59] With his usual degree of perceptiveness, Rosenne envisaged that the problem might have a deeper dimension than the ILC seemed to

---

[55] So, e.g., Castrén, 685th meeting, p. 79; Lachs, 687th meeting, p. 87; De Luna, 687th meeting, p. 89.

[56] Yasseen, 687th meeting, p. 88.

[57] In particular, Fitzmaurice had tried to come to terms with this distinction, but to little avail: the ILC rejected a draft article classifying treaties because it saw no need for such an article. See draft article 8, contained in Sir Gerald Fitzmaurice, 'Report on the Law of Treaties', *Yearbook of the International Law Commission* (1956/II), and the subsequent discussion at the Commission's 482nd meeting, in *Yearbook of the International Law Commission* (1959/I), pp. 14–15.

[58] Van Panhuys, writing before the Vienna Conference took place, astutely observed 'a kind of sliding scale', ranging from Lauterpacht via Fitzmaurice to Waldock and the ILC: 'Whereas in Lauterpacht's draft the main rule is nullity, although qualified in some respects, Sir Gerald's approach seems to be more cautious. Eventually, in accordance with Sir Humphrey's suggestions, the I.L.C. itself adopted a text which completely abandons the concept of nullity and in which the matter is viewed solely from the angle of the *application* of treaties.' See H. F. van Panhuys, 'Conflicts between the Law of the European Communities and Other Rules of International Law', *Common Market Law Review*, 3 (1965–66), 420–49, p. 421 (emphasis in original).

[59] The same two members were highly instrumental in creating the Vienna Convention's regime on reservations. For a discussion, see Klabbers, 'On Human Rights Treaties', pp. 149–82.

realise, and argued that as a result, the ILC should make clear that the rule on treaty conflict would be but a residual rule. Instead of relying on 'too general a rule', states should be encouraged to include, in their treaties, rules relating to past and future treaties.[60] Tunkin, in turn, felt that the substance had remained unclear, and remained unconvinced that treaty conflict would raise only issues of responsibility and none of validity.[61]

After the discussion had been postponed at the 687th meeting, the Commission renewed its attention for treaty conflicts at its 703rd meeting. The main reason for doing so was to discuss whether, even though it would seem the topic was best served by a priority rule, it would still need something on validity as well, therewith picking up on Tunkin's suggestion made at the 687th meeting.[62]

At the outset, Sir Humphrey and Radhabinod Pal introduced an amendment taking Tunkin's point into consideration, to the effect that:

> if the later treaty necessarily involves for the parties to it action in direct breach of their obligations under the earlier treaty, of such a kind as to frustrate the object and purpose of the earlier treaty, then any party to it whose interests are seriously affected shall be entitled to invoke the nullity of the second treaty.[63]

In line with his earlier position, this new amendment proposal still left matters very much in the hands of the parties concerned: no automatic nullity was envisaged, and thus the door remained open for arguments based on acquiescence or estoppel.

Still, the proposal met with a lukewarm response, probably because it introduced a few novel problems. For instance, as Rosenne pointed out, through what procedure could invalidity be invoked?[64] Castrén, for his part, wondered about the viability of the notion that a state's interests (not just rights) were being 'seriously affected'.[65] And Yasseen perceptively argued that nullifying the later in time would seriously risk impeding the development of international law: surely, a multilateral treaty to protect individuals ought to survive any conflict with an earlier treaty.[66]

---

[60] Rosenne, 687th meeting, p. 89.   [61] Tunkin, 687th meeting, p. 93.
[62] This was probably fairly typical for Sir Humphrey's attitude. As Brownlie puts it: 'An important part of Waldock's success on the Commission undoubtedly lay in his capacity to reconsider his first view and to avoid insisting on some preconceived personal or national viewpoint.' See Brownlie, 'The Calling', p. 41.
[63] See 703rd meeting, in *Yearbook of the International Law Commission* (1963/I), p. 196.
[64] *Ibid.*, p. 198.   [65] *Ibid.*   [66] *Ibid.*, p. 199.

Others repeated their view that all practically relevant consequences could be left to the law on state responsibility; hence, there was no real need to introduce nullity as a consequence.[67] In the end, further discussion was postponed again, after Waldock had indicated his personal position on the matter. Waldock thought 'the idea of nullity attractive from the academic point of view, but it did not reflect the present position in international law.'[68]

The Commission devoted two more meetings to treaty conflict during its 1964 session, discussing what had become draft article 65, laid down in Waldock's third report.[69] As noted, any reference to nullity had by now vanished from Waldock's report; the matter was treated as one of priority pure and simple. The Commission by and large shared this view – even Tunkin noted that 'on the whole he could accept' the approach focusing on priority rather than invalidity.[70] As a result, the discussions at this stage were not so much on matters of principle, but rather on the drafting.

Still, two worries kept nagging some of the ILC members. One of them was how to overcome the theoretical difficulty of the notion that treaties are *res inter alios acta*, leading to the problem that a conflict can never really be resolved without breaking in into something one has no involvement with.[71] In other words: a principled solution only seemed possible by means of ousting the *res inter alios acta* notion, but that in turn would be close to unthinkable. While this was raised, the Commission did not pursue this line of thought any further.

The second worry was the more familiar one about there being various sorts of treaties. Apart form contractual arrangements (which would make it relatively easy to apply principles of responsibility in cases of conflict), the Commission realised all too well that the real problems would arise in respect of what it referred to, following Fitzmaurice's analysis, as integral and interdependent treaties.

In essence, three different ideas were floated in order to come to terms with (or downplay, perhaps) the problems arising out of a conflict between such treaties, or between such treaties and contractual undertakings. Sir Humphrey argued, making explicit what was arguably already implicit

---

[67] Most vocally Briggs (*ibid.*, p. 199), and Ago (*ibid.*, pp. 199–200), although the latter was willing to identify the possible nullity of later treaties if the states concerned (or one of them) had been neutralised and had lost the capacity to conclude certain treaties.

[68] *Ibid.*, p. 202.   [69] See Waldock, 'Third Report'.

[70] ILC 743rd meeting, in *Yearbook of the International Law Commission* (1964/I), p. 129.

[71] The issue was raised by Castrén, 742nd meeting, in *Yearbook of the International Law Commission* (1964/I), p. 120 and, with less worries, also by Ago, 743rd meeting, p. 131.

in draft article 65 of his 1964 draft, that integral and interdependent treaties contain an implied undertaking not to depart from them by means of concluding a conflicting treaty.[72] It follows that any contracting out would breach the earlier undertaking and thus give rise to issues of responsibility.

Two other strategies were raised by Rosenne. First, he pointed out that often conflicts do not cover entire treaties, but only parts thereof. In this light, it might be useful to consider separability of treaty provisions as an option.[73] Rosenne's other suggestion was to focus on the application of treaties rather than on conflict in the abstract, for '[w]hen treaty provisions apparently in conflict came to be applied, it might well be found that there was no incompatibility'.[74] Both proposals downplay the scope of treaty conflict, almost to the vanishing point. As a result, treaty conflict could be regarded as a relatively minor problem, perhaps more suitable for academic reflection than creative of real-life problems.

And indeed, why not? There is a sense in which the entire ILC discussion oozes the theme that treaty conflict may be a problem, but is not a big problem, and that actual occurrences will be easily solvable in good faith. And that sentiment was perhaps further strengthened by a feeling that the one category where things really could get problematic (normative multilateral instruments) was still numerically not terribly important. Moreover, and perhaps more importantly, it could be expected that precisely when it came to normative instruments, states would be careful not to create any conflicts. Perhaps Gilberto Amado summed up the general feeling best when proclaiming that states just would not engage in treaty conflicts.[75]

The problem with that view, of course, is not so much that it is mistaken, for with the possible exception of military alliances, it is probably the case that treaty conflicts are rarely knowingly created. The problem with Amado's position, instead, is that it presupposes that treaty conflict can only result from bad faith action, and does not account for the possibility that treaty conflict may result from such things as negligence, carelessness, or information gaps. Neither of these became major themes running through the discussions; understandably so, as the problem would appear much more manageable when limited to bad faith acts.

---

[72] Waldock, 742nd meeting, p. 121.   [73] Rosenne, 742nd meeting, p. 124.
[74] Rosenne, 743rd meeting, p. 129.   [75] See Amado, during the 687th meeting, p. 92.

The topic came to be discussed in depth for the last time before the Vienna Conference during the 857th and 858th meetings of the ILC, in May 1966, this time under the heading 'Application of treaties having incompatible provisions', following a proposal Rosenne had made in 1964.[76] Nothing much of substance happened, however. Perhaps the most eye-catching development was that the discussion revolved to a large extent on questions of state responsibility, possibly due to a proposal made by Eduardo Jiménez de Aréchaga to spell out the consequences of concluding a treaty in violation of interdependent or integral treaties.[77] Matters were taken furthest, arguably, by Paul Reuter, who wondered whether the state with whom a later, incompatible treaty was concluded ought to be regarded as an accomplice in the breach of the earlier treaty, and therewith be penalised.[78]

More important perhaps was a second element: the slowly dawning realisation that, ultimately, treaty conflicts involving different parties would ultimately be unsolvable. Pessou was the first to express this, in somewhat lapidary terms, when observing that 'the incompatibility of treaty provisions raised problems which mainly involved political factors'.[79] Tunkin observed that analogies with private law would have little to offer;[80] Ago felt it would be extremely difficult to justify giving priority to either treaty,[81] and Bartos even doubted, somewhat late in the process, whether the Vienna Convention should have a rule on conflict between treaties after all.[82]

Perhaps as a consequence of this dawning realisation, again some effort went into downplaying the relevance of treaty conflicts. One emanation thereof was the reminder, by Alfred Verdross, that often 'the problem to be solved was one of interpretation, and not of compatibility'.[83] The second was, somehow, to limit the problem of treaty conflict. As Briggs brilliantly put it, 'the real point at issue' was:

> not the incompatibility of provisions of successive treaties when the parties were not identical, but the incompatibility of obligations assumed by a particular State in successive treaties.[84]

---

[76] See ILC, 743rd meeting, p. 129. The Drafting Committee had already honoured this later in 1964, when it presented a draft under that heading at the 755th meeting. See *Yearbook of the International Law Commission* (1964/I), p. 205.

[77] See 857th meeting, *Yearbook of the International Law Commission* (1966/I) pt. 2, p. 96.

[78] *Ibid.*, p. 97.   [79] *Ibid.*, p. 97.   [80] *Ibid.*, pp. 98, 100.   [81] *Ibid.*, p. 102.

[82] *Ibid.*, p. 101.   [83] *Ibid.*, p. 101.

[84] See 858th meeting, *Yearbook of the International Law Commission* (1966/I) pt. 2, p. 105.

The focus thus shifted from treaties and parties, to obligations, and this thought would be reproduced in the title of subsequent drafts.[85] That would do little to solve the underlying problem, of course, but would at least make the problem appear more limited and, therewith, more manageable. Moreover, it made perfect sense in terms of the Commission's decision to focus on the treaty as instrument rather than on treaties as obligations: by redefining treaty conflict as conflict of obligations, the ILC could be forgiven for not solving the issue. After all, any attempt to settle conflict of obligations would have rendered the Commission vulnerable to the charge of inconsistency: any solution would have looked out of place in a convention premised on the concept of treaties as instruments.[86]

The Vienna Conference's acceptance

Discussions during the Vienna Conference were mainly about drafting issues; yet, as so often, drafting issues can only hide more fundamental issues for so long. The two most prominent issues, both suggesting how difficult the topic of treaty conflict in a non-hierarchical system really is, were both introduced by the representative of the UK, Ian Sinclair. It will be recalled that the title of draft article 26 (as it then was) refers to successive treaties relating to the same subject matter. This, Sinclair argued, raises two difficult issues: what does the phrase 'same subject-matter' mean? And how to determine which treaty succeeds which? How to determine which is the earlier, and which is the later in time?[87] While some opinions would be voiced, none of them proved consequential, and it would seem that many eventually set their hopes once again on the idea, hinted at by US representative Richard Kearney, that many conflicts could possibly be overcome by means of a reconciliatory interpretation.[88]

Sir Humphrey, in the meantime, while answering Sinclair's question on the meaning of 'same subject-matter' under oblique reference to the

---

[85] Starting with the draft present at the 875th meeting, which was headed 'Application of successive treaties relating to the same subject-matter'. See *Yearbook of the International Law Commission* (1966/I), pt. 2, p. 211. This became the title of the article as it appears in the Vienna Convention.

[86] On this premise, see Chapter 2 above.

[87] See Vienna Conference on the Law of Treaties 1968, Committee of the Whole, 31st meeting, p. 165. Sinclair raised the same two issues a year later, at the 1969 Vienna Conference, Committee of the Whole, 85th meeting, pp. 221–2.

[88] Vienna Conference on the Law of Treaties, 1969, thirteenth plenary meeting, p. 56. See also Kearney's earlier remarks, Committee of the Whole, 85th meeting, p. 222.

lex specialis maxim, did provide something of a reply to the question as to how to determine which treaty was the earlier, and which the later. His response displayed a great deal of ambivalence, coming up, as he did, with two contradictory answers. At first, he argued vehemently in favour of choosing the date of adoption of a treaty, rather than date of entry into force, as the relevant date. After all, so Sir Humphrey explained, the adoption signifies the moment of legislative intent; entry into force, so the argument tacitly continued, is merely a practicality.[89]

This position is difficult to sustain as a general position,[90] though, for at least two reasons. One (left undiscussed by Waldock) is that not all adopted treaties actually enter into force; and not all of them do so without further acts. Usually, there is an act of ratification required, and since a state, by ratifying a treaty, expresses its consent to be bound, one could just as well argue that the legislative moment, for each and every individual state, is the moment of ratification. Talk (adopting a text) is cheap; action is what matters. And even that might not clinch the issue, as not all ratifications eventually give rise to a legally binding instrument: some treaties may attract but a handful of ratifications and never enter into force.[91]

Eventually, Waldock would find himself in a somewhat similar position, but because of the second reason why the adoption argument would be difficult to maintain. Multilateral treaties may enter into force for different parties at different moments; here, then, entry into force would be the relevant moment, for only from that moment onwards would that party be bound by the treaty.[92]

In the end, Waldock sought refuge in underlining that any general rule on treaty conflict was best regarded as a residual rule. As paragraph 2 of the article makes clear, 'when a treaty contained specific provisions on the subject of compatibility, those provisions would prevail'.[93]

---

[89] Vienna Conference on the Law of Treaties, 1969, Committee of the Whole, 91st meeting, p. 253.

[90] It only makes sense in a bilateral setting, and given the opening words of Waldock's next statement ('Another question, however . . .'), it seems plausible that Waldock had precisely such a bilateral setting in mind.

[91] A fine, if somewhat ironic, example is the 1986 Vienna Convention on the Law of Treaties concluded with or between International Organizations.

[92] Vienna Conference on the Law of Treaties, 1969, Committee of the Whole, 91st meeting, p. 253.

[93] *Ibid.*

Conclusion: ambivalence

In the end, then, the drafters of the Vienna Convention, both within the ILC and during the two conferences in 1968 and 1969, fought rather unsuccessfully to come to terms with the ambivalence inherent in the very attempt to create something of a hierarchy in a horizontal legal system and without having the possibility of invoking substantive values. The rule of article 30 (in conjunction with article 59) works well when it is not needed (where treaty partners are identical); yet where it is needed the most (when partners are varied), it does not offer much of a solution, beyond seeking refuge in further interpretation, taking matters outside the scope of the law of treaties altogether by invoking the rules on state responsibility, or leaving it to the treaty partners themselves to deal with. This may be useful for some purposes, as the next chapter will make clear, but in the meantime, it does not make practice any easier.

5

Post-Vienna Convention developments

Zuleeg and the principle of political decision

Since judicial decisions can be found supporting the rule that the earlier treaty in time prevails,[1] as well as the later in time,[2] it is probably no coincidence that the vast majority of academic authors writing on treaty conflict has come to adhere to the formula of the Vienna Convention: in the end, if a treaty conflict occurs and it cannot be resolved through interpretation, then the state facing irreconcilable commitments will simply have to choose which one to honour, while engaging state responsibility towards the state losing out. As German doctrine refers to it, in a term apparently coined by Manfred Zuleeg,[3] this is the 'principle of political decision' (*'Das Prinzip der Politischen Entscheidung'*): the state concerned simply has to make a political decision which commitment to prefer.

Zuleeg came to formulate the principle of political decision by and large by default: a systematic analysis of various situations and of the various possible maxims (*lex prior, lex posterior, lex specialis*; hierarchy; the 'principle of pith and substance', and the principle of legislative intent) revealed that no single rule could satisfactorily be applied to situations involving varied partners. Either it was the case that the rule appealed to things which were difficult to realise in a horizontal system such as international law (think of a hierarchy principle), or they would run counter to the third party rule (*pacta tertiis nec nocent nec prosunt* – no obligations or rights shall be created for third parties without

---

[1] An example is the decision of the District Court of The Hague in *In re B.*, judgment of 26 May 1952, reproduced in 19 *International Law Reports* 318.

[2] For an example, see the decision of Argentina's Cámara Nacional Especial in *Cía. Territorial de Seguras (S.A.)* v. *The* Clara Y., judgment of 4 May 1953, reproduced in 20 *International Law Reports* 429.

[3] See Manfred Zuleeg, 'Vertragskonkurrenz im Völkerrecht. Teil I: Verträge zwischen souveränen Staaten', *German Yearbook of International Law*, 20 (1977), 246–76.

their consent.[4] It followed that there was only one possible conclusion left:

> Aus der Erkenntnis, dass beide einander widersprechenden Verträge unter divergierenden Partnern nach dem Grundsatz *pacta sunt servanda* binden, und aus der vergeblichen Suche nach einer allgemein gültigen objektiven regel kann nur der Schluss gezogen werden, dass es der politischen Entscheidung des Staates überlassen bleibt, welchem Vertrag er den Vorzug gibt, wenn sich die Erfüllung beider Verträge nicht mit einander in Einklang bringen lässt.[5]

There is not just the fact that none of the applicable rules is fully satisfactory; Zuleeg also points out that the oft-preferred escape into harmonising interpretation is, really, no escape at all but instead reproduces the problem. For to argue that conflicting provisions in different treaties can be harmonised will normally entail that one will be brought into line with the other. But on what basis can an objective decision be made to interpret treaty A so as to accommodate treaty B, rather than the other way round? Doing so goes (*in abstracto*, at any rate) against the interests of the parties to A that are not parties to B, and therewith stumbles, once again, on the idea that treaties are ever so many *res inter alios acta*.[6] And continuing the same thought: a true reconciliation of the commitments in treaties A and B, watering down the provisions of both treaties, runs into the same problem, but doubly so, as it digresses by necessity from both treaties A and B.

Apart from Zuleeg's negative reasons, however, there are also some good positive reasons for adhering to the Vienna Convention's formula. For one, it is, after all, the Vienna Convention's formula, and for that reason alone authoritative. It may be true – and possibly a good thing too, as Sinclair suggested[7] – that article 30 of the Vienna Convention is a

---

[4] For a brief discussion of treaty conflict from this perspective, see Chinkin, *Third Parties in International Law*, pp. 73–80.

[5] Zuleeg, 'Vertragskonkurrenz', p. 267: 'From the fact that both contradictory treaties will be binding diverging parties in accordance with the principle *pacta sunt servanda*, and the fruitless search for a generally applicable objective rule can only be concluded that it is left to the political decision of states which treaty to prefer, when the fulfillment of both treaties is not to be harmonized.' (translation by JK).

[6] *Ibid.*, pp. 271–74. He observes that the only way to ground the supremacy of harmonising interpretation over the *pacta tertiis* rule would be by pointing to the unity of the international legal order (p. 271). He does not, however, develop this, and one senses he would not be too convinced himself.

[7] See Sinclair, *The Vienna Convention*, p. 98.

residual rule and that states are free to agree on something else, but still: it carries the stamp of approval which inclusion in the Convention entails.

For another, the principle of political decision avoids all the drawbacks of a mechanistic application of a single, more determinate rule. The *lex posterior* rule, useful as it is in quite a few circumstances, runs the risk of sacrificing normative instruments on the altar of later departures. The *lex prior* does the same in reverse, and interferes, as many have held, with the progressive development of international law.[8] The *lex specialis* rule is not only absent from the Convention, but has the drawback that the distinction between special versus general treaties is itself hopelessly uncertain.[9]

The principle of political decision, by contrast, allows states and in particular decision-makers (think of judges) to choose the treaty they deem the most worthy in the circumstances. Sometimes this may well be the later in time; sometimes perhaps the earlier in time may be preferred. What is more, it allows others to pressure the state or the tribunal concerned into making the right choice: human rights advocates, for example, may use the principle of political decision in advocating that in a conflict between a human rights convention and another treaty, the state concerned ought to give preference to the human rights treaty; environmentalists may invoke it to advocate the priority, in any given case, of an environmental treaty over a conflicting treaty. Put thus, it is precisely the indeterminacy of the principle of political decision that allows for flexible and responsive politics and makes it possible for society at large (civil society, if you will) to participate in international decision-making processes.[10]

Narrowing the scope

Zuleeg (and the Vienna Convention) have had quite a few followers, all emphasising with greater or lesser degrees of urgency that in the end, it

---

[8] The argument is also listed in Zuleeg, 'Vertragskonkurrenz', e.g. p. 263.

[9] For a recent positive appraisal, see Anja Lindroos, 'Addressing Norm Conflicts in a Fragmented Legal System: The Doctrine of *Lex Specialis*', *Nordic Journal of International Law*, 74 (2005), 27–66.

[10] Vranes too concludes, in rather abstract manner, that an abstract ranking of treaties is impossible. To him, conflict rules inhere in the legal order (and thus need not be explicitly granted), but may themselves lead to conflicting results. Interestingly, he reaches this conclusion on the basis of a discussion of AB:AB conflicts. The same would apply then, *a fortiori*, to the far more difficult AB:AC conflicts. See Erich Vranes, '*Lex Superior, Lex Specialis, Lex Posterior* – Zur Rechtsnatur der "Konfliktlösungsregeln"', *Zeitschrift für ausländisches öffentliches Recht und Völkerrecht*, 65 (2005), 391–405.

often boils down to a political decision which commitment to honour.[11] Many, however, deplore this, and therefore aim to narrow down the possible scope of application of the principle of political decision. Mus, for example, while accepting that some treaty conflicts are ultimately unresolvable, urges states to be careful when concluding treaties: 'states should take into account other treaties to which they are a party.'[12] He also suggests, somewhat implausibly perhaps, that the principle of political decision is a general principle of law.[13] While this suggestion that the principle is a legal principle may seem a matter of mere semantics, it may also seem that by claiming the principle as legally ordained, he implicitly presumes limits to its applicability and thus narrows its scope of application.[14]

Sadat-Akhavi also follows Zuleeg, and concludes that 'when a State is unable to comply with its obligations towards two different States under two treaties, it is free to conform with either of the treaties.'[15] Still, if only in order to mitigate unpleasant practicalities (and in order, quite possibly, to avoid 'an embarrassing situation'[16]) he posits the maxim *lex posterior derogat priori* as a general rule for the solution of treaty conflicts. The *lex posterior* rule, he suggests, derives its importance from being a 'system rule'; a rule necessary for the smooth functioning of the legal system. After all, the *lex posterior* rule 'make[s] it possible for a legal system to change'.[17] In addition, he finds that in limited circumstances, other rules may also play a role, such as the 'principle of the more favorable provision'[18] or the 'principle of maximum effectiveness'.[19]

---

[11] Writing during the drafting of the Vienna Convention, Salmon already despaired that 'la question est en droit international dominée par la politique'. See Salmon, 'Les antinomies en droit international public', p. 319.

[12] See Jan B. Mus, 'Conflicts between Treaties in International Law', 45 *Netherlands International Law Review*, 45 (1998), 208–232, p. 227.

[13] Zuleeg made no such claim, but merely stated that such a principle is inherent ('angemessen') in a legal order such as international law with its horizontal ordering of equal legislators. See Zuleeg, 'Vertragskonkurrenz', p. 267. Elsewhere, Mus stays closer to Zuleeg's text, and does not explicitly speak of a legal principle. See Mus, *Verdragsconflicten voor de Nederlandse rechter* (Zwolle: Tjeenk Willink, 1996), p. 62. It is also highly doubtful whether Dworkin, the leading legal theorist on principles, would recognise the principle of political decision as a legal principle; see Dworkin, *Taking Rights Seriously*.

[14] Indeed, others suggest that the principle of political decision implies that the law is 'stepping back'. So, e.g., Karl, 'Treaties, Conflicts between', p. 938.

[15] See Sadat-Akhavi, *Methods of Resolving Conflicts*, p. 66.   [16] *Ibid.*, p. 1.

[17] *Ibid.*, p. 211. The writing contains an almost Freudian typo, referring as it does to *lex posterior derogat posterior*.

[18] *Ibid.*, pp. 213–32.   [19] *Ibid.*, pp. 240–4.

While those additional principles will typically evoke interpretation issues (how to figure out which provision is the more favourable, and for whom it is favourable), the reasoning as far as the *lex posterior* rule goes fails to convince. As much as legal systems may need rules relating to change, they also need rules (which we might call 'system rules') to guarantee stability: to favour change over stability is a respectable political position, but is not something that can easily be argued as a matter of law. Indeed, this has been the problem when drafting the Vienna Convention's provisions on treaty conflict: it turned out to be impossible to make that choice in a neutral manner. Moreover, change may not always be change for the better: that too is a matter of political judgment. In short, Sadat-Akhavi presumes a conception of historical progress in international affairs; that presumption, however, is untenable.

For Wilting, the principle of political decision is activated once multilateral treaties cannot be bilateralised: in other words, with what Fitzmaurice referred to as integral and interdependent treaties. For Wilting, the divisibility of multilateral treaties is the premise underlying article 30 of the Vienna Convention; with bilateral bundles of rights and obligations, article 30, paragraph 4 may be able to solve conflicts.[20] With integral and interdependent treaties, however, this will not work, with the result that with those treaties, it remains to be seen whether another solution can be found. While generally sympathetic to giving priority to integral and interdependent treaties, he does observe that such a solution is of little help when it concerns a conflict between different integral or interdependent treaties.[21] Here, though, a survey of practice reveals that provisions in treaties themselves, as well as the concretisation of norms by means of interpretation by judicial or quasi-judicial organs, have the result of limiting the number of conflicts.[22]

Wolfrum and Matz are reluctant to embrace the principle of political decision, yet do observe that the law of treaties has little to offer by way of solutions. Instead of concentrating on the law of treaties or the law of responsibility, however, they focus on the creation of coordination mechanisms: the creation of institutions and fora where treaty conflicts can be discussed, mitigated, perhaps even settled. The one limit to their approach (other than the practical one that such institutions might end up reproducing the same conflict) is that their study is limited to treaty conflict in the sphere of environmental protection and here, *ex hypothesi*,

---

[20] See Wilting, *Vertragskonkurrenz im Völkerrecht*, pp. 99–107.   [21] *Ibid.*, p. 111.
[22] *Ibid.*, pp. 233–4.

most participants will at least share basic assumptions about the values at issue. This leaves unaddressed, however, the issue how to solve conflicts between different sets of values: between trade norms and environmental norms, or environmental norms and human rights norms. If coordination mechanisms within a distinct regime might be conceivable, they might be more difficult to realise across different regimes.[23]

Borgen,[24] finally, while acknowledging that treaty conflicts can never be fully eliminated, places great stock in interpretative devices and, in particular, a system of assurances, allowing for the possibility that states, when they observe that their partners are about to enter into a conflicting engagement, may ask assurances that no violation of the earlier treaty is intended or will result.[25]

There is room for such an approach, so Borgen suggests in part (and not without ambivalence), because article 30 only relates to treaties covering the same subject matter which, moreover, is itself a phrase that might have to be construed narrowly. As a result, article 30 does not cover cases of overlap between treaties dealing with different issues (e.g., conflicts between trade agreements and environmental agreements), leaving room for other devices, such as interpretation or a system of assurances, to be utilised.[26]

It is doubtful, however, whether a narrow construction of the scope of article 30 is all that plausible to begin with. Such a conception finds no support in the drafting history of article 30 and, moreover, makes fairly little sense in any case. Surely, the drafters could not have intended to leave the important category of overlapping commitments in treaties relating to different subject matters completely out of the scope of the Vienna Convention, and merely to satisfy themselves with an article that would not even aspire to help resolve conflicts between overlapping commitments.[27]

---

[23] See Wolfrum and Matz, *Conflicts in International Environmental Law.*

[24] See Christopher J. Borgen, 'Resolving Treaty Conflicts', *George Washington International Law Review*, 37 (2005), 573–648.

[25] *Ibid.*, esp. p. 640.

[26] His ambivalence on this point resides in the circumstance that while he thinks a narrow construction of article 30's scope is demanded by the Vienna Convention, he himself would feel such a narrow reading less than ideal. See, e.g., *ibid.*, p. 636.

[27] Moreover, it might be based on reading too much in the *lex posterior* solution suggested by article 30 VCLT. If article 30 would wholeheartedly embrace the *lex posterior* approach, then Borgen does have a point in suggesting that article 30 would 'not be well calibrated' (*ibid.*, p. 603): it would mean, after all, that an earlier human rights agreement could be set aside by a later trade agreement – and that is conclusion few would accept without more. It is however arguable that the *lex posterior* is not all that clearly embraced with respect

A different option: hierarchy?

In his doctoral dissertation, Dutch lawyer Jan Mus, while accepting (as noted above) the principle of political decision as a general matter, nonetheless suggests, carefully, that there might be one exception.[28] Basing himself on Dutch case-law in particular, he observes that, on occasion, Dutch courts seem to have given priority to human rights treaties; while he is not particularly convinced of a hierarchy of norms in international law,[29] he does make an effort to supply the possible reasoning behind this judicial attitude.

The starting point would be the circumstance that article 30 VCLT refers to article 103 UN Charter, which claims priority for obligations arising under the UN Charter. Human rights would find their basis, so the argument could continue, in articles 55 and 56 of the UN Charter, and thereby come within the scope of article 103 UN Charter. This reasoning could be bolstered by reference to two other potential factors. One of these is that human rights may typically be characterised as having an *erga omnes* character; this would, if taken seriously, elevate them over ordinary norms. Second, article 60, paragraph 5 VCLT creates a separate position for treaties 'of a humanitarian character', which would also seem to elevate human rights treaties over others.[30]

Mus himself, as noted, did not seem too convinced, and for good reason.[31] The problem is, after all, that inasmuch as human rights norms derive from the UN Charter (itself a fairly empty proposition), so do many other norms. Article 55 UN Charter holds that the UN shall promote such things as higher standards of living and economic and social progress; now there is something trade aficionados could point to as elevating trade norms over anything else. The UN shall, following the same article,

---

to the really difficult cases that article 30(4) addresses. Still, Sinclair offers some support for a narrow interpretation of the notion of 'same subject-matter' but only, so it seems, to prevent general treaties from overruling more specific ones. See Sinclair, *The Vienna Convention*, p. 98.

[28] See generally Mus, 'Verdragsconflicten'.   [29] *Ibid.*, pp. 78–82.

[30] *Ibid.*, p. 201. Some have listed this provision as an example of the growing influence of human rights on the development of international law. See Theodor Meron, *The Humanization of International Law* (Leiden: Martinus Nijhoff, 2005).

[31] Fitzmaurice and Elias also make a hierarchy argument (among environmental treaties), positing notions such as the common heritage of mankind, and agreements giving effect thereto, as having 'a different (higher) status' than other agreements. Later, though, they downplay those notions, holding 'that they could be useful in resolving conflicts between treaties as aids to interpretation, regardless of their substantive legal status'. See Fitzmaurice and Elias, *Contemporary Issues*, pp. 341, 345.

promote the solution of health problems: surely this would do much to boost the status of environmental norms, and one could argue that disarmament too contributes to the solution of health problems although, admittedly, the ICJ refused to go this far in its opinion on the use of nuclear weapons during armed conflict.[32] In short, reliance on articles 55 and 56 of the UN Charter does not substantiate the elevated status of human right norms alone, but would apply equally to a fair amount of other values. Surely, one could even capture extradition treaties under the notion of 'solutions of international . . . social . . . problems' (in terms of article 55 UN Charter); and if that is so, than pretty much all norms can boast some form of UN pedigree and thus come under the ambit of article 103 UN Charter.

In addition, it is generally recognised that articles 55 and 56 of the UN Charter are not themselves directly creative of rights or obligations. Article 55 UN Charter suggests a number of values that the UN 'shall promote', with article 56 UN Charter merely adding that the UN's member states shall work together with the organisation in promoting those values. It does not follow, however, that those values themselves can somehow be considered as 'obligations under the [UN] Charter', in the words of article 103 UN Charter. At best, the duty to cooperate may qualify as such, but not the substantive values themselves.

Likewise, the references to *erga omnes* obligations and article 60 can be countered. The notion of *erga omnes* obligations, as the ICJ found out in its 1971 *Namibia opinion*,[33] cannot be applied coherently while simultaneously adhering to the *pacta tertiis* rule;[34] and, surely, the fact that article 60, paragraph 5 VCLT is the only provision in the entire Vienna Convention singling out treaties of a humanitarian character can also be taken to mean, *a contrario*, that the distinction was never contemplated as applying to other provisions of the Vienna Conventions.[35]

---

[32] See *Legality of the Use by a State of Nuclear Weapons in Armed Conflict*, advisory opinion [1996] *ICJ Reports* 66, para. 26 (suggesting that health and disarmament are tasks given to different actors within the broader UN system).

[33] See *Legal Consequences for States of the Continued Presence of South Africa in Namibia (South West Africa) Notwithstanding Security Council Resolution 276* (1970), advisory opinion [1971] ICJ Reports 9.

[34] See Jan Klabbers, 'The Scope of International Law: *Erga Omnes* Obligations and the Turn to Morality', in Matti Tupamäki (ed.), *Liber Amicorum Bengt Broms* (Helsinki: Finnish ILA Branch, 1999), pp. 149–79.

[35] The drafting history of article 60, paragraph 5, bears this out: paragraph 5 was added at the last moment, when the Red Cross realised that allowing breach as a ground for termination

Indeed, authors are generally reluctant to confirm a hierarchy of treaties without more. The starting point, for most, would appear to be the absence of hierarchy, often theorised under reference to the horizontal nature of the international legal order. At best, then, states could intentionally create limited hierarchical relationships, as has been done in article 103 UN Charter, or might result from relations between a basic treaty and subsequent implementing agreements.[36]

On a more theoretical level too, a hierarchy of norms cannot be all too lightly assumed. For one thing, as Hobbes reportedly already knew, positing a higher and a lower order presupposes that the higher order rules over the lower order: that some people rule over other people – and that is something many find unpalatable.[37]

Moreover, various approaches to law all typically posit some form of hierarchy but, equally typically, usually propose that different norms be found at the apex. As Koskenniemi once put it: 'Law continues to set up hierarchies and provide the resources for reversing them.'[38] The naturalist may propose human rights norms at the top, but is unable to respond coherently to the realist who would, instead, propose that power realities find their proper place at the high end of the hierarchy. By the same token, the realist is unable to reply to the positivist positing a formal rather than substantive *Grundnorm*: the snake inevitably ends up biting itself in the tail.[39]

A different option: *lex specialis?*

A more complicated form of dissatisfaction with the principle of political decision is displayed by Joost Pauwelyn. Pauwelyn, a former WTO employee, sets out to demonstrate that, contrary perhaps to popular opinion within the WTO and amongst trade observers, the WTO is not isolated

---

might be counterproductive with treaties of a humanitarian character. See, e.g., Meron, *The Humanization*, pp. 210–11.

[36] A useful example is Seidl-Hohenveldern, 'Hierarchy of Treaties', pp. 7–18.

[37] See Carl Schmitt, *The Concept of the Political* (Chicago: University of Chicago Press, 1996, first published 1932, Schwab trans.), p. 67: 'The rule of a higher order, according to Hobbes, is an empty phrase if it does not signify politically that certain men of this higher order rule over men of a lower order.'

[38] See Martti Koskenniemi, 'Hierarchy in International Law: A Sketch', *European Journal of International Law*, 8 (1997), 566–82.

[39] In a similar vein, see J. H. H. Weiler and Andreas L. Paulus, 'The Structure of Change in International Law or Is There a Hierarchy of Norms in International Law?', *European Journal of International Law*, 8 (1997), 545–65.

from general international law. Instead, on the basis of the reference in its own Dispute Settlement Understanding, WTO panels and its Appellate Body ought to take international law into account whenever warranted. In doing so, however, the question might arise as to how this applicable non-WTO law relates to WTO law itself. In other words, to say that the WTO is not a self-contained system is one thing; it requires another step though to pinpoint the connections between WTO law and other norms, and this becomes particularly urgent in case of treaty conflict.

Pauwelyn rightly suggests that interpretation cannot solve all problems; at best, in his terminology, it can solve 'apparent conflicts'.[40] While covering a lot of ground, Pauwelyn is at his most interesting when positing that perhaps the easiest way to solve certain conflicts is to disregard ('disapply'[41]) article 30 VCLT. This is based on the observation that many multilateral treaties are, as he puts it, of a living nature: their contents evolve constantly through interpretation, application by judicial bodies, or accession of new states. In such a case, it would be silly to insist that the treaty be frozen in time; as a consequence, precisely because of this evolution, it becomes difficult to associate such a treaty with any particular date (the UN Charter, anno 2007, is a different instrument from the one that was signed in 1945), and if that is the case, then one cannot meaningfully use article 30 VCLT which, after all, in speaking of 'successive treaties' and in generally favouring the *lex posterior* approach, presupposes that treaties can be fixed to a certain date.

Instead of thus applying article 30 VCLT, it might be more useful, Pauwelyn suggests, to apply the *lex specialis* maxim: the more special norm ought to prevail over the more general norm.[42] And this finds its rationale, he continues, in the idea that being a special norm, the *lex specialis* 'reflects most closely, precisely and/or [sic] strongly the consent or expression of will of the states in question'.[43] Which is, come to think of it, rather the same as with the *lex posterior* maxim, for this too relates to the most 'current expression of state consent'.[44] In the end, then, substituting *lex specialis* for article 30 VCLT is a methodological shift (applying the speciality factor rather than the time factor), not a principled shift: 'It is not a shift in the underlying legal norm applied to resolve conflict. This norm remains the principle of contractual freedom of states.'[45]

In the end, then, Pauwelyn plays down the relevance of the *lex specialis* maxim: the *lex posterior* of article 30 VCLT should remain the avenue of

---

[40] See Pauwelyn, *Conflict of Norms*, p. 272.   [41] *Ibid.*, p. 378.   [42] *Ibid.*, p. 385.
[43] *Ibid.*, p. 387.   [44] *Ibid.*, p. 388.   [45] *Ibid.*, p. 388.

first resort, if only because that is what the Vienna Convention suggests – the Convention, after all, does not specifically incorporate the *lex specialis* maxim. *Lex specialis* cannot, dixit Pauwelyn, overrule *lex posterior*, but it can take its place with 'living' treaties.[46]

There are good grounds for presuming that Pauwelyn has been a bit over-optimistic concerning the chances of success for his approach. For one thing, one can probably classify all (literally *all*) multilateral treaties as living treaties, constantly evolving through acts of interpretation, judicial application, non-judicial practical application, withdrawal or modification of reservations or interpretive declarations, and accession of new states (or perhaps withdrawal of original parties). Indeed, one can probably say the same of most bilateral treaties, and to the extent that one cannot, those bilateral treaties may well have fallen into *desuetudo* and be considered terminated. If this is plausible, then under Pauwelyn's approach, article 30 VCLT would be a dead letter itself: a treaty provision for which no practical situations could possibly arise because no treaty is frozen in time.

More importantly though, to the extent that the *lex specialis* rule gives effect to the most recent or special expression of state consent, it can only mean state consent between the same states. Pauwelyn's approach is of little avail in case the treaty conflict concerns different obligations towards different parties: he is unable to overcome the *pacta tertiis* rule,[47] and is forced to resort, like so many others, to the principle of political decision, concluding that 'the law of treaties does not provide a solution for AB/AC conflicts in the sense that it does not direct state A to give preference to either one of the two norms.'[48]

Inescapable

It would seem, then, that resort to the principle of political decision is well-nigh inescapable, at least for the really problematic cases, those where A has different commitments towards B and C which cannot be reconciled. Interpretation is of limited help, and is, moreover, as a matter of principle, bound to do injustice towards either B or C – or both. The

---

[46] *Ibid.*, p. 409.
[47] Instead, he claims to have incorporated it, in that his approach rests on three traditional principles: the contractual freedom of states, the *pacta sunt servanda* maxim, and the rule that one cannot create rights or obligations for third parties without their consent. Together, these 'offer a coherent theory on conflict of norms' (*ibid.*, p. 490).
[48] *Ibid.*, p. 427.

flight into hierarchy would seem attractive (not in the least because it would make international law look like a real legal system; given that all real legal systems have a hierarchy of norms) but turns out to be untenable, and Pauwelyn's *lex specialis* solution works only when treaty partners are the same. All that is left, it seems, is the flight into state responsibility: state A should simply choose which of its conflicting commitments to honour, and compensate the partner losing out.

A first-order explanation for this state of affairs (an explanation on the basis of the law of treaties itself) resides in the interplay, as Pauwelyn suggests, between three traditional notions. States are free to contract as they please (barring *jus cogens* considerations, but those are not very interesting here[49]); once a treaty enters into force, it 'is binding upon the parties to it and must be performed by them in good faith', as article 26 VCLT phrases the classic *pacta sunt servanda* norm; and such a treaty can only create rights and obligations for its parties: it is and remains a *res inter alios acta.*[50]

But, contrary to Pauwelyn's suggestion, the three notions together do not make for a coherent theory of treaty conflict; after all, the three together are unable to solve the really problematic cases, precisely because a treaty remains a thing between its parties: it cannot transcend the identity of its parties. And this finds its cause, in turn, in the circumstance that the Vienna Convention conceptualised treaties as instruments, rather than as collections of rights and obligations. As a consequence, nothing of great import could possibly be said about conflicting obligations; the Vienna Convention is simply not equipped to do so. It is no accident, then, that the law of state responsibility (which does think in terms of obligations rather than instruments, but was purposefully left out of the Vienna Convention) has to come to the rescue.

Even so, though, the law of state responsibility is itself inconclusive, in that it does not say which of the partners should be given preference; it leaves this decision to the one party that has brought the problems on to itself. Hence, neither the law of treaties nor the law of state responsibility is capable of providing an abstract answer to the question which treaty

---

[49] A treaty concluded in violation of a *jus cogens* norm would, following article 53 VCLT, be void. Hence, conflict with another treaty could not possibly arise, despite occasional suggestions in the literature to the contrary (see, e.g., Mus, *Verdragsconflicten*).

[50] Likewise, Paolillo suggests that paragraphs 3 and 4 of article 30 VCLT 'ne sont rien d'autre que des formulations de principes traditionnels du droit international tels que les principes *lex posterior derogat priori* et *pacta tertiis nec nocent nec prosunt*'. See Paolillo, 'Convention de Vienne de 1969' (emphasis in original).

prevails in case of conflict. In a brilliant study (often overlooked, curiously enough[51]), Guyora Binder explains why this is the case.[52] Starting from the oft-recognised tension between sovereignty and the very existence of international law, Binder puts forward the idea that treaties can be conceptualised in two different ways. On one view, a treaty creates something like a property right,[53] something that, even if it arises out of the will of states, assumes an objective existence and cannot simply be set aside; on another view, however, it creates a more limited liability. On the first view, a later conflicting treaty would be void; on the second, it would merely lead to, quite literally, a liability.[54]

These two different conceptualisations, in turn, tap into deeper, incompatible, sentiments and, crucially, do so simultaneously: nationalism and internationalism. The treaty as property right has to appeal both to nationalism (it is, after all, an emanation of state consent) and internationalism (it creates something objective). In turn, the treaty as liability does the same thing: it hooks up with internationalism (it is binding) as well as with nationalism (in that it results from state consent). As a result, treaty conflicts are forever caught between two stools: if one insists on the *lex prior*, any dynamics will be lost; however, to give preference to the *lex posterior*, is to invite and reward breaches of the earlier treaty.

Like Pauwelyn, Binder covers a lot of ground. He does so in a mere 130 pages, and it is possible to argue that not all of his argument is necessary to make the central point (there is, for instance, a lengthy excursion into the links with the market economy). Even so, his explanation seems fully plausible: international law cannot solve treaty conflicts without choosing one value over another. Yet, as others have suggested, the condition of international law is precisely that it cannot justify giving priority to some values over others, in the absence of agreement on what constitutes the good life.[55]

---

[51] It is missing from the bibliographies of all the recent monographs on the topic: see Mus, *Verdragsconflicten*; Wilting, *Vertragskonkurrenz*; Sadat-Akhavi, *Methods*; Pauwelyn, *Conflict of Norms*; and Wolfrum and Matz, *Conflicts*.

[52] See Binder, *Treaty Conflict*.

[53] This finds a belated (and somewhat distorted) echo in José E. Alvarez, *International Organizations as Law-Makers* (Oxford: Oxford University Press, 2005), esp. pp. 361–2, arguing that treaties give rise to property rights and, as a consequence, that their breach entails responsibility. Binder might be justified in finding that this conflates the distinction he draws (incidentally: Alvarez does not rely on Binder), as responsibility would not be attached to the property conception but only to the liability conception.

[54] See Binder, *Treaty Conflict*, p. 27.

[55] See generally Koskenniemi, *From Apology to Utopia*.

Avoidance strategies: conflict rules

The obvious question then is, of course, how to overcome the indeterminacy of general international law. One possible answer would be, to resort to specific conflict rules, and provide when concluding treaties how those treaties shall relate to other treaties, and in a sense, article 307 TEC is an emanation thereof.

This too, however, despite being a popular suggestion in the literature,[56] will not always solve conflicts, and again it is precisely where values clash that problems will resurface. A wonderful example is contained in article 22, paragraph 1 of the UN Convention on Biological Diversity. This provides:

> The provisions of this Convention shall not affect the rights and obligations of any Contracting Party deriving from any existing international agreement, except where the exercise of those rights or obligations would cause serious damage or threat to biological diversity.[57]

But that is, of course, precisely where and when the article would be expected to do its work: when there is a serious conflict between another treaty, and the protection of biodiversity. As it is, the Biodiversity Convention actually claims priority in cases of 'serious damage or threat', which raises the obvious question, as ever, why this would apply to parties to treaties in conflict with the Biological Diversity Convention but not to the Biological Diversity Convention itself.[58]

A related document is the Cartagena Protocol on Biosafety, which deals with possible conflicts in its preamble. The Protocol 'shall not be interpreted as implying a change in the rights or obligations of a Party under any existing agreements'; this would suggest that it grants priority to other agreements. However, the next preambular paragraph holds that this 'is not intended to subordinate this Protocol to the other international agreements'. As some commentators have dryly observed, those 'two recitals appear to cancel one another out to some degree'.[59]

---

[56] See, e.g., Mus, 'Conflicts between Treaties', p. 231; a useful overview of such rules is Sadat-Akhavi, *Methods*.

[57] See the 1992 Convention on Biological Diversity, as reproduced in 31 *International Legal Materials* (1992) 818.

[58] For a general discussion see Martti Koskenniemi, 'The Fate of Public International Law: Between Technique and Politics', *Modern Law Review*, 70 (2007), 1–30.

[59] See Mitsuo Matsushita, Thomas J. Schoenbaum and Petros C. Mavroidis, *The World Trade Organization: Law, Practice, and Policy* (Oxford: Oxford University Press, 2003), p. 517.

Other conventions too often leave things undecided. For instance, the International Convention for the Suppression of the Financing of Terrorism provides, in article 21, that nothing in that convention 'shall affect other rights, obligations and responsibilities of States and individuals under international law, in particular the purposes of the Charter of the United Nations, international humanitarian law and other relevant conventions'.[60] The question then presents itself whether humanitarian law applies to terrorism to begin with; and it is this question to which an easy answer would seem to be impossible.[61]

Interestingly, the article dealing with conflicting obligations in the 2005 Council of Europe Convention on the Prevention of Terrorism[62] (article 26) is one of the lengthier articles of that Convention, demonstrating that if a conflict rule is to be taken seriously, it will have to be precise and will have to address various different situations. Its first paragraph specifies that it 'supplements' other treaties, multilateral as well as bilateral, between the parties.

The second paragraph is also limited, in its own terms, to relations between the parties to the Convention, and both grants and establishes priority. It grants priority to existing agreements, but claims priority with respect to later treaties: these must be 'not inconsistent with the Convention's objectives and principles'.

Paragraph 3 does likewise. On the one hand, it gives priority to EU law for those parties that are members of the EU; yet, on the other hand, it also claims priority by positing that the EU rules in question must be 'without prejudice to the object and purpose of the present Convention and without prejudice to its full application with other Parties.'[63]

This, then, suggests strongly that the Convention wants to have its cake and eat it too: it simultaneously claims and grants priority, both generally (in paragraph 2) and with respect to EU law (paragraph 3).

More interesting still are paragraphs 4 and 5, as their scope is not expressly limited to the parties to the Convention itself. Paragraph 4 specifies that: '[N]othing in this Convention shall affect other rights, obligations and responsibilities of a Party and individuals under international

---

[60] Taken from Malcolm Evans (ed.), *Blackstone's International Law Documents*, 7th edn (Oxford: Oxford University Press, 2005), p. 537.

[61] See Jan Klabbers, 'Rebel with a Cause? Terrorists and Humanitarian Law', *European Journal of International Law*, 14 (2003), 299–312.

[62] Text in Evans (ed.), *Documents*, p. 583.

[63] For further discussion of this aspect, see Chapter 9.

law, including international humanitarian law'. This, in turn, may be difficult to reconcile with paragraphs 1–3, unless it builds on the presumption
that other treaties between the parties are excluded and that EU law is not
to be considered part of international law.

Paragraph 5, finally, would seem to give priority to international
humanitarian law and to international law generally, at least as far as
the behaviour of armed forces goes, while positing the Convention as the
fall-back regime.[64] Again, though, the question is begged: to the extent
that other rules of international law apply, the Convention does not. But
that either means that it rarely, if all, applies (there will often be a different
rule applicable), or it means, equally implausibly, that the drafters have
worked on a fairly limited notion of what constitutes international law,
excluding competing treaties.

Article 26, in all its length, is therewith a fine example of the complicated
nature of treaty conflicts: dealing with it will generally entail preferring
one treaty over another, and it is difficult to specify in the abstract which
treaty ought to be ignored. As a result, article 26 has a hard time making
up its mind, and keeps the door wide open for all sorts of arguments.

The general point to make, of course, is that such provisions are of
limited use. Often enough, they merely reproduce the uncertainties that
are associated with treaty conflict, and for precisely the same reason: it
is well-nigh impossible to choose coherently in favour of one value over
another. The Vienna Convention's provisions on treaty conflict suggest as
much, and so do incidental provisions in individual treaties. It is no coincidence then that, under some agreements, coordination mechanisms are
being developed: instead of applying a single legal rule, the idea behind
these is to reach compromises about how to give effect to conflicting
treaties.[65] In other words, treaty conflict is taken as inescapable; instead of
solving the conflicts, the emphasis switches to managing those conflicts
and mitigating their worst effect. And this in turn, while seemingly salu-
tary, does have one considerable drawback: it presumes – and endorses –
the idea that political decisions best be taken by non-political experts or
managers.[66]

---

[64] Paragraph 5 reads: 'The activities of armed forces during an armed conflict, as those terms
are understood under international humanitarian law, which are governed by that law,
are not governed by this Convention, and the activities undertaken by military forces of a
Party in the exercise of their official duties, inasmuch as they are governed by other rules
of international law, are not governed by this Convention.'
[65] See generally Wolfrum and Matz, *Conflicts*.   [66] See also Koskenniemi, 'The Fate'.

Avoidance techniques: judicial escapism

It should come as no surprise that courts are not overly keen on being confronted with a serious treaty conflict, and will do their best to avoid having to deal with such issues. Indeed, there is nothing particularly troubling about this: courts ought to be in tune with the idea that while legal problems may be solved legally, serious treaty conflicts are essentially political conflicts that the law has proved unable to deal with in a plausible manner. As a result, it seems only fitting that courts are generally reluctant to specify their own preference for one solution over the other, and do their best to dissolve the disputes before them.

Courts have developed various techniques for doing so. One of these, and perhaps the most obvious, is to try and reconcile the conflicting norms or, alternatively, try and define any conflict away. Sometimes this is made possible by the provisions in question, which might be sufficiently flexible or open-ended to accommodate such an exercise. Sometimes also the treaties at issue, or one of them, allows for discretion under certain circumstances. Other techniques are different in kind, and may include finding that the court in question has no jurisdiction to address the case before it or, alternatively, that its jurisdiction is limited to only applying one of the two treaties concerned.

A. Using discretion

A relatively straightforward example of judicial use of discretion created by a treaty provision is the well-known *Soering* case before the European Court of Human Rights, involving the fate of a young German awaiting extradition from the UK to the US and the near certainty of this leading to the death penalty and its accompanying death row phenomenon. On the one hand, the existence of an extradition treaty between the US and the UK would seem to warrant extradition; on the other, the UK's commitment to the European Convention on Human Rights might prevent the UK from extraditing Mr Soering, as such extradition could well conflict with the prohibition of inhuman or degrading treatment embodied in article 3 of the European Convention. In the end, the Court could easily escape from dealing with the issue of conflict, as the extradition treaty allowed for discretion in cases involving the death penalty. As long as the UK used this discretion, there was, in other words, no real treaty conflict.[67]

---

[67] See *Soering* v. *United Kingdom* European Court of Human Rights, judgment of 7 July 1989, application no. 14038/88, in *Publications of the ECHR*, vol. 161 (1989), and helpfully

B. Alternative options

Domestic courts too often try hard to escape from having to deal with treaty conflict; and sometimes, like the European Court of Human Rights in *Soering*, they do not have to try all that hard. This is particularly true in many cases involving recognition and enforcement of foreign judgments. A myriad of treaties exist to deal with such issues (both bilateral and multilateral), but these are rarely such as to exclude each other's application: often enough, the courts are left some measure of discretion as to which convention to apply; they can pick and choose, so to speak.

A fairly typical example would be the situation which arose in *X v. Jugendamt Tempelhof, Y, and Z and De Raad voor de Kinderbescherming te Zwolle*, a case making its way through the Dutch courts in the 1980s and ending up before the Dutch High Court (de Hoge Raad).[68] Mr X, residing in the Netherlands, had been ordered by a German court to pay child support to his children living in Germany. The Dutch authorities recognised this decision in accordance with a 1962 bilateral treaty. Mr X objected that, instead, the Hague Child Maintenance Convention of 1958 ought to have been applied. Hence, the decision had been taken on a flawed legal basis, and thus ought to be quashed.

The Dutch courts addressing the issue were unanimous though on this point. The two treaties did not create mutually exclusive regimes, but instead merely created alternatives. As the High Court would eventually put it, the treaties were not creative of 'peremptory self-elimination': the fact that several treaties can be applied does not mean that either of them excludes all alternatives.[69]

C. Non-conflict

Conflicts can also be denied, of course, when they do not exist in the first place. Obvious as this may sound, it does on occasion happen that applicants invoke rights under treaties which are simply not applicable.

reproduced in 98 *International Law Reports* 270. Tellingly, at no point does the Court discuss treaty conflict and how to solve it. The UN Human Rights Committee did not seem to think of the tension between extradition of someone facing the death penalty and the right to life as guaranteed in article 6 of the International Covenant on Civil and Political Rights as a problem involving treaty conflict, suggesting that the existence of the right to life does not result in the illegality of the death penalty. See *Kindler* v. *Canada* (Communication no. 470/1991), decision of 30 July 1993, reproduced in 98 *International Law Reports* 426.

[68] High Court (Hoge Raad), decision of 5 January 1990. See the report in *Netherlands Yearbook of International Law*, 22 (1991), 422.

[69] *Ibid.*, p. 430.

Such a case reached the Dutch High Court in 1988. *In Re P. K.* involved a nationality claim. Mr K., born in Surinam in 1946 with Dutch nationality, had been given Surinamese nationality (and stripped of his Dutch nationality) after Surinam became independent, on the basis of the 1975 Dutch-Surinamese Agreement on Assignment of Nationality. He contended that this violated his liberty of movement as secured in various human rights treaties, but this, so the Court held, was simply not at issue.[70]

D. Declining jurisdiction

Perhaps the most obvious, or most practiced, technique for dealing (or not) with treaty conflicts is to decline jurisdiction. On this line of thought, courts and tribunals typically have a limited jurisdiction, usually limited to applying a specific treaty or set of treaties, and usually with further limitations as well (regarding time, persons or substance matter).

The *Slivenko* case, decided in 2002, provides a fairly straightforward example of a court declining jurisdiction altogether.[71] Here the European Court of Human Rights was confronted with a claim that Latvia's commitments under the European Convention of Human Rights were incompatible with a 1994 treaty between Latvia and Russia on withdrawal of Russian armed forces. This treaty formed the basis of the involuntary removal of some Russian military as well as, initially, their offspring (despite the latter having been born in Latvia). Here the Court could find solace in the circumstance that the removal of one of the applicants preceded the entry into force of the European Convention for Latvia, and thus could easily conclude that the Convention was not yet applicable at the relevant moment, with respect to that applicant.[72] In anticipation, some of the applicants argued that removal from Latvia resulted in a continuing violation of the Convention, but this the Court simply (and

---

[70] *In Re P. K.* High Court (Hoge Raad), the Netherlands, decision of 4 March 1988, as reported in *Netherlands Yearbook of International Law*, 21 (1990), 431.

[71] See *Slivenko* v. *Latvia*, Application no. 48321/99, judgment of 21 January 2002 (admissibility), in *ECHR Reports of Judgments and Decisions* (2002/II) 467.

[72] A similar decision was reached by the European Commission of Human Rights in a case involving a claim involving a refusal to allow an appeal to a conviction for murder decided before the entry into force of the European Convention. See *X* v. *Federal Republic of Germany* application no. 655/59, decision of 3 June 1960, reproduced in 30 *International Law Reports* 326.

inevitably perhaps) chose to ignore, and felt justified in doing so by the applicant's failure to exhaust domestic remedies.[73]

The limited jurisdiction idea works from two angles. Typically, a tribunal's jurisdiction is limited to a specific set of treaties, and typically, its jurisdiction over those treaties is exclusive. In other words, those subject to its jurisdiction are not entitled to submit their disputes elsewhere. While understandable as a method of avoiding forum-shopping, it does on occasion make disputes more difficult to resolve.

The technique of limited jurisdiction is employed with particular relish, or so it seems, within the WTO. The WTO's Dispute Settlement Understanding provides, in article 23, that issues arising under the WTO agreements may only be submitted to the jurisdiction of the WTO and, in article 3, paragraph 2, that the WTO's panels and Appellate Body only have jurisdiction to address issues arising under the WTO agreements. As a result, a case involving conflict between WTO law and, say, a human rights agreement, must be submitted to the WTO which, in turn, is not allowed to apply the human rights norm in question.

Pauwelyn makes a powerful argument to the contrary, suggesting that while the WTO's jurisdiction is limited, this does not mean that it has to limit itself in finding out which law to apply: jurisdiction is analytically distinct from applicable law.[74] That is, generally, a fine point to make, but precisely in the specific context of the WTO it is not entirely persuasive: the WTO's Dispute Settlement Understanding (DSU), after all, specifies that the main task of its dispute settlement system is limited to clarifying the scope of rights and obligations under WTO law, and to preserving those rights and obligations. It would be stretching things, or so it seems, to hold that obligations under, say, a labour agreement somehow assist in preserving rights or obligations under the WTO.

Elsewhere Pauwelyn seems to realise as much, and adds another distinction: between interpretation of a norm, and application of that norm.[75] According to him, a panel's possibilities to interpret WTO law would remain limited (in accordance with the DSU) while the potentially applicable law would still be broad. This, however, fails to convince, for two reasons. The first of these is that the distinction between interpretation of

---

[73] See *Slivenko*, esp. paras. 66–70.   [74] See Pauwelyn, *Conflict of Norms*, esp. pp. 460–63.

[75] See Joost Pauwelyn, 'Bridging Fragmentation and Unity: International Law as a Universe of Inter-connected Islands', *Michigan Journal of International Law*, 25 (2004), 903–16. To be sure, the distinction also appears in Pauwelyn, *Conflict of Norms*, esp. pp. 203–4, but less systematically worked out.

a norm and application of that same norm is highly artificial: any appli-cation involves interpretation.[76] Second, the interpretation/application dichotomy still leaves unresolved the problem that on paper, at least, the DSU seals off WTO law from most other things: the only opening it leaves is by reference to the customary rules of treaty interpretation. It is clearly defensible to argue that this reference to rules of treaty interpretation facil-itates a reading of the WTO that is not in clinical isolation from public international law,[77] but this presupposes that panels have jurisdiction to begin with, and it is this jurisdiction which is limited by the DSU. While Pauwelyn's argument is appealing in that it aims to connect trade law to other branches of international law and thereby aims to protect non-trade interests, it does not manage to overcome the very hurdles it was designed to overcome.

The unique jurisdiction of the WTO is borrowed from the EC Court of Justice which, under the EC Treaty, is designated as the sole guardian of the EC Treaties. The Court of Justice has gone so far as to prohibit a member state from submitting a dispute to a different tribunal in a case involving EC law;[78] and an arbitral tribunal felt compelled, in the 2005 *Iron Rhine* arbitration between the Netherlands and Belgium, to devote quite a bit of attention to defusing the possible impact of EC law on the rights and obligations of the parties.[79]

Courts and the principle of political decision

On occasion, courts may, all avoidance techniques aside, be willing to bite the bullet and actually decide a case involving treaty conflict. One such case is *Charles D. Short* v. *The State of the Netherlands*, a 1990 decision of the Dutch High Court (Hoge Raad).[80] Mr Short, a member of the US

---

[76] On interpretation generally, see Stanley Fish, *Doing What Comes Naturally: Change, Rhetoric, and the Practice of Theory in Literary and Legal Studies* (Oxford: Clarendon Press, 1989).

[77] See Koskenniemi, *Fragmentation*, esp. pp. 87–91. See also Campbell McLachlan, 'The Prin-ciple of Systemic Integration and Article 31(3)(c) of the Vienna Convention', *International and Comparative Law Quarterly*, 54 (2005), 279–320.

[78] See Case C-459/03, *Commission* v. *Ireland (Mox Plant)* [2006] ECR I-4635.

[79] *Arbitration regarding the Iron Rhine ('Ijzeren Rijn') Railway* (Belgium/The Netherlands), award of 24 May 2005. A useful discussion, suggesting that the arbitral tribunal recognised the precedence of the ECJ, is Ineke van Bladel, 'The Iron Rhine Arbitration Case: On the Right Legal Track?', *Hague Justice Journal*, 1 (2006), 5–21.

[80] Decision of 30 March 1990, as reported in *Netherlands Yearbook of International Law*, 22 (1991), 432. For extensive commentary, see Steven J. Lepper, 'Short v. The Kingdom of the

military based in the Netherlands, was accused of (and had pleaded guilty to) murdering and dismembering his wife. Under the 1953 NATO Status of Forces Agreement (SOFA, to which both the US and the Netherlands were parties), there was little doubt that he should be transferred to the US authorities; however, the possibility of the death penalty being awarded in the US meant, quite possibly, a conflict with the European Convention on Human Rights. The Netherlands was not just bound by this Convention itself, but also by its Sixth Protocol, which prohibited the death penalty in all circumstances and which, arguably, takes precedence over the possibility of applying the death penalty left open in article 2 of the European Convention itself.

The Dutch Court of Appeal had attempted to escape from the treaty conflict by feebly arguing that since under the SOFA, the US would have primary jurisdiction over Sergeant Short, therefore he would not be within the jurisdiction of the Dutch authorities and hence outside the protection of the European Convention on Human Rights.[81] However, the High Court rightly made short shrift of this argument, suggesting that the jurisdiction mentioned in the Convention meant something like actual control and responsibility, rather than whether or not someone would be subject to the jurisdiction of a state's court system.

The High Court openly acknowledged the existence of a conflict, and openly acknowledged that there were no legal rules available to solve it. As the Dutch authorities were perfectly willing to hand Mr Short over to the US while relying on the SOFA, the question arose, as the Court put it:

> whether, in view of all the circumstances of the case, when the relevant interests are weighed – including the national and international interests that are involved in the performance of both sets of treaty obligations – the treaty obligation in question constitutes such a serious impediment to the State's compliance with its obligation to the relevant individual that it cannot be required to perform this obligation towards the individual and cannot therefore be ordered to do so.[82]

The way the question was phrased already suggested the prevalence of the individual right not to be exposed to the death penalty, and indeed the

---

Netherlands: Is it Time to Renegotiate the NATO Status of Forces Agreement?', *Vanderbilt Journal of Transnational Law*, 24 (1991), 867–943.

[81] Lepper, 'Short', esp. p. 903, rather endorsed this point of view.

[82] *Short v. Netherlands*, p. 437. Lepper, 'Short', e.g. p. 877, somewhat deceptively construes this weighing of interests as the Court merely invoking a public policy argument.

Court would hold that its balancing 'inevitably' resulted in a decision in favour of Mr Short.[83] The interest of the Netherlands in complying with its SOFA obligations, and the international interest in properly observing the terms of the North Atlantic Alliance, could not begin to match Mr Short's interest in staying alive.

While the Court acknowledged the existence of various interests, it made clear that, in its view, there was no real clash of values involved; the national and international interest were set at such a high level of abstraction that they would apply to each and every agreement. After all, states, and international society at large, have something of an interest in keeping even the most mundane treaties; confronted with a concrete human rights claim, however, such abstract interests would 'inevitably' have to give way.

What is perhaps relevant to note (as in the Sherlock Holmes story about the dog that did not bark) is that the Court did not seek refuge in any principle of political decision. It did not mention this as the general academic construction relating to treaty conflict, nor did it hint more specifically at compensation for the US, or that the Netherlands, by breaching the SOFA, would incur responsibility.

Conclusion

Courts and tribunals, typically, tend to prevent having to decide serious treaty conflicts: they may invoke a lack of jurisdiction, or they may aim to reconcile or balance the various instruments before them. Either way, they are unlikely to meet the conflict head on.

They might find inspiration and support in the work of the International Law Commission. The ILC's Study Group on the Fragmentation of International Law produced its final report in the spring of 2006 and broadly advocates that a 'principle of systemic integration' be taken into account.[84] Starting from the premise that international law is meant not only as an instrument to reach particular specific goals, but also is somehow supposed to serve the general interest, the report notes that giving automatic preference to the values embedded in certain regimes, at the expense of other considerations or values, is bound to

[83] *Short* v. *Netherlands*, p. 437.   [84] See Koskenniemi, Fragmentation, esp. part F.

remain unsatisfactory. In doing so the report adopts a pluralist stand:[85] it works on the basis of the thought there might be irreconcilable political differences between various actors, differences that cannot be bridged by means of a simple appeal to common values. As the Study Group's chair-person has written elsewhere, grasping at values in a world on fire 'is to throw gas on the flames'.[86]

The Study Group's principle of systemic integration may find expres-sion in particular in article 31(3)(c) of the Vienna Convention on the Law of Treaties, which suggests that interpreters of a treaty should take into account 'any relevant rules of international law applicable in the rela-tions between the parties'.[87] It is not always self-evident what precisely this might mean. In particular, the question arises whether the term 'par-ties' refers to the parties to the dispute, or to the treaty to be taken into account.[88]

Nonetheless, the principle of systemic integration finds some support in the case-law of the International Court of Justice, which held in the 2003 *Oil Platforms* case[89] that a bilateral Friendship, Commerce and Navigation Treaty between Iran and the US had been concluded against the back-ground of general international law. Nevertheless, the Court's phrasing is not entirely free from ambiguities. It held that it could not accept that

---

[85] Note, though, that it remains far removed from the curious judicial pluralism advocated by Burke-White: leave things to judges and all will work out fine. See William W. Burke-White, 'International Legal Pluralism', *Michigan Journal of International Law*, 25 (2004), 963–79.

[86] See Koskenniemi, 'The Fate', p. 16.

[87] For a discussion, see Jan Klabbers, 'Reluctant *Grundnormen*: Articles 31(3)(c) and 42 of the Vienna Convention on the Law of Treaties and the Fragmentation of International Law', in Matthew Craven, Malgosia Fitzmaurice and Maria Vogiatzi (eds.), *Time, History and International Law* (Leiden: Martinus Nijhoff, 2007), pp. 141–61. See also McLachlan, 'Systemic Integration'.

[88] The latter, narrower version was endorsed by a WTO panel discussing the legality of an import ban on genetically modified organisms which was justified, in part, by reference to the 1992 Biodiversity Convention and its 2000 Cartagena Protocol. See *European Communities – Measures Affecting the Approval and Marketing of Biotech Prod-ucts*, WT/DS291.292.293, decision of 29 September 2006, para. 7.68. As the US was not a party to either instrument, this argument proved to be of little avail. As the panel put it, 'it is not apparent why a sovereign State would agree to a mandatory rule of treaty interpretation which could have as a consequence that the interpretation of a treaty to which that State is a party is affected by other rules of international law which that State has decided not to accept'. (*Ibid.*, para. 7.71).

[89] See *Case concerning Oil Platforms* (Islamic Republic of Iran v. United States of America) [2003] ICJ Reports 161.

a certain provision of the bilateral FCN treaty 'was intended to operate wholly independently of the relevant rules of international law on the use of force', which by stressing the role of intent could be read as suggesting that it would be possible, intentionally, to deactivate those background rules.[90] Such deactivation, however, would make little sense. In Koskenniemi's graphic language, one 'cannot just take one finger out of [the international legal order] and pretend it is alive. For the finger to work, the whole body must come along'.[91]

So far, I have outlined, in this part of the study, how the conflict rules embodied in the Vienna Convention may not be very effective: they work well when they are least needed, but have serious problems addressing the situation where a state has conflicting commitments towards different treaty partners. That may not be a bad thing, as it opens up a space for politics and civil society involvement, and should not come as a surprise: the theoretical discussion in Chapter 2 suggests that there are good reasons why the law of treaties is incapable of solving or dissolving serious treaty conflicts.

The focus of this study will now come to rest upon the EC, and in particular the case-law of its courts. What will become obvious is that the ECJ (and, to a lesser extent, because less involved) the CFI have yet to internalise the principle of systemic integration. By contrast, many of the cases seem to be based on the thought that the jurisdiction of the EC courts is limited to applying EC law, and nothing else: other considerations, including treaties in force under international law, so it transpires, are given little or no attention. It is to this that I will now turn.

---

[90] *Ibid.*, para. 41. It may also be relevant that as the main rules on the use of force typically are shared by all states (barring discussions on details, however exemplary perhaps) no state could successfully argue that any of those rules are not applicable to it.
[91] See Koskenniemi, 'The Fate', p. 17.

PART III

EC law

6

The EC and anterior treaties

Introduction

There is a variety of ways in which conflicts between treaties and EU law might occur. The most obvious perhaps, and at any rate the only one which the EC Treaty makes provision for, is that obligations under EC law may come into conflict with commitments entered into by the EC's member states before the creation of the EC or, alternatively, before the date they acceded to the EC. This has found regulation in article 307 TEC, which will be discussed extensively in the remainder of this chapter.

Additionally, however, other scenarios are also possible, and in fact do occur. One is where commitments under EC law come into conflict with later commitments entered into by individual member states with third parties, either because those individual member states wittingly ignored Community law (though this is rare, perhaps non-existent) or because of the continuous development of Community law: what may still be legally possible on Monday may turn out to be prohibited on Tuesday. Alternatively, as will be discussed in Chapter 8 in particular, in many cases it is not exactly clear from the outset what Community law still leaves to its member states, and what the Community institutions can lawfully claim as falling within their proper competences.

A third category, somewhat special if technically falling either under anterior or posterior treaties, relates to two treaties that can boast some claim to supremacy: the UN Charter prevails, on its own terms, over commitments under other treaties, and the European Convention on Human Rights, while lacking a supremacy clause, has been described, by its own monitoring court, as being of constitutional character. If taken seriously, it would seem to follow that the ECHR too can claim supremacy, perhaps even supremacy over EC law. Either way, the situations concerning these two treaties is so specific that they cannot meaningfully be discussed under the heading of either anterior or posterior treaties, and thus will be addressed separately, in Chapter 7.

In addition, the category of posterior treaties (i.e. treaties concluded after the creation of the EC, or accession thereto) shows itself in a number of variations. Some of those treaties are concluded by individual member states, with third parties. Some others may be concluded between member states *inter se*. Yet others are concluded by the EC and its member states (as mixed agreements) or by the EC going solo. Still, even in that case a possible conflict between EC law and the EC agreement cannot fully be excluded; as a result, many such treaties contain clauses safeguarding the sanctity of EC law, as will be discussed in Chapter 9.

Article 307

Figuring out what to do with conflicting treaty commitments often will involve a political decision. The EC has taken its own political decision on the matter, in the form of article 307 TEC. Article 307 grants a priority (of sorts) to treaties concluded by its member states with third parties prior to the entry into force of the EC treaties or, for those who joined later, prior to the date of accession. It remains silent, however, on treaties concluded after the entry into force of the EC treaty.

Article 307 (formerly article 234) reads in full:

> The rights and obligations arising from agreements concluded before 1 January 1958 or, for acceding States, before the date of their accession, between one or more Member States on the one hand, and one or more third countries on the other, shall not be affected by the provisions of this Treaty.
>
> To the extent that such agreements are not compatible with this Treaty, the Member State or States concerned shall take all appropriate steps to eliminate the incompatibilities established. Member States shall, where necessary, assist each other to this end and shall, where appropriate, adopt a common attitude.
>
> In applying the agreements referred to in the first paragraph, Member States shall take into account the fact that the advantages accorded under this Treaty by each Member State form an integral part of the establishment of the Community and are thereby inseparably linked with the creation of common institutions, the conferring of powers upon them and the granting of the same advantage by all the other Member States.

In the literature, article 307 is sometimes described as giving effect to a principle of integration in conformity with international law (*Grundsatz der völkerrechtskonformen Integration,* in German).[1] This may be a mite overly generous, but nonetheless does emphasise the point that, as a matter of principle, EC law recognises that it cannot interfere with treaties previously concluded by its member states with third states. After all, as far as the EC is concerned, such treaties are *res inter alios acta*: in particular the first paragraph of article 307 stresses as much.[2]

While the ECSC Treaty never contained a similar provision,[3] the Euratom Treaty, concluded at the same time as the original EEC Treaty, did: its articles 105 and 106 protect anterior treaties of the member states relating to cooperation in the field of nuclear energy, but only to the extent that those treaties have been reported to the Commission and were not intended to circumvent the Euratom treaty, and under the proviso that the Community should ideally substitute itself for its member states as treaty partner.[4]

---

[1] So Petersmann, 'Artikel 234', p. 5728; Koen Lenaerts and Piet van Nuffel, *Constitutional Law of the European Union* (London: Sweet & Maxwell, 1999), p. 561. Elsewhere, Lenaerts describes the protection of the rights of third states as the *ratio legis* of article 307. See Lenaerts and de Smijter, 'The European Union as an Actor', p. 114. Less sanguine is Jean Boulois, 'Le droit des Communautés Européennes dans ses rapports avec le droit international général', *Recueil des Cours,* 235 (1992/IV), 9–80, pp. 67–9 (noting how agreements with non-member states are to be regarded as *res inter alios acta*). See also Koutrakos, *EU International Relations Law,* pp. 301–28 (who ends up discussing article 307 as aiming to achieve a balance between the Community interest and that of third parties).

[2] Dowrick puts it nicely: 'A layman might be forgiven for inferring from the wording of this Article that all prior treaty obligations of member States survived after the coming into operation of the E.E.C.' See Dowrick, 'Overlapping International and European Laws', p. 75.

[3] See MacLeod, Hendry and Hyett, *External Relations,* p. 229.

[4] Article 105 Euratom reads: 'The provisions of this Treaty shall not be invoked so as to prevent the implementation of agreements or contracts concluded before its entry into force by a Member State, a person or an undertaking with a third State, an international organization or a national of a third State where such agreements or contracts have been communicated to the Commission not later than 30 days after the entry into force of this Treaty. Agreements or contracts concluded between the signature and entry into force of this Treaty by a person or an undertaking with a third State, an international organization or a national of a third State shall not, however, be invoked as grounds for failure to implement this Treaty if, in the opinion of the Court of Justice, ruling on an application from the Commission, one of the decisive reasons on the part of either of the parties in concluding the agreement or contract was an intention to evade the provisions of this Treaty.' Article 106 provides: 'Member States which, before the entry into force of this Treaty, have concluded agreements with third States providing for cooperation in the field of nuclear energy shall be required to undertake jointly with the Commission the necessary negotiations with these third States in order to ensure that the rights and obligations arising out of such agreements shall as far as possible be assumed by the Community. Any new agreement ensuing from such negotiations shall require the consent of the Member State

118 TREATY CONFLICT AND THE EUROPEAN UNION

This would seem to suggest that the main point of these provisions is not so much to protect anterior treaties. These would most likely be protected under international law at any rate, as article 30 of the Vienna Convention would be reluctant to apply the *lex posterior* rule in full in cases involving third parties. As a result, it would seem that Article 307 TEC first and foremost aims to strike a balance between the protection of anterior treaties, and the integrity of Europe's integration process or, as some would have it, the protection of the *acquis communautaire*.[5] Articles 105 and 106 Euratom point in this direction, as does the third paragraph of article 307 TEC, with its reference to the interdependence created by the TEC. The aim of this chapter, then, is further to explore this thesis: article 307 does not protect anterior treaties *tout court*,[6] but aims to balance respect for anterior treaties with the demands of Community law.[7]

A similar argument is put forward by Koutrakos, in what is the most detailed recent treatment of article 307. While he starts by saying that the upshot of article 307 is that Community law cannot undermine the time-honoured international law maxim *pacta sunt servanda* (which would thus have international law prevail), he acknowledges that in the end, article 307 'requires member States to find a way of accommodating their international law obligations within the Community legal order'.[8] One way of realising this, he further suggests, is by involving domestic courts and positing a duty to interpret the international agreement at issue as much as possible in harmony with Community law.[9]

The Draft Treaty establishing a Constitution for Europe, signed in December 2004 but, at the time of writing, defeated by means of referenda in France and the Netherlands, would have left the system of article 307

---

or States signatory to the agreements referred to above and the approval of the Council, which shall act by a qualified majority.'

[5] For an analysis in these terms (though not specifically focusing on article 307), see Loïc Azoulai, 'The *Acquis* of the European Union and International Organisations', *European Law Journal*, 11 (2005), 196–231; see also the excellent discussion in Rass Holdgaard, 'Principles of Reception of International Law in Community Law', *Yearbook of European Law*, 25 (2006), 263–314.

[6] For such a position, see Julie M. Grimes, 'Conflicts Between EC Law and International Treaty Obligations: A Case Study of the German Telecommunications Dispute', *Harvard International Law Journal*, 35 (1994), 535–64, p. 564 (article 307 entails 'that prior treaty obligations are not meant to be affected by Community law').

[7] So also Roucounas, who points out that article 307 sees to 'la co-existence d'engagements parallèles et contradictoires'. See Emmanuel Roucounas, 'Engagements Parallèles et Con-tradictoires', *Recueil des Cours*, 206 (1987/VI), 9–288, p. 264 (emphasis omitted).

[8] See Koutrakos, *EU International Relations Law*, p. 304.   [9] *Ibid.*, esp. pp. 309–12.

essentially intact. Article III-435 reproduced almost verbatim the terms of article 307, except for substituting references to the Constitution where article 307 makes reference to the Treaty, and except for some minor drafting changes in the third paragraph. The Reform Treaty, concluded in Lisbon in late 2007, confirms this approach: it does not amend article 307.

Under the Constitution, moreover, no regime was envisaged for dealing with later treaties concluded between member states *inter se* or between member states and third parties, with one exception: under protocol 21, member states were explicitly left with the competence to conclude agreements on external border crossings, 'as long as they respect Union law and other relevant international agreements'.[10] This protocol is fraught with interpretative difficulties. One could argue, first, that since it is the only example where the member states were left with competence, all other fields have been arrogated by the Union. This, however, would not appear to be the most realistic assessment of the drafters' intentions.

Perhaps more to the point is that this was the only example where the constitutional authority (i.e., the member states) made clear that in concluding agreements with third parties, Union law ought to be respected. In other words, it was the only point where Union law explicitly claimed supremacy over later agreements concluded by or between member states, and that provides some food for thought.[11]

The 2007 Reform Treaty adds a few documents, mainly concerning security and defence, confirming that EU law shall not affect the obligations of the member states under the North Atlantic Treaty or under the United Nations Charter.[12] Highly intriguing also is article 6, paragraph 10 of the Acts relating to the last two rounds of accessions (2004 and 2007), which is reminiscent of paragraph 2 of article 307 but not of paragraph 1 of that article. The Act of Accession relating to the accession of ten new member states in 2004 reads, in article 6, paragraph 10:

---

[10] See Protocol 21, on External Relations of the Member States with Regard to the Crossing of External Borders. An earlier version was adopted at Amsterdam, referring to respect for Community law rather than Union law. The 2007 Reform Treaty leaves the Protocol substantially unaffected.

[11] A more modest provision is article I-40, para. 5, urging member states to consult with each other before taking unilateral action in foreign and security policy. Article 16 TEU already states much the same, but without the reference to unilateral action.

[12] See the Protocol on Permanent Structural Cooperation Established by Article 28A of the Treaty on European Union (preamble and article 2(d)), as well as Declarations 13 and 14 of the Final Act.

> To the extent that agreements between one or more of the new Member States on the one hand, and one or more third countries on the other, are not compatible with the obligations arising from this Act, the new Member State shall take all appropriate steps to eliminate the incompatibilities established.[13]

This adds fodder to the proposition that the Community's main interest resides not so much with the protection of the legal rights of third parties, but rather with fencing off Community law from international law, especially perhaps in light of the circumstance that the earlier Acts of Accession did not go quite this far: they merely provided a *renvoi* to article 307.[14]

Still, the main relevant provision to be found in the EC Treaty is article 307. Article 307 raises a number of legal questions: What exactly is the scope of the protection offered by its first paragraph? Who is protected by paragraph 1? What does the term 'all appropriate steps' in the second paragraph mean? Many of these issues have been clarified (or at least addressed) by the Court of Justice.[15]

Setting the standard: *Commission* v. *Italy*

On one reading, article 307 TEC could be interpreted as simply giving priority to anterior treaties over the later EC Treaty,[16] even to the extent that such anterior treaties would have to be applied between member states *inter se*, as long as the treaties concerned would also count non-members among their parties. This was the argument made by Italy in the first case to invoke article 307 TEC (article 234, as it then was) before the Court of Justice.

In this case,[17] Italy applied a fixed customs duty on radio tubes and valves coming from other member states, and used this sum as the basis

---

[13] See the Act of Accession of the Czech Republic and nine other states, *Official Journal*, 23 September 2003, L 236. See also the Act of Accession of Bulgaria and Romania, *Official Journal*, 21 June 2005, L 157. In both cases it concerns article 6(10).
[14] See, e.g., the Act concerning the conditions of accession of Norway, Austria, Finland and Sweden, *Official Journal*, 29 August 1994, C 241.
[15] Less interesting for present purposes is the procedural question whether article 307 can be invoked on appeal if it was not relied on in earlier proceedings. The ECJ answered in the negative in Case C-355/04 P, *Segi and others* v. *Council* [2007] ECR I-1657, paras. 29–32.
[16] But only in relation to states that are parties to the anterior treaty at the relevant time: see Joined Cases C-364/95 and C-365/95, *T. Port GmbH & Co.* v. *Hauptzollamt Hamburg-Jonas* [1998] ECR I-1023.
[17] See Case 10/61, *Commission* v. *Italy* [1961] ECR 1.

for calculating later reductions. Italy claimed that this was proper, as this was the duty agreed to under the General Agreement on Tariffs and Trade (GATT) prior to the conclusion of the EC Treaty. In other words, the issue arose whether Italy could rely on GATT obligations in its relations with other member states of the EC, all of them parties to GATT.[18]

Advocate-General Lagrange, following the Commission's argumentation, would set the tone both for the Court's eventual decision and for the way in which article 307 TEC has since been approached. From the injunction in the second paragraph that member states should take steps to eliminate incompatibilities, he derived the proposition that, where a right of the member state under such an anterior treaty was concerned, the most appropriate step would simply be to renounce the right in question. Where, instead, a right of the third party or an obligation of the EC member state, would be concerned, the advocate-general became a bit less precise: the member state would 'have to resort to the procedures necessary to eradicate the incompatibility by lawful means'.[19]

Those are interesting words, for two reasons. One is that the Advocate-General worked on the basis of the assumption that a treaty can typically be divided into bundles of rights and corresponding obligations between the parties. Otherwise, it would have made fairly little sense to distinguish between the rights of member states, and their obligations, or the rights of third parties.[20] The problem, however, is that this particular conception excludes the (growing) class of treaties concluded with a view to the community interest: human rights treaties are often cited as the most conspicuous example of treaties that cannot be conceptualised as bundles of bilateral rights and obligations applicable between states. Instead, many would hold that with a human rights treaty (and likely with environmental and disarmament treaties as well), states commit themselves and create obligations not only towards each other, but also towards their citizens or even towards the world community at large, as is sometimes suggested.[21]

---

[18] Or rather, applying GATT on a provisional basis, in accordance with GATT's Protocol on Provisional Application. GATT would never actually enter into force.

[19] *Commission* v. *Italy*, Advocate-General Lagrange, p. 17.

[20] As a contemporary commentator noted, the eventual decision 'is built upon the assumption that the legal relations created by the earlier agreement are separable into "rights" and "obligations"'. See van Panhuys, 'Conflicts', p. 428.

[21] See, e.g., Bruno Simma, 'From Bilateralism to Community Interest in International Law', *Recueil des Cours*, 250 (1994/VI), 221–384; Matthew Craven, 'Legal Differentiation and the Concept of the Human Rights Treaty in International Law', *European Journal of International Law*, 11 (2000), 489–519; Theodor Meron, *Humanization*.

The second noteworthy aspect of Advocate-General Lagrange's position is that, unwittingly perhaps, he seemed to presuppose the prevalence of the EC Treaty. If a right pertaining to a member state under an external agreement needs to be eliminated, the result will be that the contractual balance created under that external agreement will be upset. That might pose no problems under a bilateral treaty; indeed, the treaty partner might be happy that the EC member renounces its right while the partner's right remains intact. This happiness is less obvious, though, with multilateral treaties. Treaties may fairly typically be based on mutual concessions, and with multilateral treaties those mutual concessions would be captured in a complex web of obligations. The balance thus struck will inevitably be upset as soon as one of the parties renounces a right pertaining to it: the result will not be that all parties are automatically better off and thus willing to accept the renunciation; the result, instead, is that some may have made greater sacrifices than others on the point now being renounced, and will thus have a legitimate grief even if, technically, their rights remain intact. This, in turn, is necessarily based on the idea that the EC Treaty is somehow superior to the anterior treaty; otherwise, there would be no valid ground for supposing that EC members have to renounce their rights under the anterior treaty. Why not, instead, the other way around? Why not have the member state renounce its rights under the EC Treaty?

The Court would follow the Commission's and Advocate-General Lagrange's position. It cited the Commission's position (under which the word 'rights' in article 307 refers solely to the rights of third parties, whereas the term 'obligations' refers to the obligations of EC member states), and held this position to be 'well-founded'.[22] It also added a more general consideration, one which indeed spells out what was implicit in Advocate-General Lagrange's approach: 'In fact, in matters governed by the EEC Treaty, that Treaty takes precedence over agreements concluded between Member States before its entry into force, including agreements made within the framework of GATT'.[23]

This then was to become the standard position. Article 307 TEC has a fairly limited protective role: it protects only the rights of third parties under anterior treaties; the rights of member states themselves under such treaties are to be considered renounced by virtue of concluding the EC Treaty. And while the Court remained silent on the obligation to terminate agreements incompatible with EC law (it could afford to remain silent,

---

[22] *Commission* v. *Italy*, p. 10.   [23] *Ibid.*

given the facts of the case), it is nonetheless clear that at the very least, member states would be expected to do their utmost.

The doctrine established in *Commission* v. *Italy* is an understandable compromise between the exigencies of the common market and the protection of the interests of third parties, but it is important to realise that it is a compromise: it does not completely protect the position of third parties, and may be difficult to apply with treaties aiming to protect the community interest. Moreover, it is useful to remember that, ultimately, *Commission* v. *Italy* was relatively easy case: Italy was claiming the applicability of an anterior treaty in its relations with other EC members. There were, in other words, no concrete rights of third parties at stake; at worst, those third parties could complain that Italy treated others (i.e., its EC partners) more favourably than those third parties.

There is another interesting aspect of *Commission* v. *Italy* that must be addressed. At first sight, the Court seemed perfectly happy to consider itself as merely applying general international law. The Commission had argued (as it is phrased in the judgment) that under general international law, the *lex posterior* rule applies: 'by assuming a new obligation which is incompatible with rights held under a prior treaty a State *ipso facto* gives up the exercise of these rights to the extent necessary for the performance of its new obligations'.[24] The Court then concludes, without too much argument, that the Commission's position is 'well founded',[25] but its subsequent words are a bit ambivalent.

Those subsequent words hold that 'in matters governed by the EEC Treaty, that Treaty takes precedence over agreements concluded between Member States before its entry into force, including agreements made within the framework of GATT'.[26] The ambivalence resides in the words 'in matters governed by the EEC Treaty'. On one reading, this could simply mean that whenever the EEC Treaty would be applicable, international law says that it should overrule earlier agreements. This is what, in effect, the Commission, argued, and what the Court, at first sight, seemed to endorse.

However, taken seriously, this analysis could become vulnerable itself in later years. For if the matter is solely governed by international law, and international law simply upholds the *lex posterior* rule, then it would follow that the EEC Treaty itself can also be superseded by a later treaty. Under such a scenario, it would be perfectly possible for two member states to

---

[24] *Ibid.*   [25] *Ibid.*   [26] *Ibid.*

conclude a treaty departing from Community law and point to the validity and supremacy of the later in time under international law. It is uncertain whether the Court was already aware of this risk in *Commission* v. *Italy*, but it is possible to argue that the reference to 'matters governed by the EEC Treaty' was intended to place that Treaty at the apex. On this reading, the supremacy of EC law over an earlier agreement would not just follow from international law, but also from EC law itself.

As noted, it is uncertain whether the Court actually intended to make this point (and if so, it could have spelled it out more clearly), but there is something in Advocate-General Lagrange's opinion which suggests that the Court may have been well aware of the risk. Lagrange agreed that the first paragraph of article 307 merely restated an established rule of international law, suggesting that this was done as much for psychological effect as anything else. The real heart of article 307, Lagrange suggested, was to be found in the second paragraph, which lays down an obligation on the member states to eliminate any incompatibilities with an earlier agreement. This obligation now clearly stems from EC law itself, and informs the application of the opening paragraph.

Indeed, while it would be possible that the resulting situation would make a distinction between member states and non-member states (leading, e.g., to a distortion of competition), this was, as Lagrange argued, merely the consequence of there being an EEC Treaty to begin with. And, perhaps in order to dispel any remaining doubts, Lagrange pointed out that between themselves, the member states of the EC can do as they please, provided their behaviour does not negatively affect the rights of third states under anterior agreements.[27]

Much of the subsequent case-law follows the Court's decision in *Commission* v. *Italy*, with only minor variations.[28] And such variations as exist are usually, and typically, the result of diverging circumstances. As already noted, important though *Commission* v. *Italy* was (and is), it decided a

---

[27] *Ibid.*, p. 18.

[28] Van Panhuys, 'Conflicts', pp. 428–31, reports some political debate concerning a regulation which might have come to affect the Mannheim Act on navigation on the river Rhine (to which also Switzerland, a non-EC member, is a party, and which goes back to the nineteenth century). Apparently, some governments defended the opinion that the Act was protected under article 307, possibly based on a conception of the Act as multipolar. This has never come before the ECJ, although the obligation to cooperate (in article 307) helped justify the participation of a number of member states, alongside the Community, in establishing a Fund covering amongst other things shipping on the Rhine. See Opinion 1/76 *(Laying-up Fund)* [1977] ECR 754, para. 7.

relatively easy case where no concrete rights of third parties were being threatened, and where the underlying anterior agreement (tariff bindings under the General Agreement on Tariffs and Trade) could fairly easily be conceptualised as a bundle of bilateral agreements.[29]

While the second part of this chapter will explore the second paragraph of article 307 in greater detail, the remainder of this first part will be devoted to the study of those various different circumstances. Several different situations can be distinguished: at issue may be an anterior treaty concluded between member states *inter se*; or an anterior treaty involving concrete rights of a third party; or an anterior treaty involving a newer member state; or an anterior treaty concluded with the common interest in mind and not reducible to sets of bilateral rights and obligations (I shall typically refer to such treaties as 'multipolar'). All these situations are distinct, but they do raise at least one common problem: the time factor. How to determine when exactly a treaty has been concluded for purposes of the treatment of anterior treaties?

Application between member states *inter se*

Since *Commission* v. *Italy*, the case-law is unanimous in holding that the provisions of an anterior treaty cannot be invoked in relations between member states *inter se*, even if the treaty concerned also has non-members amongst its parties.[30] In the interesting *Matteucci* case,[31] the Court went a step further or, more accurately perhaps, outlined how far this position goes really.

In 1956, Belgium and Germany had concluded a cultural cooperation agreement providing, amongst other things, for a scheme of scholarships for each other's nationals. Ms Matteucci, living and working in Belgium but of French nationality, was not deemed eligible, and objected to that

---

[29] The *Italy* v. *Commission* construction, to once more quote van Panhuys, 'can only be applied where the rights and duties arising under the prior treaty are separable'. van Panhuys, 'Conflicts', p. 448.

[30] See in particular Cases 34/79, *Regina* v. *Henn and Darby* [1979] ECR 3795 (discussed below); 121/85, *Conegate* v. *HM Customs and Excise* [1986] ECR 1007; 286/86, *Ministère Public* v. *Gérard Deserbais* [1988] ECR 4907 (para. 18); Joined Cases C-241/91 P and C-242/91 P, *RTE and ITP* v. *Commission* [1995] ECR I-743 (para. 84); C-147/03, *Commission* v. *Austria* [2005] ECR I-5969, para. 73. Less explicitly, also C-324/95, *Evans Medical and MacFarlan Smith* [1995] ECR I-563. The same applies presumably also to Joined Cases 56/64 and 58/64, *Consten & Grundig* v. *Commission* [1966] ECR 299, at p. 346 (ex-article 234 not applicable in proceedings).

[31] Case 235/87, *Matteucci* v. *Communauté Francaise of Belgium* [1988] ECR 5589.

decision, claiming that it was irreconcilable with her rights as a worker under the EC Treaty. The Court agreed, holding in effect that even though the EC treaty did not confer any powers in the cultural field to the EC, nonetheless EC law was superior to the bilateral 1956 agreement. The Court made clear that article 307 did not apply to anterior bilateral agreements concluded solely between member states[32] and reached the position that 'the application of Community law cannot be precluded on the ground that it would affect the implementation of a cultural agreement between two Member States'.[33]

As so often, the Court provided little or no argument.[34] Perhaps the most obvious reasoning could have been that when concluding the EC treaty, the member states abrogated, implicitly or explicitly, all bilateral agreements between them which would be incompatible with EC law.[35] This, however, is a tall order to prove. While it might be plausible with respect to issues and treaties over which the EC was given competences, it would be less obvious, and less plausible, with regard to those walks of life left outside the reach of the EC. On such topics, one might just as easily have concluded, as France did, that 'the pursuit of legitimate objectives of bilateral cooperation in [the cultural] sphere may not be frustrated by the development of Community law'.[36]

Even though the Court was plainly correct in noting that a bilateral agreement concluded solely between member states would fall outside the scope of article 307, its approach is nonetheless characteristic: in case of conflict, it simply places EC law as hierarchically superior, without bothering to add much argument or to analyse the situation in the light of international law.

Application involving actual, non-abstract rights

Since *Commission* v. *Italy* merely concerned the position of third parties in the abstract, it must be distinguished from situations where actual,

---

[32] *Ibid.*, para. 21.   [33] *Ibid.*, para. 14.

[34] Neither did Advocate-General Lord Slynn, merely claiming that even though topics might not be specifically referred to in the Treaty, provisions thereof may still affect such topics. See *ibid.*, Advocate-General Lord Slynn, p. 5603.

[35] This seems to be the basis of the decision in Case C-475/93, *Thévenon* v. *Landesversicherungsanstalt Rheinland-Pfalz* [1995] ECR I-3813 (suggesting that an EC regulation on social security has come to replace a 1950 treaty between France and Germany).

[36] *Matteuci*, para. 13.

concrete rights of third parties are at issue. The leading case involving actually existing rights of third parties and their nationals was decided in 1980: *Attorney General* v. *Burgoa*.[37] Mr Burgoa was the master of a Spanish fishing vessel prosecuted in Ireland for fishing within Irish waters. The scope of Irish waters was determined by Community law following Ireland's accession to the EC, but Mr Burgoa claimed antecedent rights under the 1964 London Fisheries Convention, to which both Spain and Ireland were parties.[38] This Convention would be protected, so Mr Burgoa argued, under article 307 TEC (article 234 TEC, as it was at the time). The London Convention allowed for the continuation of traditional fishing rights in the so-called Contiguous Zone; being caught twenty miles off the baseline, he was well within his rights under the Convention, even though Ireland (following EC law) had proclaimed a so-called Exclusive Economic Zone of 200 miles.

Both the Court and Advocate-General Capotorti disagreed with Mr Burgoa, both suggesting that the 1964 London Convention was no longer in force.[39] Interestingly, however, they radically differed on how it had ceased to be in force. Advocate-General Capotorti launched the thesis that ever since the London Convention had been concluded in 1964, the law of the sea had undergone rapid developments, in particular as manifested by the emergence of the concept of the Exclusive Economic Zone. This had resulted in the formation of a new set of rules of customary international law which, so Capotorti suggested, had 'abrogated the rules agreed on in London in 1964'.[40]

This must have seemed too risky a thesis to the Court, knowing very well that to find the existence of a new customary rule of international law would involve a great amount of research and would always be controversial, in particular if the new custom would be expected to have replaced an earlier treaty. Instead, the Court opted for a different avenue, and faintly suggested that, at least as far as Spain was concerned, a new agreement between the Community (succeeding Ireland as treaty partner) and Spain had been concluded. This, however, was not

[37] Case 812/79, *Attorney General* v. *Burgoa* [1980] ECR 2787.
[38] Note that at the relevant time, Spain had not yet joined the EC: it would only do so in 1986.
[39] The Court, incidentally, does not spell this out in so many words, but its analysis (to be discussed below) would seem to suggest that at least as far as Spain was concerned, the London Convention was no longer in force.
[40] *Burgoa*, Advocate-General Capotorti, p. 2818.

unproblematic.[41] True enough, negotiations had taken place, but the resulting agreement would only enter into force in 1981. At the relevant time (10 July 1978, the date Mr Burgoa's vessel had been seized), the agreement had not even been initialed, let alone signed.[42] In the end then, the Court decided the case on the basis of secondary Community law, hinting that Spain had been perfectly happy with the development of an interim regime by the Community, and had fully cooperated.[43]

One may entertain serious doubts about the Court's reasoning. Surely, to consider an agreement in force to be abrogated by what is at best an example of informal cooperation preceding any expressions of consent to be bound runs the risk both of not taking the sanctity of existing treaties too seriously, as well as making a mockery of such acts as signature and ratification. That raises the question why the Court was so keen to uphold the relevant Community legislation in the face of the 1964 London Convention, and the only plausible answer would seem to be that finding the London Convention to be applicable and able to protect the rights of individual Spanish fishermen[44] might end up undermining the still fragile Community regime on fisheries.

Either way, the Court, even though it did not honour Mr Burgoa's position, made a few important remarks on the interpretation of article 307. First, it confirmed the doctrine earlier set out in *Commission* v. *Italy* and added, for good measure, that the protection afforded to anterior treaties implied that the Community institutions would not make the performance under anterior treaties impossible: article 307 implies 'a

---

[41] Note also that it is difficult to reconcile with the finding, earlier in the judgment, that the London Convention was protected under article 307. If abrogated, it would need no protection. See *Burgoa*, para. 11(c).

[42] The agreement was initialed on 23 September 1978, and signed on 15 April 1980. It entered into force, upon approval by the Community and ratification by Spain, on 22 May 1981.

[43] See *Burgoa*, especially paras. 23 and 24. The same approach was followed in Case 181/80, *Procureur Général près la Cour d'Appèl de Pau and others* v. *José Arbelaiz-Emazabel* [1981] ECR 2961, and Joined Cases 180/80 and 266/80, *José Crujeiras Tome* v. *Procureur de la République* and *Procureur de la République* v. *Anton Yurrita* [1981] ECR 2997. In these cases, the ECJ never once mentioned article 307 (not even its existence) and in the latter it suggested that the Community measures concerned were part of 'the progressive creation of new reciprocal relations between the Community and Spain' (para. 19).

[44] In terms of the London Convention, Mr Burgoa would have been fishing on the high seas. There is no recognition of this in either the judgment or the Advocate-General's opinion, possibly because Burgoa's lawyer invoked the much weaker argument of having rights by analogy. See *Burgoa*, Advocate-General Capotorti, p. 2818.

duty on the part of the institutions of the Community not to impede the performance of the obligations of Member States which stem from a prior agreement'.[45]

Dogmatically more importantly perhaps, the Court also recognised that article 307 would not merely protect the rights of treaty partners, but should also find application with treaties creating rights for individuals. While, sensibly, it held that article 307 would not create direct effect where this would not follow from the treaty itself,[46] nonetheless it did recognise that EC member states might have obligations under an agreement not just to their treaty partners, but to individuals as well.[47] Indeed, it spoke more neutrally of the 'obligations of the Member States' under anterior agreements,[48] rather than of the rights of third states under such agreements.

The Court followed a similar line of reasoning in *Levy*.[49] At issue here was the compatibility of a directive on equal treatment of men and women with a French law prohibiting women from doing night work. The French law, in turn, implemented a 1948 ILO Convention. As in *Burgoa*, the Court sketched how international law had developed, by pointing in particular to the 1979 New York Convention on the Elimination of All Forms of Discrimination against Women and a few later ILO Conventions (including a Convention on night work).[50] Moreover, it strongly hinted that international law recognises the possibility that states abrogate an older treaty by concluding a newer one, as codified in article 59 of the Vienna Convention on the Law of Treaties.[51] However, perhaps in light of some of the comments following *Burgoa*,[52] the Court stopped short of drawing any conclusions as to whether indeed the 1948 ILO Convention

---

[45] *Burgoa*, para. 9.
[46] *Ibid.*, para 10: '. . . cannot have the effect of altering the nature of the rights which may flow from such agreements.' See also Case C-307/99, *OGT Fruchthandelsgesellschaft mbH v. Hauptzollamt Hamburg St-Annen* [2001] ECR I-3159, para. 30; Case T-3/99, *Banatrading GmbH v. Council* [2001] ECR II-2123, para. 78.
[47] *Burgoa*, para. 10: article 307 does not 'adversely affect the rights which individuals may derive . . . .' Similarly, para. 11(b).
[48] *Ibid.*, para 11(a).
[49] Case C-158/91, *Criminal Proceedings against Jean-Claude Levy* [1993] ECR I-4287.
[50] *Ibid.*, para. 18.   [51] *Ibid.*, para. 19.
[52] See, e.g., R.R. Churchill & N.G. Foster, 'European Community Law and Prior Treaty Obligations of Member States: The Spanish Fishermen's Cases', *International and Comparative Law Quarterly*, 36 (1987), 504–24, esp. p. 522 (the idea of an earlier treaty being replaced by a later one was 'incorrectly applied' with incidents happening before the provisional entry into force of the EEC-Spain agreement, in 1980).

had been abrogated: it played this ball back to the referring national court.[53]

Again, the Court and its advocate-general were not in full agreement. Advocate-General Tesauro made a point of noting that, although there were developments which suggested that at some point the 1948 Convention might be considered as taken over by events, nonetheless 'at the material time ILO Convention No 89 had binding force and hence Article 234 [now 307 – JK] of the Treaty was and is applicable to it'.[54] He too, however, would leave the final decision with the referring national court.

Of some theoretical interest is Advocate-General Tesauro's conceptualisation of the sort of rights at issue. Instead of accepting the possibility that an ILO Convention might create individual rights which could find protection under article 307 (as *Burgoa* had, albeit fleetingly perhaps, suggested), Tesauro fell back on the more classic notion that treaties are compacts between states and article 307 merely protects the rights of states. In the case at hand, so he claimed, 'the rights of the contracting parties undeniably consist in ensuring night work for women in industry is prohibited . . .'[55]

Anterior treaties with new member states

The leading case in this category is, perhaps, the 1992 *Exportur* case.[56] In 1973, France and Spain (then still outside the EC) concluded an agreement on protection of designations of origin, article 3 of which provided that certain product names ('Turrón de Alicante' and 'Turrón de Jijona') could, in France, only be used with respect to Spanish products. When the respondent started to use those product names for products made in France, applicant brought proceedings. This provoked an analysis of the EC rules on free movement of goods and the bilateral 1973 Convention.

The Court started, without devoting a lot of words to the matter, from the premise that the provisions of the 1973 Convention could not apply in Franco-Spanish relations if they were found to be incompatible with the

---

[53] See *Levy*, para. 21.   [54] *Ibid.*, Advocate-General Tesauro, para. 9.

[55] *Ibid.*, Advocate-General Tesauro, para 5. It has been suggested that the Advocate-General might have placed greater emphasis on reciprocity in treaty relations than the Court eventually did. For such a suggestion, see Christoph Vedder and Hans-Peter Folz, 'A Survey of Principal Decisions of the European Court of Justice Pertaining to International Law in 1993', *European Journal of International Law*, 5 (1994), 448–63, pp. 460–1.

[56] Case C-3/91, *Exportur SA* v. *LOR SA and Confiserie du Tech* [1992] ECR I-5529.

EC Treaty.[57] It then moved on to analyse the substance of the Convention which, it held, could potentially form an obstacle to intra-Community trade, and found that this obstacle could be justified under reference to the necessity, laid down in article 30 TEC (then article 36), to protect intellectual property rights.

Here then the Court appeared to honour an anterior treaty, even in relations between member states, but appearances can be deceptive. What the Court did, eventually, was to deny that there was any conflict between the terms of the 1973 Convention and EC law, aided by the circumstance that the Community had no legislative powers in the field of intellectual property protection. The 1973 Convention could continue to be applied, but only by virtue of what is now article 30 TEC; not by virtue of article 307 TEC, much less any law of treaties consideration. The basic principle, then, remained the same as in other cases: in case of conflict between EC law and the 1973 Convention, EC law prevails. Advocate-General Lenz quickly explained why: 'This follows from the primacy of Community law'.[58]

Multipolar treaties

The question of whether a treaty would be bipolar or multipolar came up most elaborately in the opinion of Advocate-General Warner in *Henn and Darby*.[59] Messrs Henn and Darby were accused of importing pornographic materials into the UK, and while they maintained that a limitation on the import of pornography amounted to a restriction of the free movement of goods, the Court nevertheless felt that such restriction was justifiable in light of the protection of public morals. As something of an afterthought, the Court had also been asked whether the law on the issue was in any way influenced by two earlier conventions: one on postal traffic, and one dating back to 1923 and dealing with the suppression of traffic in obscene publications. The Court, justifiably,[60] chose the easy way out and, handling the issue in a few brief paragraphs, simply found that there was little chance of conflict between applying the public morals exception of the EC Treaty, and meeting obligations under the 1923 Convention.[61]

The Advocate-General, however, engaged in a deeper analysis of the sort of obligations which the 1923 Convention could create. One possible interpretation, he found, was that the Convention merely created bundles

---

[57] *Ibid.*, para. 8.   [58] *Ibid.*, Advocate-General Lenz, para. 11.   [59] *Henn and Darby*.
[60] The materials had, after all, not been sent by means of postal traffic.
[61] *Henn and Darby*, paras. 26–7.

of bilateral relationships and, thereby, bilateral rights and obligations between the parties. On such a reading, the *Commission* v. *Italy* formula would apply, and a member state would not be allowed, in relations with other member states, to rely on the 1923 Convention, in much the same way as Italy, in *Commission* v. *Italy*, was not allowed to rely on GATT in its dealing with other EC members.[62]

There was, however, a second possible reading, according to Advocate-General Warner. On such an alternative reading, the 1923 Convention was multipolar in nature, creating an interlocking and interdependent network of rights and obligations. On such a reading, non-EC members could be affected by a more liberal intra-EC regime: 'a flourishing trade in obscene material within the Community could prejudice other States' efforts to suppress the traffic in it'.[63] Which of the two interpretations to prefer, however, was a matter of interpretation of the 1923 Convention, and thus best left to the national courts concerned: interpreting a non-EC law instrument such as the 1923 Convention was outside the jurisdiction of the EC Court.[64]

Advocate-General Warner also made a principled point about the other treaty invoked in *Henn and Darby*, the Universal Postal Convention. This is an example of a convention where the basic treaty is not so much amended as simply replaced by a new treaty on a more or less regular basis. The version at issue was concluded in 1974 in Lausanne and entered into force in 1976, replacing the previous Tokyo Convention of 1969, which in turn can be traced back to the original constitutional document of the Universal Postal Union, concluded in 1874.[65] Without much argument, Warner

---

[62] See also *Deserbais* (with respect to application of the 1951 International Convention on the Use of Designations of Origin and Names of Cheeses as between France and Germany).

[63] *Henn and Darby*, Advocate-General Warner, p. 3833.

[64] The same two conventions made an appearance a few years later in *Conegate*. Without having to apply either of them, the Court merely affirmed that at any rate, anterior treaties cannot 'be relied upon in relations between Member States in order to justify restrictions on trade within the Community' (para.25). It is tempting to read this statement, unnecessary as it was for deciding the case at hand, as a belated reply to Advocate-General Warner's speculations on multipolar treaties. The Universal Postal Convention was also mentioned, but not used in any meaningful way, in Joined Cases C-147/97 and C-148/97, *Deutsche Post AG* v. *Gesellschaft für Zahlungssysteme mbH and Citicorp Kartenservice GmbH* [2000] ECR I-825.

[65] A brief discussion of the UPU and the phenomenon of 'serial' treaties more generally is G. W. Maas Geesteranus, 'Recht en praktijk in het verdragenrecht', in E. W. Vierdag and G. W. Maas Geesteranus, *Spanningen tussen recht en praktijk in het verdragenrecht* (Deventer: Kluwer, 1989, Mededelingen Nederlandse Vereniging voor International Recht, No. 99), pp. 89–122.

seemed to endorse the Commission's position that, because the treaty had been renewed in 1974, it could no longer be regarded as having pre-dated the EC (or the UK's accession), even though the relevant provisions had remained identical.[66]

When is a treaty concluded?

Advocate-General Warner's discussion of the time factor refers to a recurring question: when exactly must an agreement be considered as having been concluded? This is an open issue under the law of treaties generally,[67] where there might be a gap between adoption of a text and signature, and even more so between signature, ratification and entry into force.[68]

Before the EC Court the problem appears most of all in respect of 'serial' treaties, treaties that originally may have been concluded prior to the EC Treaty, but which have been amended, revised, or replaced since. The positions will be fairly evident: if an amendment is regarded as, essentially, a new treaty, then chances are that article 307 is not even formally applicable. If, on the other hand, the amendment is regarded as continuing the anterior treaty, there is at least an argument in favour of applying article 307. The Court has been less than generous, and tends to regard amendments, revisions and replacements as so many abrogations of the anterior treaty. This was already visible in Advocate-General Warner's opinion in *Henn and Darby*, and has found some confirmation in later cases.

Where treaties themselves provide that a new version abrogates the previous version, such is no doubt justifiable. Thus, the 1994 WTO Agreement specifies that the GATT 1994 is legally distinct from GATT 1947,[69] even though in parts it reproduces the substantive law of GATT 1947. Decisions

---

[66] *Henn and Darby*, Advocate-General Warner, pp. 3832–3. Either way, since the importation in *Henn and Darby* had not involved postal services, the argument remained purely hypothetical. The *RTE/ITP* case likewise contains a hint (but no more than that) concerning treaty revision in para. 85.

[67] See E.W. Vierdag, 'The Time of the Conclusion of a Multilateral Treaty: Art. 30 of the Vienna Convention on the Law of Treaties and Related Provisions', *British Yearbook of International Law*, 59 (1988), 92–111.

[68] The existence of that gap is recognised in article 18 of the Vienna Convention. For a discussion with respect to multipolar treaties, see Jan Klabbers, 'How to Defeat a Treaty's Object and Purpose'.

[69] It does so in article II, para. 4.

then holding that article 307 does not apply to GATT 1994 seem perfectly justifiable.[70]

Things get more difficult when there is no such specific clause, as was the case in some of the *Open Skies* cases.[71] In one of them, a specific abrogation clause was inserted (the later treaty, even if in substance mostly amending the earlier treaty, was deemed to replace the earlier agreement). Here then, the Court had little difficulty in maintaining a strict line and holding that article 307 was not applicable.[72]

In some of the other *Open Skies* cases, however, the matter was less clear-cut. Denmark, for example, argued that its 1995 bilateral agreement with the US was, in effect, little more than an amendment of the earlier treaty, concluded in 1944. Many of the older provisions had remained unaffected, and some had merely been subjected to drafting changes. As a result, the 1944 agreement could not have been said to be transformed into a new agreement.[73]

Advocate-General Tizzano was not without sympathy for this sort of reasoning. Placing a premium on the role of the parties' intentions, he found the Commission's position that any amendment turns an older agreement into a new treaty untenable. In the absence of evidence that a later treaty is intended to terminate an earlier one, a conclusion to that effect may not lightly be reached.[74] The amendments themselves would, of course, no longer fall within the scope of article 307, but the 'untouched' parts of the anterior agreement would remain unaffected.[75]

The Court would eventually opt for a stricter approach, holding in effect that even a non-amended provision had nonetheless been confirmed during renegotiations and (without putting it in so many words) was thus

<hr/>

[70] See *Banatrading*, paras. 74–75; see also Case T-2/99, *T. Port GmbH & Co. v. Council* [2001] ECR II-2093, paras. 79–81.
[71] For a useful overview (though not concentrating on article 307), see Piet-Jan Slot and Jacqueline Dutheil de la Rochère's case-note, *Common Market Law Review*, 40 (2003), 697–713. See also Frank Hoffmeister, 'Annotation' (*Open Skies* cases), *American Journal of International Law*, 98 (2004), 567–72.
[72] See Case C-466/98, *Commission v. United Kingdom* [2002] ECR I-9427. The *Open Skies* cases will be discussed in greater detail in Chapter 8.
[73] See case C-467/98, *Commission v. Denmark* [2002] ECR I-9519, para. 34.
[74] See Advocate-General Tizzano's opinion to Cases C-466/98, *Commission v. United Kingdom*; C-467/98, *Commission v. Denmark*; C-468/98, *Commission v. Sweden*, C-469/98, *Commission v. Finland*; C-471/98, *Commission v. Belgium*; C-472, *Commission v. Luxembourg*; C-475/98, *Commission v. Austria*, and C-476/98, *Commission v. Germany*, para. 111.
[75] *Ibid.*, para. 112.

to be considered as falling outside the scope of article 307.[76] On the Court's reading, an amended anterior treaty contains both new provisions and provisions which, though going back into time, have been 'renewed', and are thus to be regarded as new provisions as well.[77]

On this reading, each and every amended treaty will constitute a new treaty for purposes of article 307, regardless of the parties' intentions, regardless in particular also of the third party's stance.[78] That may be acceptable from the point of view of Community law but, as Advocate-General Tizzano suggested, may be less obvious under international law, with its emphasis on the parties' intentions.[79]

A separate story: the second paragraph

The early cases involving article 307 focused solely on its first paragraph: the scope of the notion of protected treaties. The second paragraph, on the member state's obligation to bring its treaty commitments into conformity with EC law, received but scant treatment. There are a number of possible explanations for this state of affairs. One is, as Roucounas points out, that often enough the treaty partner (the third party) is offered a better deal: in commercial cases, typically, a bilateral agreement will be replaced with one with the Community at large. Hence, it has not proved too difficult to persuade treaty partners to accept a denunciation of the earlier bilateral agreement.[80]

In addition, most of the earlier cases (the early *Commission* v. *Italy* case was an exception) were brought by domestic courts in cases involving the

---

[76] *Commission* v. *Denmark* (Open Skies), para. 39.
[77] To bolster its conclusion, the Court also invoked Advocate-General Tizzano's more moderate finding that the provisions at hand, though formally left untouched, had nonetheless been changed due to the changing scope of the bilateral agreement itself. *Ibid.*, para. 41, referring to Advocate-General Tizzano's opinion, paras. 136–138.
[78] The same conclusion is drawn by Christian N.K. Franklin, 'Flexibility vs. Legal Certainty: Article 307 EC and Other Issues in the Aftermath of the Open Skies Cases', *European Foreign Affairs Review*, 10 (2005), 79–115, p. 94. Franklin also cites the Commission to this effect: *ibid.*, footnote 47.
[79] See also Chapter 8 below.
[80] See Roucounas, 'Engagements', pp. 266–7. Likewise, it has been pointed out that the *Open Skies* decisions owed some of their political acceptability to the circumstance that the US was willing to renegotiate its existing agreements, this time with the Community. See Liz Heffernan and Conor McAuliffe, 'External Relations in the Air Transport Sector: The Court of Justice and the Open Skies Agreements', *European Law Review*, 28 (2003) 601–19, pp. 615–6. Koutrakos reports, however, that initially the US was not at all cooperative: EU International Relations Law, pp. 316–7.

legal position of private parties. Typically, those private parties invoked an anterior treaty in their defence; doing so would prompt the Court to investigate whether their defence would hold up, but would not necessitate an analysis of the member state's obligations under the second paragraph of article 307.[81]

Moreover, in many of those cases, the Court typically found that the issue at hand remained limited to EU member states, or that the anterior treaty was, for some reason or other, no longer in force. In those circumstances, too, there is no need for an analysis of the second paragraph. As a result, the precise scope of the second paragraph of article 307 only seriously came to be analysed in the year 2000, in two cases with a long and complicated background.

The groundwork for the two cases leading up to the first analysis of the second paragraph of article 307 was done in a few cases involving a number of bilateral treaties concluded between the Belgium-Luxembourg Economic Union (BLEU) and a handful of African states, involving maritime transport.[82] In the mid-1980s, the EC had adopted a Regulation (Regulation 4055/86), envisaging a phasing out of anterior bilateral commitments.[83] Instead, however, the BLEU maintained anterior bilateral agreements on maritime transport services with Côte d'Ivoire and Senegal, and saw later agreements with Mali and Togo enter into force in 1987. The Commission brought proceedings under article 226 TEC (then article 169 TEC), and the Court agreed that the BLEU had violated the terms of Regulation 4055/86. Importantly, however, article 307 was not thought

---

[81] There has been some speculation in the earlier literature that article 307 could also be used so as to question the validity of EC acts under article 230 TEC (formerly article 173), as forming part of the rules of law relating to application of the EC Treaty whose violation could result in invalidity of Community acts. This, however, has never happened. See, e.g., Van Panhuys, 'Conflicts', p. 446. Even so, in the literature a plea of illegality is sometimes treated as coming close to treaty conflict. See, e.g. (and note the title), Meinhard Hilf and Frank Schorkopf, 'WTO und EG: Rechtskonflikte vor den EuGH?', *EuropaRecht*, 35 (2000), 74–91.

[82] Joined Cases C-171/98, C-201/98 and C-202/98, *Commission v. Belgium and Luxembourg* [1999] ECR I-5517. See also, concerning a similar agreement with Malaysia, Joined Cases C-176/97 and C-177/97, *Commission v. Belgium and Luxembourg* [1998] ECR I-3557.

[83] To make things more complicated: this regulation served itself to implement an international convention (the UN Code of Conduct on Liner Conferences) into Community law. Not all EC members were parties to this Convention. For more details, see Pieter Jan Kuyper, 'The European Communities and the Code of Conduct for Liner Conferences: Some Problems on the Border-line between General International Law and Community Law', *Netherlands Yearbook of International Law*, 12 (1981), 73–112.

to be at issue just yet; the Court could decide on the basis of the Regulation.[84] Also, importantly, the Court did not yet specify what behaviour was expected from Belgium and Luxembourg; it merely specified that the two had failed to fulfil their obligations under EC law by concluding or retaining unchanged the bilateral agreements at issue.[85]

Where the Court decided solely on the basis of the Regulation in the cases involving Belgium and Luxembourg (the agreements in question were concluded long after Belgium and Luxembourg had helped to found the EC), two cases brought somewhat later against Portugal required the Court to analyse the second paragraph of article 307.[86] The factual circumstances were similar: Portugal had concluded, or retained without adjustment, a number of bilateral agreements on maritime transport services, with Senegal, Cape Verde, Angola, and Sao Tomé e Príncipe. The Commission felt that these were in conflict with Regulation 4055/86, and initiated proceedings on that basis.

Portugal retorted that the relevant instrument was not so much this Regulation, but rather article 307 TEC, and under this article, so Portugal suggested, its behaviour was perfectly defensible: the second paragraph of article 307 requires member states to take all appropriate steps to bring their international commitments in line with their commitments under Community law, but 'does not impose the obligation to achieve a specific result in the sense of requiring [member states], regardless of the legal consequences and political price, to eliminate the incompatibility'.[87]

Portugal, in other words, could not be expected simply to denounce treaties without more, and it advanced two arguments to bolster this thesis. First, paragraph 2 had to be read in conjunction with paragraph 1 of article 307; surely, a duty to denounce would render the protection

---

[84] It followed by and large the analysis of Advocate-General La Pergola, who had also not invoked article 307.

[85] In a separate case, an agreement concluded between Belgium alone with Zaire was at issue, leading to a similar decision. See Case C-170/98, *Commission* v. *Belgium* [1999] ECR I-5493.

[86] Case C-62/98, *Commission* v. *Portugal* [2000] ECR I-5171 and Case C-84/98, *Commission* v. *Portugal* [2000] ECR I-5215. The two cases raise similar issues, the latter involving an agreement with Yugoslavia; I shall concentrate on the former decision. For a brief discussion, see Jan Klabbers, 'Moribund on the Fourth of July? The Court of Justice on Prior Agreements of the Member States', *European Law Review*, 26 (2001), 187–97. See also, equally briefly, Pietro Manzini, 'The Priority of Pre-existing Treaties of EC Member States within the Framework of International Law', *European Journal of International Law*, 12 (2001), 781–92.

[87] See Case C-62/98, para. 24.

offered by the first paragraph a dead letter. Second, paragraph 2 refers to the member states assisting each other; this too would be a dead letter if the second paragraph were to be taken as involving an absolute obligation to denounce, for, after all, such an unilateral act of will does not require any assistance.[88]

Strong as those arguments are, Portugal subsequently deflated them itself when pointing out that denunciation might nonetheless be required under article 307, albeit under limited and extreme circumstances. Two conditions would have to be met: 'total incompatibility between a provision of a pre-Community convention and Community law and the impossibility of safeguarding, by political or other means, the Community interest involved'.[89]

Having thereby undermined its own position, Portugal presented one final, practical argument: considering its treaty relations with Angola, the Court should remember that the state of war in Angola made the regular conduct of diplomatic relations that much harder. In the circumstances, surely, renegotiation might be difficult to accomplish.[90] This latter point was swiftly, and perhaps somewhat harshly, dismissed by the Court: 'the existence of a difficult political situation in a third State which is a contracting party . . . cannot justify a continuing failure on the part of a Member State to fulfil its obligations under the Treaty'.[91]

Here the Court merely repeated its earlier holding in *Commission* v. *Belgium*, in which Belgium had argued that the political situation in Zaire complicated political negotiations.[92] In that case it had added, somewhat thoughtlessly perhaps, another sentence: 'If a Member States encounters difficulties which make it impossible to adjust an agreement, it must denounce the agreement'.[93]

This sentence now was not repeated in *Commission* v. *Portugal*; instead, the Court engaged in a more subtle argument, arguing that under article 307, paragraph 1, Portugal 'must in all cases respect the rights which the Republic of Angola derives from the contested agreement'.[94] However, the treaty at hand contained a denunciation clause, so a Portuguese denunciation could not be regarded as violating Angola's rights.

Having established as much, the Court continued by arguing that the duty to denounce, *in casu*, followed from Regulation 4055/86, not from

---

[88] *Ibid.*, paras. 26–27.   [89] *Ibid.*, para. 28.   [90] *Ibid.*, para. 31.   [91] *Ibid.*, para. 39.
[92] See Case C-170/98, para. 42.   [93] *Ibid.*   [94] Case C-62/98, para. 45.

article 307.[95] Even so, as Article 307 obligates member states to eliminate any incompatibilities, it could not be excluded that an obligation
to denounce might also follow from article 307, even though article 307
leaves the member states the choice as to the appropriate steps to be
taken.[96]

What is striking about these cases is how they accord primacy to EC
law, in two ways.[97] One is, in *Commission* v. *Belgium*, how the Court can
simply posit an obligation to denounce, regardless of the circumstances
and, more importantly, regardless of what international law has to say
about it.[98] Second, more ingeniously, is how the Court construes the
connection between Regulation 4055/86, and article 307. To suggest, as
it does, that the obligation to denounce follows from the regulation, is
to place the regulation above article 307. This is unsatisfactory from the
point of view of the systematics of EU law (which would normally do the
opposite: treaty provisions prevail over secondary legislation, *lex specialis*
considerations notwithstanding), and undermines the protection offered
by article 307: surely, if article 307 can be trumped by a regulation, then the
protection of the interests of third parties runs the risk of being rendered
nugatory.[99] Additionally, there is the ironic point that if, indeed, internal
EC legislation is decisive, it may become opportune to analyse the relation
with international law no longer from the point of view of article 30 of
the Vienna Convention, but rather from article 27 of that convention: a
state shall not invoke its domestic law as an excuse to violate its treaty
commitments.[100]

Later case-law initially followed the same type of analysis,[101] but appears
to have become somewhat more mindful of international legal commitments. Thus, in *Commission* v. *Austria*, decided in 2005, the Court accepts
the circumstance that an ILO convention adhered to by Austria despite
its incompatibility with EC law, can only be denounced after a ten-year
period.[102]

---

[95] *Ibid.*, para. 48.   [96] *Ibid.*, para. 49.

[97] See, however, Manzini, 'Pre-existing Treaties', pp. 790–2, who suggests that the ECJ gives
pride of place to international law in the cases under discussion.

[98] *Commission* v. *Belgium*, para. 42.

[99] So also Grimes, 'Conflicts', p. 547, speaking of an 'absurd effect' which would arise if
article 307 would not cover secondary legislation.

[100] This will be explored in greater detail in Chapter 8.

[101] See, e.g., some of the *Open Skies* cases, such as Case C-467/98, para. 39.

[102] See Case C-203/03, *Commission* v. *Austria* [2005] ECR I-935, paras. 63–64.

Possible explanations

What, then, explains this Eurocentric attitude on the part of the ECJ? Why can the Court satisfy itself by conjuring up a world in which international law hardly exists? Two possible explanations present themselves, one sociological, the other more technical. According to the sociological explanation, the ECJ would lack expertise in matters of international law and be institutionally predisposed to stimulate the project 'Europe'. The more technical explanation would hold that the Court has little choice but to apply EC law, and to apply it to the exclusion of anything else: it would simply lack the jurisdiction to apply international law, or even merely interpret it. Neither of the two explanations is fully convincing.

The sociological explanation seems attractive, at first sight. Obviously, so one could argue, ECJ judges and advocates-general (the latter form part of the Court) are not selected due to their merits in international law. It follows that, as a group, they cannot be expected to be particularly well versed in matters of international law, and might thus be reluctant to venture into an area where their expertise is limited, perhaps even non-existent. This, however, fails to convince upon closer scrutiny. At the time of writing (October 2007), of the 35 members of the Court (judges and advocates-general), no fewer than eight, i.e. some 23 per cent., have a documented background in international law, typically manifested by having been a professor of international law (often in combination with some other discipline, such as EU law or constitutional law).[103] There is no reason to presume that this percentage has been subject to wild fluctuations: there have, in all likelihood, always been judges and advocates-general at the ECJ with some background in international law.[104]

---

[103] This applies to Rosas, Kokott, Makarczyk, Küris, Malenovsky, Klucka, Mengozzi, and Lindh. The latter is exceptional in that her international law background stems from Sweden's Foreign Ministry rather than Academia. The biographical information used in this section is largely culled from the website of the various courts, available at www.curia.europa.eu (last accessed 26 October 2007).

[104] Some indeed are quite prominent regarding the topic of this study, such as Manfred Zuleeg (at the ECJ between 1988 and 1994). Others include Riccardo Monaco, Max Sörensen, Paul Kapteyn (who held a chair in international organisations law), Pieter VerLoren van Themaat (a chair in economic law, but with a strong emphasis on the international in his work) and Jean-Pierre Puissochet (a former legal adviser at the French Foreign Ministry). Others had a background in trade law (Leif Sevón is an example), and it is perhaps useful to note that Advocate-General Maurice Lagrange, who wrote the conclusions to the seminal *Commission* v. *Italy* case, himself had been involved in the negotiations leading up to the conclusion of the ECSC Treaty.

What is noteworthy, however, is that those members of the Court with a background in international law tend to come from the newer member states where, it might be hypothesised, EU law is still predominantly regarded as a branch of international law rather than an independent discipline in its own right. The two exceptions would be Mengozzi and Kokott, Italian and German respectively, but they hail from traditions where EU and international law are often seen together as well: Italian chairs often comprise international and EU law, whereas German chairs may include both international law and EU law under the broader heading public law.[105]

More to the point, perhaps, some of the advocates-general most closely concerned in the relevant cases on article 307 have some background in international law. Advocate-General Capotorti, for instance, taught international law at the University of Bari from 1955 to 1968 and moved on to teach international organisations law at the University of Naples. He also gave lectures to the prestigious Hague Academy of International Law,[106] where being invited to teach a general course is considered by some as the greatest possible honour that can be bestowed upon an international lawyer.[107] By the same token, one of the many things the highly influential Advocate-General Francis Jacobs has to his credit is that he co-authored one of the leading textbooks on the European Convention on Human Rights which, while not conclusive perhaps, does suggest a familiarity with bits and pieces of international law and a sensitivity to matters other than strict EU law.[108]

In short, it seems difficult to sustain the (somewhat simple) sociological argument that the ECJ as a whole lacks expertise in international law, or

---

[105] That said, the international presence is decidedly less marked at the Court of First Instance, where at best three of the current judges can be said to have something of a background in international law, albeit in conjunction with EU law (this applies to Dehousse, Vadapalas and Nielsen). Former CFI judges with international law exposure would include Lindh and Mengozzi (now at the ECJ) and possibly Hubert Legal, who spent some time as legal advisor at the French mission to the United Nations.

[106] Two of these involved public international law. See Francesco Capotorti, 'L'extinction et la suspension des traités', *Receuil des Cours*, 134 (1971/III), 417–587, and Francesco Capotorti, 'Cours général de droit international public', *Receuil des Cours*, 248 (1994/IV), 9–343. His third course addressed private international law.

[107] The characterisation is from the preface to Rosalyn Higgins, *Problems and Process: International Law and How We Use it* (Oxford: Clarendon Press, 1994) at p. v. Higgins's book is a revised version of just such a general course.

[108] See Clare Ovey and Robin White, *Jacobs and White: The European Convention on Human Rights*, 3rd edn (Oxford: Oxford University Press, 2002). The work was first published by Jacobs and White in 1975.

could not be expected to have some sensitivity to it. A more complicated version of the argument may, however, be more plausible. It has been noted that the community of EU lawyers forms a tight-knit group, whose members include academics, EU officials, members of the two courts, plus a handful of others (government lawyers, private practitioners). This community of lawyers 'identifies with the project of European integration both intellectually and socially [and] that identification expresses itself in a widely shared conception of law and what law can and should do'.[109]

EU lawyers, in other words, form an interpretive community, to use the term developed by the literary theorist Stanley Fish. Fish describes the notion as follows: it concerns 'not so much a group of individuals who share a point of view, but a point of view or way of organizing experience that share[s] individuals in the sense that it assume[s] distinctions, categories of understanding, and stipulations of relevance and irrelevance . . .'.[110] Different interpretive communities will have different perspectives on the same phenomena and, what is relevant for present purposes, it would not seem too far-fetched to suppose that newcomers will only be taken seriously once they have adopted the basic categories and frameworks of understanding prevailing within the interpretive community concerned. Hence, even those members of the ECJ or the CFI with a background in international law are asked and expected to bracket their international law exposure when functioning within the context of EU law, as within the community of EU lawyers different assumptions apply than within the community of international lawyers.[111]

Be that as it may, EU lawyers themselves would rather refer to technical reasons for the myopia of EU law, and the most prominent amongst these is the argument that the EC courts simply lack the jurisdiction to interpret (let alone apply) instruments other than EU instruments. Perhaps the clearest endorsement of this position is *Vandeweghe*,[112] where

---

[109] See Harm Schepel and Rein Wesseling, 'The Legal Community: Judges, Lawyers, Officials and Clerks in the Writing of Europe', *European Law Journal*, 3 (1997), 165–88, p. 176.

[110] See Fish, *Doing What Comes Naturally*, p. 141. Usefully applying the notion to international law is Iain Johnstone, 'Treaty Interpretation: The Authority of Interpretive Communities', *Michigan Journal of International Law*, 12 (1991), 371–419.

[111] This is also, incidentally, why interdisciplinary academic collaboration is so difficult to achieve: different disciplines utilise different vocabularies and form different communities, each vying for prominence. For a discussion along these lines, see Jan Klabbers, 'The Relative Autonomy of International Law or The Forgotten Politics of Interdisciplinarity', *Journal of International Law and International Relations*, 1 (2004–05), 35–48.

[112] It is mentioned, with apparent approval, by Manzini, 'Pre-existing Treaties', p. 787, and by former ECJ Judge Paul Kapteyn as authority for the position that the ECJ should

the Court held, in no uncertain terms, that in cases brought under article 234 TEC it 'has no jurisdiction . . . to give a ruling on the interpretation of provisions of international law which bind member states outside the framework of Community law'.[113] In this case, the referring German court had been asked to interpret, in the course of interpreting a Community Regulation on social security, also a bilateral social security agreement between Germany and Belgium. The Court declined to do so, and was probably correct in doing so on the facts of the case.

Still, *Vandeweghe*'s scope is limited, in two ways. First, the Court explicitly connected its lack of jurisdiction to article 234 TEC, suggesting that in cases brought on a different basis, jurisdiction may well be present. Second, the Community Regulation contained corresponding terms, and these the Court could, and did, interpret, and it suggested, moreover (following the referring court) that the interpretation of the Regulation's terms could well be relevant to the interpretation of the bilateral agreement.[114]

Thus, at best, *Vandeweghe* is authority for the proposition that the Court has no jurisdiction, in cases brought under article 234 TEC, to address matters of international law when there are corresponding Community provisions available. *Vandeweghe* cannot, however, be authority for the thesis that the Court also lacks jurisdiction, even in a case brought under article 234, where the question at issue involves a conflict between an international agreement and Community law.[115]

---

not interpret international agreements. See P. J. G. Kapteyn, 'The Role of the ECJ in Implementing Security Council Resolutions', in Erika de Wet and André Nollkaemper (eds.), *Review of the Security Council by Member States* (Antwerp: Intersentia, 2003), pp. 57–62, p. 59, note 7.

[113] See Case 130/73, *Magdalena Vandeweghe and others* v. *Berufsgenossenschaft für die Chemische Industrie* [1973] ECR 1329, para. 2. See also Joined Cases 267/81, 268/81 and 269/81, *Amministrazione delle Finanze dello Stato* v. *Società Petrolifera Italiana (SPI) and SpA Michelin Italiana (SAMI)* [1983] ECR 801 (suggesting that jurisdiction to interpret GATT obligations only took effect from the date at which GATT became binding on the Community; para. 19).

[114] *Ibid.*, para. 3. Advocate-General Ruiz-Jarabo Colomer, in para. 86 of his conclusions to Case C-62/05 P, *Nordspedizionieri di Danielis Livio & C. Snc and others* v. *Commission* (not yet reported) interprets this, not unreasonably, as 'the Court has held that it has jurisdiction in respect of a bilateral treaty unconnected with the Community, even after maintaining the contrary'.

[115] In cases brought on a different basis, the courts happily interpret international agreements, even those without Community involvement. For recent illustrations involving a 1965 Agreement between Italy and the (then) Socialist Federal Republic of Yugoslavia on Mutual Administrative Assistance for the Prevention and Suppression of Customs Fraud, see Case T-322/02, *Nordspedizionieri di Danielis Livio & C. Snc and others* v. *Commission*

It is true, of course, that the text of article 234 suggests a fairly narrow scope. Article 234 reads, in relevant part, that the Court has jurisdiction to give preliminary rulings concerning the interpretation of the EC Treaty and the validity and interpretation of acts of the institutions of the Community.[116] An agreement between a member state and a third party falls in neither category; hence, one could conclude, no jurisdiction.[117] This, however, is too facile. Surely, it cannot be excluded that in the course of interpreting Community law, the Court must sometimes have a close look at other law as well, and indeed, this is what it regularly does. It could not, for example, have decided *Ebony Maritime* without taking into account the Security Council resolution which formed the basis of the Community provision concerned (to be discussed in the next chapter); even the classic *International Fruit Company* cases involved the Court looking into (and therewith interpreting) an international agreement with third parties. Indeed, in the latter cases the Court held unequivocally that since its jurisdiction under article 234 TEC 'extends to all grounds capable of invalidating' Community measures, 'the Court is obliged to examine whether their validity may be affected by reason of the fact that they are contrary to a rule of international law'.[118] In other words, nothing would prevent the Court from interpreting an international agreement if such were necessary to address the interpretation or validity of a Community Act or the interpretation of the EC Treaty.

[2004] ECR II-4405, para. 79, and Case C-62/05 P, *Nordspedizionieri di Danielis Livio & C. Snc and others* v. *Commission* (judgment of 18 October 2007, nyr), paras. 42–46.

[116] This includes acts of purportedly non-binding effect, such as recommendations emanating from international bodies of which the EC is a member. See Case C-188/91, *Deutsche Shell AG* v. *Hauptzollamt Hamburg-Harburg* [1993] ECR I-363.

[117] It is perhaps for this reason that Advocate-General Ruiz-Jarabo Colomer, in *Nordspedizionieri* argues in para. 82 that the Court would have jurisdiction in case the development of Community powers has been such so as to have come to encompass the topic of the earlier agreement with a third party. In such a scenario, he suggests, the agreement's conclusion can best be regarded as a member state implementing a Community power. While this fails to convince (quite simply because when it concluded the agreement, the member state was acting within its own powers), it does point to *Vandeweghe* being of limited value; indeed, the Advocate-General goes so far as to say that a refusal to look at a treaty with a third party might amount to a denial of justice (para. 92).

[118] See Joined Cases 21–24/72, *International Fruit Company* v. *Produktschap voor Groenten en Fruit* [1972] ECR 1217, para. 6. Koutrakos sums up the Court's attitude in *International Fruit Company* as follows: as article 234 did not limit the Court's jurisdiction 'by the grounds on which the validity of Community measures might be contested, its jurisdiction extended to all grounds capable of invalidating those measures. These include international law.' See Koutrakos, *EU International Relations Law*, p. 192.

The Court confirmed as much in its judgment in *Hurd*. Mr Hurd was headmaster at the European School in Culham, Oxfordshire, and claimed tax immunities, partly on the basis of Community law, and partly on the basis of the documents setting up the European School. The Court pointed out that the latter documents were, really, not EC instruments, but agreements between the member states, and therewith falling outside the scope of article 234. However, so the Court continued, in order to interpret the relevant Community instruments, it could be necessary to have a look at the non-Communtiy instruments as well. This would now be perfectly possible under article 234: the jurisdiction to interpret the international agreements concerned arose 'by virtue of' its jurisdiction to interpret the relevant Community instruments.[119]

A variation on the argument that the ECJ would lack jurisdiction is the position, more subtle, that in proceedings for a preliminary ruling it is for the referring national courts eventually to decide on the scope of an international agreement: the ECJ has the jurisdiction to interpret, while jurisdiction to apply rests with the referring national court. This is most clearly phrased in *Levy*: 'in proceedings for a preliminary ruling, it is not for this Court but for the national court to determine which obligations are imposed by an earlier international agreement on the Member State concerned and to ascertain their ambit so as to be able to determine the extent to which they constitute an obstacle to the application' of the Community measure at issue.[120] Unfortunately, the Court provided no reasoning whatsoever concerning its assertion, nor did it provide any reference.

The general approach to interpretation and application of Community law in preliminary ruling proceedings was laid down by the Court as early as 1963. In *Da Costa and Schaake*, the Court suggested that its power under article 234 was limited to interpreting the Community law measure at hand, leaving application thereof to the referring national

---

[119] See Case 44/84, *Derrick Guy Edmund Hurd* v. *Kenneth Jones (Her Majesty's Inspector of Taxes)* [1986] ECR 29, paras. 21–2. Likewise, in one of its *Eurocontrol* cases, the Court happily interpreted the Eurocontrol Convention, despite this encompassing a number of third parties. See Case C-364/92, *SAT Fluggesellschaft mbH* v. *Eurocontrol* [1994] ECR I-43. And as far as mixed agreements go, the Court has not hesitated to claim the jurisdiction to interpret the parts falling outside the scope of EC powers. Hence, the Court seems to have generally embraced a wide understanding of the reach of its jurisdiction in requests for preliminary rulings.

[120] See Case C-158/91, para. 21.

court.[121] This found its reason, the Court suggested, in a number of considerations. Perhaps most importantly, such procedures were characterised by the absence of parties: hence, a regular litigation context was missing. Moreover, under the Court's Statute, the member states and institutions would participate in proceedings, and under the treaty, the Court would sit in plenary. All this together suggested that the function of the Court in such proceedings was not so much to decide the case at hand (this was reserved for the referring court), but rather to present an interpretation of Community law, with a view to guaranteeing its uniformity.[122]

While this general reasoning is plausible enough as it is, two considerations are of relevance. First, the reasoning applies to the interpretation and application of Community law; it does not apply to interpretation or application of treaties concluded by member states with third parties, for the good reason (apart from the text of article 234, which singles out Community law) that in such cases, the uniformity of EC law is not at issue, or rather: is not the only thing at issue.

Second, as has been observed in the general context of article 234 proceedings (without there being an international agreement with third parties in the background), the Court tends to manipulate the distinction between interpretation and application, which is dangerously thin at any rate.[123] In some cases, the Court has presented such a detailed interpretation of the Community measure at issue, that the referring Court had nothing left to apply itself: the Court's interpretation had lapsed into application.[124] As one prominent observer puts it: 'The precise distinction between interpretation and application is . . . very elastic and the European Court appears to make use of this elasticity for its own purposes.'[125]

---

[121] This is still the position, according to the 2005 Information Note on references from National Courts for a Preliminary Ruling, published in *Official Journal*, 11 June 2005, C 143/1, para. 5.

[122] See Joined Cases 28–30/62, *Da Costa and Schaake N.V. and others* v. *Netherlands Inland Revenue Administration* [1963] ECR 61 (French edn.).

[123] This is all the more so as the Court suggests that it 'does have jurisdiction to provide the national court with all the elements of interpretation under Community law to enable it' to decide a case. See, e.g., Case C-186/90, *Giacomo Durighello* v. *Istituto Nazionale della Previdenza Sociale* [1991] ECR I-5773, para. 10.

[124] See, e.g., Paul Craig and Gráinne de Búrca, *EU Law: Text, Cases, and Materials*, 3rd edn (Oxford: Oxford University Press, 2003), pp. 472–3 ('The willingness of the ECJ to provide very specific answers to questions serves to blur the line between interpretation and application').

[125] See Trevor C. Hartley, *The Foundations of European Community Law*, 6th edn (Oxford: Oxford University Press, 2007), pp. 293–4.

This elasticity is clearly observable in the context of treaty conflict and again, the *Levy* case is a strong example. In *Levy*, the Court strongly suggested that the ILO Convention had been overruled by later international law, in which case article 307 TEC would not be applicable. Given this strong suggestion, the referring French court would have had a hard time claiming that the ILO Convention had remained in force and warranted the protection of article 307 TEC.

More generally, when the Court concludes that its analysis of a case (including the contents of an international agreement invoked under article 307) discloses 'no factor of such a kind as to affect the validity' of a Community instrument, it is also clear that the referring national court would have little choice left.[126] In light of such a finding, it would be difficult for the referring national court not to apply the Community measure at issue.

The jurisdictional picture is further complicated by the ECJ's insistence in its 2006 *MOX Plant* judgment that disputes with a Community law element not be submitted elsewhere, in accordance with article 292 TEC. To the extent that a matter is covered by a Community competence, there is always the risk, so the Court suggested, that a decision taken by a different tribunal might touch on the EC's legal order; consequently, there is always the risk that 'the autonomy of the Community legal system may be adversely affected'.[127] And as Advocate-General Maduro explains, this reaches far: there is no 'threshold' for Community law to apply. As soon as a dispute touches upon Community law, the ECJ's jurisdiction is exclusive.[128]

MOX Plant was truly, as one observer put, a 'stunning' decision; it 'falls squarely on the oldest, and most conservative trajectory of European thinking about the role of international law and its relations with national law'.[129] One potential consequence might be that it leaves a gap in the

---

[126] This was the formula used, e.g., in *Tome and Yurrita*. See also Case C-344/04, *R v. Dept of Transport (IATA, ELFAA)* [2006] ECR I-403 (testing, inter alia, the legality of an EC regulation against the Montreal Convention for the Unification of Certain Rules for International Carriage by Air).

[127] See Case C-459/03, *Commission v. Ireland (MOX Plant)* [2006] ECR I-4635, para. 154.

[128] *Ibid.*, Advocate-General Maduro's opinion, paras. 13–14.

[129] See Martti Koskenniemi, 'International Law: Constitutionalism, Managerialism and the Ethos of Legal Education', *European Journal of Legal Studies*, 1 (2007). Perhaps because this is an electronic journal, no page numbers are given; the quote can be found on the first page of the printed version. Interestingly, Koskenniemi likens the ECJ position to that of the old Soviet Union, prohibiting its dissidents, 'seeking . . . to break out of the hermetic absolutism of the Soviet order' (*ibid.*, 2nd page), from appealing to international human rights covenants.

system of judicial protection: if a dispute having a Community element but involving international law can only be submitted to the ECJ, yet the ECJ would be reluctant to interpret or apply international law, then the result would be a gap, creating the possibility ('spectre' being too strong a word, perhaps) that while various legal orders would potentially have a bearing on the dispute, only EC law could actually be applied.

This is, admittedly, something of a worst case scenario. After all, the *MOX Plant* reasoning was based on the convention at hand being a mixed agreement (thus falling within the Court's jurisdiction to interpret[130]), and the scope of *Vandeweghe* should be narrowly construed, as suggested above. Still, the Court's attitude is worrisome: it does aspire to build a fence around EU law, therewith running the risk of placing the EU outside international law.

To conclude: some general issues

Following the cases, one can only reach the conclusion that article 307 TEC is more about balancing Community law with international law than that it affords outright protection to international commitments.[131] Admittedly, article 307 does protect anterior treaties in the abstract, but it just so happens that the Court can often find a reason not to apply article 307 in the concrete case before it. In some cases the agreement would be applied between two member states and thus, so the dominant reasoning goes, not involve the rights of the third parties under the agreement concerned. Advocate-General Warner's careful hypothesis that not all treaties are reducible to bilateral sets of rights and obligations (bipolar, that is) in *Henn and Darby* has been all but ignored in later cases.

In other cases, the Court defined away the existence of any possible conflict between an anterior convention and the EC Treaty (as in *Exportur*) or, more dubious, somehow reached the conclusion (or, with much innuendo, hinted at that conclusion) that the anterior convention had somehow stopped being in force. And that, of course, also means that there is no longer any conflict.

After the curious *Burgoa* decision, in which the Court itself concluded that the London Fisheries Convention had been replaced by a highly

---

[130] See *MOX Plant*, para. 84.
[131] The Commission put it (inadvertently, no doubt) very well when claiming (in the Court's rendition) that article 307 TEC 'does not establish that public international law obligations prevail over Community law, but rather the reverse'. See *Banatrading*, para. 63.

informal interim regime, the Court's tactic has been not to burn its own fingers, but remand the case to the referring court. While, in and of itself, this makes sense in terms of judicial economy and can properly be said to follow from the EC Treaty's very system of preliminary references, it nonetheless smacks a bit of 'passing the buck', in particular if the Court includes strong suggestions as to what decision the referring Court is expected to reach.[132] More sensibly perhaps, the Court has also developed the common position that where an anterior treaty leaves the member states discretion, those members are supposed to choose the policy option prescribed by EC law.[133]

The cases also seem to suggest a shift in approach. Whereas the earlier cases were mostly concerned with the interpretation of paragraph 1 of article 307 and thus with the question whether it would be possible to protect an anterior treaty, the more recent cases focus on paragraph 2 and detail the exigencies of terminating or denouncing the anterior treaty. This is possibly best regarded as resignation: there is no longer any point in trying to squeeze an anterior treaty into paragraph 1; the best a member state can hope for is that it will not be asked to immediately denounce the anterior treaty, so that a failure to denounce will not be regarded as a violation of Community law by the Court.[134]

To some extent this may be a matter of the structure of proceedings. However, it may also mark a policy shift: even if, as the *Budvar* case suggests, an agreement falls within the scope of article 307, then nonetheless paragraph 2 quickly enters the picture: in case of incompatibilities which prove impossible to adjust with the treaty partner or partners concerned, 'an obligation to denounce that agreement cannot therefore be excluded'.[135]

---

[132] Early observers might have been disappointed. Witness Van Panhuys' optimism: '. . . it is not likely that the Court of Justice will ever give a ruling on the compatibility of the law of the Communities with another treaty in such a way that . . . the liberty of national courts is thwarted.' See van Panhuys, 'Conflicts', p. 436.

[133] See, e.g., *Evans Medical and MacFarlan Smith*, para. 32; Case C-124/95, *The Queen, ex parte Centro-Com/HM Treasury and Bank of England* [1997] ECR I-81, para. 60.

[134] An example is Case C-203/03, paras. 61–5.

[135] Case C-216/01, *Budejovicky Budvar* v. *Rudolf Ammersin GmbH* [2003] ECR I-13617, para. 170.

7

The UN Charter and the European Convention

Introduction

It has become standard practice for the Court of Justice, at least since *Burgoa*, to hold that article 307 'is of general scope and applies to any international agreement, irrespective of subject-matter, which is capable of affecting application' of the EC Treaty.[1] All treaties are equal, but some, as they say, are more equal than others: there are good reasons to devote separate treatment to the relationship between two specific treaties and EC law.

First, there is the relationship with the UN Charter to consider. Not only is the UN Charter sometimes considered as a constitution for the world community,[2] it also has its own clause on treaty conflict: it demands priority, and does so in no uncertain terms. These two characteristics together warrant a special investigation into the attitude of the Community courts when confronted with UN law.

Second, there is the European Convention on Human Rights and Fundamental Freedoms which, at least in the eyes of the Court overseeing its implementation and application, is also of a special nature, creative as it is of 'objective obligations'.[3] Indeed, the same Court has even qualified it as

---

[1] See, e.g., Case C-466/98, *Commission* v. *United Kingdom* [2002] ECR I-9427, para. 23.

[2] See, e.g., Bardo Fassbender, 'The United Nations Charter as Constitution of the International Community', *Columbia Journal of Transnational Law*, 36 (1998), 529–619.

[3] The ECtHR puts it as follows: 'Unlike international treaties of the classic kind, the Convention comprises more than mere reciprocal engagements between contracting States. It creates, over and above a network of mutual, bilateral undertakings, objective obligations which, in the words of the Preamble, benefit from a "collective enforcement".' See *Ireland* v. *United Kingdom*, application no. 5310/71, judgment of 18 January 1978, *Publications of the European Court of Human Rights*, Series A, no. 25, para. 239. Incidentally, while the paper versions of decisions of the Strasbourg institutions are organised somewhat messily, the electronic collection is excellent and easy to navigate. See http://cmiskp.echr.coe.int/tkp197/search.asp?skin=hudoc-en (last visited 22 January 2008).

'a constitutional instrument of European public order'.[4] If that claim is to be taken seriously, it too could perhaps demand to be given priority over conflicting EC law. Moreover, an analysis of the Convention in terms of article 307 TEC might be problematic, as not all EU members had ratified the Convention when joining the EU,[5] with France being the textbook example.[6]

Both the UN Charter and the European Convention, then, could provide a strong argument as to why, in case of conflict, conflicting EC law should give way. As will be demonstrated below, however, the EC courts have a somewhat different approach: instead of simply and overtly granting priority to either the Charter or the Convention, they seem first and foremost concerned to protect the primacy of EC law: to the extent that priority is granted to the UN Charter or the European Convention, it is in the guise of EC law, and by virtue of EC law.

The UN Charter before the EC Court

The UN was established in the aftermath of the Second World War, with its constituent document, the UN Charter, concluded in 1945.[7] Most of the EU's member states were members of the UN before joining the EU, with the single exception of Germany, which joined the UN only in 1973. For any member state but Germany, then, the UN Charter would qualify as an anterior treaty which, under article 307, would deserve protection.[8]

The UN Charter also demands to be protected by virtue of its own article 103. This article provides:

---

[4] See *Loizidou* v. *Turkey*, preliminary objections, judgment of 23 February 1995, para. 75. Notably, however, when citing this passage, former ECtHR president Wildhaber sometimes omits the adjective 'constitutional'. See Luzius Wildhaber, 'The European Convention on Human Rights and International Law', *International and Comparative Law Quarterly*, 56 (2007), 217–32, e.g. pp. 220, 229.

[5] This circumstance seems to have been overlooked by Tawhida Ahmed and Israel de Jesús Butler, 'The European Union and Human Rights: An International Law Perspective', *European Journal of International Law*, 17 (2006), 771–801, esp. pp. 784–7.

[6] As Chaltiel delightfully notes, the French felt that as the home of human rights, there was nothing they could learn from Europe. See Florence Chaltiel, *Naissance du peuple européenne* (Paris: Odile Jacob, 2006), p. 31.

[7] The drafting is pleasantly recorded in Stephen C. Schlesinger, *Act of Creation: The Founding of the United Nations* (Boulder, CO: Westview, 2003).

[8] Kapteyn seems happy to extend the protection of the UN Charter under Article 307 to all member states. See Kapteyn, 'Implementing Security Council Resolutions'.

> In the event of a conflict between the obligations of the Members of the United Nations under the present Charter and their obligations under any other international agreement, their obligations under the present Charter shall prevail.

The UN's functional predecessor, the League of Nations,[9] had introduced a similar clause in its Covenant, in article 20.[10] This article 20 of the Covenant had survived the various drafting stages of the Covenant in virtually unchanged form,[11] which strongly suggests that, early on, the Covenant's drafters already thought that an organisation with ambitions of global governance requires such a clause, subordinating other treaties to it. Otherwise, those global ambitions could easily be undermined.

Article 103 UN is generally held to grant priority not just to Charter provisions, but also to lawful decisions of UN organs, and perhaps even to agreements concluded by the UN to the extent that these can find a basis in the Charter.[12] One would expect that, on this basis, Article 103 UN would also provide UN law with entry into the Community's legal order,[13] but Community law itself contains two provisions which may also serve that purpose. One is, not surprisingly (if little used in this context), article 307; the other is article 297 (formerly article 224).

---

[9] In strictly legal terms, the UN cannot be considered as the successor to the League: both co-existed for some nine months in 1945 and 1946, until the League's dissolution. See generally Jan Klabbers, *An Introduction to International Institutional Law* (Cambridge University Press, 2002), ch. 15.

[10] This read: '1. the Members of the League severally agree that this Covenant is accepted as abrogating all obligations or understandings *inter se* which are inconsistent with the terms thereof, and solemnly undertake that they will not hereafter enter into any engagements inconsistent with the terms thereof. 2. In case any Member of the League shall, before becoming a Member of the League, have undertaken any obligations inconsistent with the terms of this Covenant, it shall be the duty of such Member to take immediate steps to procure its release from such obligations.' Note the limitation to *inter se* agreements.

[11] See C. A. Kluyver (ed.), *Documents on the League of Nations* (Leiden: Sijthoff, 1920), esp. pp. 63–115.

[12] See Rudolf Bernhardt, 'Article 103', in Bruno Simma *et al.* (eds.), *The Charter of the United Nations: A Commentary*, 2nd edn (Oxford: Oxford University Press, 2002), pp. 1292–302.

[13] So, e.g., Dowrick, writing in the early 1980s before the activation of the Security Council: 'Hypothetically, if a conflict between obligations under the Basic Treaties and the U.N. Charter could be pin-pointed, the European Court would hardly dare to deny supremacy to the Charter as a prior, universal, "constitutive" treaty, and would have to re-define the Basic Treaty obligation to remove the incompatibility.' See Dowrick, 'Overlapping', p. 80.

Article 297 has been dubbed a 'reservation of sovereignty'[14] ('*reserve de souveraineté*'), and provides a fall-back provision in case a member may be called upon to take measures which may come to affect the functioning of the common market. Those measures may arise in case of internal disturbances, but may also follow from a threat of war or 'in order to carry out obligations it has accepted for the purpose of maintaining international peace and security'. In short, member states may take unilateral measures in such circumstances, but 'shall consult with each other' on minimising the damage to the functioning of the common market. And as the Court held early on, article 297 deals with an exceptional situation and does not lend itself to 'any wide interpretation'.[15]

Article 297 was used by the member states to justify the unilateral implementation of UN ordered sanctions, in particular against Rhodesia. Community law, at the time, did not yet have a specific provision relating to sanctions (article 301 TEC currently fulfils that role[16]), and UN sanctions were regarded as laying down binding obligations for the individual member states of the Community.[17]

For some reason, article 297 was deemed to apply to such sanctions, rather than article 307. One can only speculate why this was so, but three possibilities present themselves. One of these possibilities is that where article 307 applies in principle to all anterior treaties, article 297 is decidedly narrower in scope, and could thus be construed as the *lex specialis* to the *lex generalis* of article 307. Second, and possibly more to the point, the position of Germany (for whom the UN Charter, as noted, is not an anterior treaty) may have made application of article 307 less obvious. Third, there is the traditionally narrow interpretation of article 307, as formulated in *Commission* v. *Italy*, limiting the scope of article 307 to protecting the rights of third states. But with sanctions, it is not so much the rights of third states that is at issue, except in the more or less abstract form of upholding the sanctity of the treaty regime (in this case,

---

[14] See Richard H. Lauwaars, 'The Interrelationship between United Nations Law and the Law of Other International Organisations', *Michigan Law Review*, 82 (1983–84) 1604–19, p. 1608. But see Pieter Jan Kuyper, 'Implementation of Binding Security Council Resolutions by the EC/EU', in Erika De Wet and André Nollkaemper (eds.), *Review of the Security Council by Member States* (Antwerp: Intersentia, 2003), pp. 39–55, at p. 41 (suggesting that article 297 can be 'harmonized away' by the Council).

[15] See Case 13/68, *Salgoil* v. *Italian Ministry of Foreign Trade* [1968] ECR 453, at 463.

[16] Article 60 TEC functions alongside it, in facilitating measures with respect to capital and payments.

[17] See generally Panos Koutrakos, 'Is Article 297 EC a "Reserve of Sovereignty"?', *Common Market Law Review*, 37 (2000), 1339–62, esp. at 1344.

the sanctions). In marked contrast, sanctions appeal, by definition, rather to a multipolar conception of treaties; yet this conception was, the odd exception notwithstanding,[18] never deemed to apply to article 307 TEC.

Since the Maastricht amendments, the TEC has its own provision on sanctions: article 301 TEC. While this has meant that article 297 can no longer be invoked as the justification for implementing UN sanctions by individual member states, there is still an open question in connection with article 307. Article 301 provides that the EC Council can take sanctions against third states. It does not state that those sanctions shall always follow UN sanctions, or that those sanctions shall be identical to UN sanctions. In other words, the question of the effect of UN sanctions in EC law may still arise, and article 307 TEC may still enter the picture.

Until the early 1990s, given the near-paralysis of the Security Council, the question of the relationship between UN law and EC law did not arise all too often. Since the end of the Cold War, however, a number of cases have forced the two Community courts to explore this relationship. In particular, these cases revolve around the implementation by the Community, under the Union's first pillar, of Security Council sanctions.[19] To the extent that action taken by the EU under its second pillar is at issue, the jurisdiction of the courts is limited.[20]

The first of these cases addressing the effects of actions taken by the reinvigorated Security Council action was *Bosphorus*,[21] involving aircraft owned by a company based in Yugoslavia during the period when Yugoslavia was under UN sanctions, even though at the relevant time the aircraft had been leased to a Turkish company. The aircraft had been seized by the Irish authorities following maintenance operations at Dublin airport, and the Irish authorities cited a Community Regulation (No. 990/93) in support. This regulation, in turn, had been adopted by the EC in order to implement a number of Security Council resolutions, in particular SC Resolution 820 (1993).

---

[18] Most notably in Advocate-General Warner's opinion in Case 34/79, *R* v. *Henn and Darby* [1979] ECR 3795. See the discussion in Chapter 6.

[19] A very useful comprehensive study of the various sanctions regimes is Jeremy Matam Farrall, *United Nations Sanctions and the Rule of Law* (Cambridge: Cambridge University Press, 2007).

[20] See e.g. Case T-299/04, *Abdelghani Selmani* v. *Council and Commission* [2005] ECR II-20, para. 56 ('. . . the Court of First Instance has jurisdiction to hear an action for annulment directed against a CFSP common position only strictly to the extent that in support of such an action the applicant alleges an infringement of the Community's powers.').

[21] See Case C-84/95, *Bosphorus* v. *Minister for Transport, Energy and Communications, Ireland and the Attorney General* [1996] ECR I-3953.

The question submitted to the EC Court by Ireland's Supreme Court explicitly asked for an interpretation of one of the articles of EC Regulation 990/93; perhaps for that reason, both Advocate-General Jacobs and the Court framed their decisions in terms of EC law. Still, the Advocate-General advocated an approach revolving around the international law aspects of the case. For him, there was no doubt that the regulation had to be interpreted in light of the initial Security Council resolutions, and he went so far as to reject an interpretation of the regulation which, although plausible in itself, he found difficult to reconcile with the Security Council's intentions.[22] What mattered, as he pointed out, was not the intention of the Community legislator, but of the Security Council: 'What is in issue is not the intention of the Community institutions themselves . . . but the purpose of the Security Council . . .'[23] He steered clear, however (and could do so, given the similarity between the Resolutions and the Regulation and given the way the Irish Supreme Court had phrased the request), of providing a clear argument as to why the Security Council's intentions should be decisive: there is no mention of either article 103 UN, or article 307 TEC. At best, there is a hint later on in his opinion, to the effect that Security Council measures reflect the opinion of the world community, and thus exercise 'a particularly strong public interest'; the Community merely implemented these measures.[24]

While the Court did not depart dramatically from the advocate-general's approach, it did tone it down considerably by staying much closer to Regulation 990/93. The Court, first and foremost, interpreted this Community Regulation, and felt compelled to note that the regulation had been taken to give effect to the foreign policy decision of the Community and its members to implement certain Security Council measures.[25] The wording of Security Council Resolution 820 (1993) was used merely to 'confirm' the proper interpretation of the Community Regulation, which suggests that in the Court's view, perhaps precisely because its main task is applying EC law, the EC Regulation was the more important instrument.[26]

The same Regulation 990/93 and Security Council Resolution 820 (1993) were also at issue a few months later in *Ebony Maritime*.[27] This case

---

[22] See *ibid.*, Advocate-General Jacobs, para. 39.   [23] *Ibid.*, para. 40.   [24] *Ibid.*, para. 64.

[25] *Bosphorus*, para 13; the wording creates an extra Community layer, suggesting some distance between the Regulation and the Security Council resolutions.

[26] *Ibid.*, para. 15.

[27] Case C-177/95, *Ebony Maritime SA and Loten Navigation Co. Ltd* v. *Prefetto della provincia di Brindisi and others* [1997] ECR I-1111.

revolved around a ship flying the Maltese flag and carrying cargo owned by a Liberian company, seized by NATO/WEU troops on the high seas, on its way to Serbia's territorial waters, and brought into the port of Brindisi, Italy. The applicants claimed that in impounding the ship after seizure, the Italian authorities had acted outside their jurisdiction proper. According to the applicants, the EC regulation could only apply to the territory of the EU's member states, EU nationals and companies incorporated in the EU. None of these elements were present, however.

This prompted the advocate-general, once again, to launch a liberal theory on resolutions and regulations; he had somehow to overcome the jurisdictional limitations of EC law, after all. Noting that the regulation had been adopted to give effect to Security Council Resolution 820 (1993), he observed that it 'plainly follows from the objectives and the provisions of that Resolution that it was intended to be applied as broadly as possible'.[28] This broad reading of the resolution, so he held, was also supported by the wording of the regulation itself,[29] and this broad reading would make it possible to rely on the notion of universal jurisdiction, implicitly relied on by the Security Council.

The Court, as in *Bosphorus*, approached the matter from the other side. It deftly sidestepped the jurisdictional question by suggesting that the regulation applied within the whole of its territory to all vessels under its territorial jurisdiction, 'even if the alleged infringement occurred outside its territory'.[30] Again, the underlying Security Council resolution was used merely to support this interpretation.[31]

As long as interpretation of the Security Council resolution and the implementing Community instrument reveal that both say the same thing, it could be argued that there is no problem, and it stands to reason that a court charged with the task of applying Community law would feel more comfortable applying Community instruments than other instruments. However, the situation may arise in which interpretations diverge or, at any rate, in which actors claim that the regulation and the Security Council resolution are at loggerheads. Such a situation occurred in *Centro-Com*, decided a month and a half before *Ebony Maritime*. Centro-Com had been delivering medical supplies from Italy (where it was registered) to Montenegro. Medical supplies were not caught by the trade embargo on Serbia and Montenegro imposed by Security Council Resolution 757 (1992), nor by the Community's implementing Sanctions Regulation. Centro-Com was to be paid from a Yugoslav account held at Barclays

---

[28] *Ibid.*, Advocate-General Jacobs, para. 20.   [29] *Ibid.*, para. 21.
[30] *Ebony Maritime*, para. 19.   [31] *Ibid.*, para. 20.

Bank in the UK, and following reports of abuse of the procedure at the UN Sanctions Committee (which had approved the sale), the Bank of England refused Barclays to transfer money to Centro-Com, only approving the sale of medical supplies originating in the UK.

The UK argued that its change in policy had been necessary so as to implement Security Council Resolution 757 effectively, even if the Sanctions Regulation did not specifically allow for it. The Court, however, following Advocate-General Jacobs, did not see any conflict between the two,[32] and simply claimed, in line with classic case-law, that member states should trust each other's administrative procedures.[33]

Indeed, in a sense the Court went further still: it found that it followed from article 133 TEC (laying down the Community's exclusive competence to engage in commercial policy) that member states could not unilaterally adopt measures to ensure effective implementation of a Security Council resolution.[34] Rephrased in more abstract terms of a conflict between EC law and UN law, the Court thereby clearly gave priority to EC law: no matter what a Security Council resolution may demand, it cannot trump EC law.

The Court then moved on, albeit without much enthusiasm, to article 307 TEC; this, after all, had been among the questions asked by the referring court. It found that it was up to the national court to determine whether or not in the specific circumstances of the case, the UK's policy was necessary to ensure that the UK could meet its obligations under the UN Charter. Still, in so doing the national court should remember that when the member state has discretion, it should refrain from taking measures which would go against Community law.[35] In the end, then, the member state could not take national measures contrary to Community law, unless those measures would be necessary to give effect to commitments towards third states under an anterior treaty.

Perhaps the most intriguing aspect of the *Centro-Com* decision is that the Court firmly kept the EC law prism in place. There is no mention of the special position that, many would agree, the UN occupies; there is no mention of the circumstance that under article 103 UN, UN law itself claims supremacy. The case is analysed purely as a matter of EC law. To some extent this 'legal parochialism' is, of course, justified by the

---

[32] See Case C-124/95, *R, ex parte Centro-Com/HM Treasury and Bank of England* [1997] ECR I-81, Advocate-General Jacobs's opinion, para. 77; the Court itself did not explicitly deny any conflict, but as much can be derived from its decision.
[33] *Centro-Com*, para. 48.   [34] *Ibid.*, para. 53.   [35] *Ibid.*, para. 60.

consideration that the EC Court's first and foremost task is to interpret and apply EC law. Yet, it is ultimately untenable: in order to reach a decision, either way, the EC Court is bound to work on the basis of some presumptions concerning international law, and cannot simply pretend that higher law does not exist if the higher law claims supremacy. It cannot escape all this by claiming to apply only EC law.

This is perhaps even more clearly visible in *Ebony Maritime*. The Court, as outlined above, deftly sidestepped the question of whether or not the EC would have jurisdiction over acts occurring on the high seas by suggesting that jurisdiction was established once the ship in question was in the hands of the Italian authorities. It was this argument that allowed the Court to ignore the underlying Security Council resolution, and only use it for interpretative support. However, the Court's judgment, on this point, remains vulnerable to the criticism that even if adjudicative jurisdiction was ensured, nonetheless accepting the seizure of a ship on the high seas also presupposes that the EC would have legislative jurisdiction: the seizure, after all, would require some justification.[36] That justification could derive from the underlying Security Council resolution (which clearly posited universal jurisdiction), and therewith by extension also attach to the EC implementing regulation, but making this argument would place the Security Council resolution in the foreground: if the EC regulation is dependent on the Security Council resolution when it comes to jurisdiction, then the only conclusion to be drawn is that this Security Council resolution is, in case of conflict, hierarchically superior. Yet it is this conclusion that the Court has been at pains to avoid – had the Court accepted the primacy of UN law, arguably the unity of Community law would have been endangered.[37]

Paradoxically, while it would perhaps seem desirable to the international lawyer for the EC's courts to be open to UN law, there is some room for finding that a more receptive attitude towards international law, and

---

[36] In a similar vein, Puissochet, 'The Court of Justice and International Action', esp. p. 1570 (claiming in no uncertain terms that cases such as *Bosphorus* and *Ebony Maritime* make clear 'that the Court views U.N. Security Council resolutions more as guides to interpretation than as binding rules whose breach should be punished.'). Interestingly, Puissochet was a Judge at the EC Court at the time he wrote these words. The attitude of using Security Council resolutions merely as interpretative aids can still be discerned in the case law. See Case C-117/06, *Gerda Möllendorf and Christiane Möllendorf-Niehuus*, judgment of 11 October 2007, nyr, paras. 54, 56.

[37] As Puissochet sums it up: 'The approach adopted enables the Court's powers of interpretation to remain unfettered, while limiting, but not eliminating, the risk of divergence between international and Community rules.' *Ibid.*, pp. 1570–1.

UN law in particular, is not without its dangers. This is well illustrated by two decisions of the Court of First Instance rendered in September 2005.[38] In both cases, applicants had been placed on the blacklist by the UN Sanctions Committee for Afghanistan, having been suspected of supplying terrorists with financial support. Their funds and bank accounts had been frozen on the basis of Community legislation adopted to implement UN Security Council resolutions. Applicants applied to have some of the relevant Community instruments annulled, citing a number of grounds including violations of human rights. The Council and the Commission responded that the Community instruments merely implemented UN law; this prompted the CFI to undertake an adventurous analysis of the relationship between UN law and EC law. The curious epistemological problem facing the Court was that, contrary to its usual experience, the applicants were doing their best to portray the EC as an independent legal order, independent from the UN and in no way subservient to it, whereas the Community institutions by contrast tried to suggest that the EC was not at all independent from the UN, and that UN law prevails over EC law.

Member states of the UN, so the CFI recalled, are bound to accept the primacy of UN law by virtue of article 27 of the Vienna Convention on the Law of Treaties.[39] As far as other treaties are concerned, the primacy of the UN follows from article 103 UN. The Court then continued by stating that article 307 TEC also was of relevance, without specifying at this point how exactly it would be of relevance.[40] To make a long story short, the CFI held that Security Council resolutions bind all the member states of the Community 'which must therefore, in that capacity, take all measures necessary to ensure that those resolutions are put into effect.'[41] Remarkably, in the next paragraph the CFI proclaimed the primacy of UN law: '... pursuant both to the rules of general international law and to the specific provisions of the Treaty, Member States may, and indeed must,

---

[38] Case T-306/01, *Yusuf and Al Barakaat* v. *Council and Commission* [2005] ECR II-3533, and Case T-315/01, *Kadi* v. *Council and Commission*, [2005] ECR II-3649. For commentary, see the case note by Christian Tomuschat, *Common Market Law Review*, 43 (2006), 537–51. For a highly critical discussion, see Robert Schütze, 'On "Middle Ground": The European Community and Public International Law', *EUI Working Papers, Law*, 2007/13. Useful background is sketched in Per Cramér, 'Recent Swedish Experiences with Targeted UN Sanctions: The Erosion of Trust in the Security Council', in De Wet and Nollkaemper (eds.), *Review*, pp. 85–104.

[39] Article 27 VCLT provides that domestic law is no excuse for failure to perform a treaty obligation.

[40] *Kadi*, para. 185.   [41] *Ibid.*, para. 189.

leave unapplied any provision of Community law, whether a provision of primary law or a general principle of that law, that raises any impediment to the proper performance of their obligations under the Charter of the United Nations.'[42] Even so, the Court felt the need to go even further, and while it accepted that generally, the Community is not bound by the Charter because it is not a member of the UN, it nonetheless posited that in those fields where the Community exercises exclusive competences, it has become bound as the successor to its member states.[43]

This reasoning is clearly based on the famous succession theory launched in *International Fruit Company*,[44] but without fully employing the test developed in that case. The CFI suggests that the intention of the member states to transfer powers related to the UN becomes apparent from in particular the inclusion of article 301 TEC, which provides the EC with the legal basis to engage in economic sanctions.[45] It does not, however, gauge the response of the UN's membership to the alleged succession, nor does it come to terms with the formality that only states can be members of the UN,[46] and the circumstance that the UN might experience some difficulty in accepting partial membership.[47] Moreover, it ignores the awkward circumstance that in the field of foreign policy narrowly construed (thus excluding commercial policy), the member states have transferred or delegated few powers to the Community, much less exclusive powers.[48] And if the reasoning is that the Community has bound itself to UN law by unilateral act, then it would have required the CFI to spell this out in some detail. Either way though, it follows from the CFI's analysis that the Community is under a twofold obligation: it must itself

---

[42] *Ibid.*, para. 190.
[43] *Ibid.*, para. 203. The CFI confirmed this approach in Case T-362/04, *Leonid Minin* v. *Commission*, nyr, judgment of 31 January 2007, para. 67.
[44] Joined Cases 21/72 to 24/72, *International Fruit Company and others* [1972] ECR 1219.
[45] See *Kadi*, para. 202.   [46] See article 4 UN.
[47] This would be the consequence: the EU being a partial member, accepting some obligations but not others. This, in turn, would reflect on the condition (see article 4 UN) that the members of the UN should be willing and able to accept the obligations arising out of membership.
[48] The treaty succession theory is also discussed by Advocate-General Kokott in Case C-308/06, *The International Association of Independent Tanker Owners and Others* (opinion of 20 November 2007, nyr, judgment pending) in connection with the 1973 International Convention for the Prevention of Pollution from Ships (MARPOL), to which the EC is not a party. She dismisses the argument because the EC's powers on the topic are not exclusive, and because there is no indication that the member states intended the EC to succeed to their obligations nor that such would have been accepted by MARPOL's other parties. See in particular paras. 40–45.

respect UN law, and it must enable its member states to fulfil their obligations under UN law.[49] Somehow, though – and it is this circumstance which diminishes the earlier statement that the EC must accept the primacy of UN law – this is said to follow not from general international law, but from Community law itself.[50] This latter remark aims to push the toothpaste back in the tube, as it were: having suggested that UN law has supremacy, the CFI now felt to need to trump this supremacy by suggesting, in marked contrast to its earlier musings,[51] that the very supremacy of UN law flowed from EC law, and thus, really, it is EC law that is supreme.

Nonetheless, in discussing its jurisdiction, the CFI goes back to its original track, at least initially. The institutions, so it held, acted 'under circumscribed powers'[52] when adopting the implementing legislation. As a result, the CFI is in reality asked to engage in judicial review of Security Council acts but this, so the CFI holds, it cannot do. Such jurisdiction would be incompatible with both the UN Charter and article 27 of the Vienna Convention on the Law of Treaties,[53] and with the EC Treaty itself.[54] Nonetheless, and without much explanation,[55] the CFI does declare itself competent 'to check, indirectly, the lawfulness of the resolutions of the Security Council in question with regard to *jus cogens*'.[56] And this, once again, however welcome in itself given the absence of any judicial review at the UN level,[57] suggests the primacy of EC law: in the final analysis, arrogating the power to test the legality of Security Council

---

[49] See *Kadi*, para. 204.   [50] *Ibid.*, para. 207.   [51] *Ibid.*, e.g., para. 190.

[52] *Ibid.*, para. 214.

[53] *Ibid.*, para. 222. It is not immediately self-evident though how article 27 of the Vienna Convention (the article suggesting the primacy of treaties over domestic law) would have any bearing on judicial review of Security Council acts by the CFI.

[54] *Ibid.*, para. 223.

[55] Unless one counts the position that *jus cogens* provides a limit to the binding effect of Security Council resolutions (see *Kadi*, para 230). This is questionable however: if the argument before was that testing the validity of Security Council resolutions does not belong to the CFI's province, then it does not all of a sudden start to belong there as soon as the magic words *jus cogens* are uttered. Testing is a power one either has or does not have; it cannot depend on the substance of the test.

[56] See *Kadi*, para. 226.

[57] Tomuschat, for example, warmly welcomes the exercise of review by the CFI over Security Council resolutions. See Tomuschat, 'Annotation', esp. p. 546: 'The Court must be congratulated on insisting that there are inalienable human rights which must be respected under any circumstances. The Security Council is an institution of the international community for which observance of human rights is a parameter the core of which must never be sacrificed.'

decisions presupposes a hierarchically superior position – or, at least, not an inferior position. As review would have to entail the power to declare norms inapplicable, or even invalid, such can only be done from a position of authority. While it is unlikely that, following *Kadi* and *Yusuf*, the CFI would test Security Council resolutions against substantive EC law (as EC law is unlikely to be elevated to *jus cogens* status), it does suggest that the CFI, organ of the EC, is willing to act as the guardian of legality within the UN.[58]

The CFI would go even further in its later judgment in *Ayadi*.[59] While the circumstances of the case were similar to those in *Yusuf* and *Kadi*, and indeed much of the judgment relies on those earlier two cases, in one way the CFI departs. It proclaims that, by virtue of EC law an obligation to exercise judicial review may rest upon domestic judicial authorities, if not of decisions taken by Sanctions Committees directly, then at least against decisions of national authorities relating to the work of Sanctions Committees. The interesting thing is that, according to the CFI, this obligation stems from Community law, and comes into play in relation to actions 'intended to safeguard the rights which individuals derive from the direct effect of Community law'.[60]

Things are different, of course, where the Community can exercise some discretion in implementing Security Council sanctions. This was held to be the case in *Organisation des Modjahedines du peuple d'Iran* v. *Council*, where the organisation at issue was blacklisted not by the Security Council itself, but by the EC Council; moreover, it was the Council which had decided on the modalities of freezing funds and judicial safeguards.[61] In those circumstances, the exercise of discretion by Community institutions is reviewable.[62]

---

[58] Indeed, a different construction is chosen by Advocate-General Maduro in his opinion on the *Kadi* appeal, suggesting that human rights are parts of EC law and taking the dualist position that Security Council resolutions themselves have no particular effect within the EC legal order. See Case C-402/05 P, *Kadi* v. *Council and Commission*, opinion of 16 January 2008, nyr, judgment pending.

[59] See Case T-253/02, *Chafiq Ayadi* v. *Council* [2006] ECR II-2139, esp. paras. 151–3.

[60] *Ibid.*, para. 151.

[61] See Case T-228/02, *Organisation des Modjahedines de peuple d'Iran* v. *Council*, judgment of 12 December 2006, nyr, paras. 100–1 (explicitly distinguishing the case from *Kadi* and *Yusuf*). See also Case T-47/03, *Jose Maria Sison* v. *Council*, judgment of 11 July 2007, nyr, esp. paras. 148–55.

[62] Perhaps as a result, the CFI, in *Organisation des Modjahedines*, did not address the legality of the underlying Security Council resolution. It would, however, annul the Community measure, to the extent it applied to the applicant.

The *Kadi* and *Yusuf* cases mark, at the very least, a departure from settled case-law in their finding that the EC itself, qua entity, is bound by UN law and that, in case of conflict, UN law reigns supreme.[63] The reasoning is not always convincing, and at times the cases show clear signs of ambivalence, perhaps even inner contradictions. What is refreshing though, if not perhaps felicitous, is their recognition of there being a world outside the Community; a world in which the Community can and does participate, but is not alone and is most assuredly not omnipotent.[64]

The European Convention before the EC Court

The story of the complicated relationship between the EC and the European Convention has been told before, sometimes with considerable brilliance and a critical eye.[65] After initially claiming that human rights and Community law had nothing whatsoever to do with each other,[66] the EC Court, under pressure from some of the member state courts, came round to the idea that perhaps it was not such a bad idea to try and get Community law to guarantee human rights.[67]

The question remained how to do this, though. Easiest, no doubt, would have been simply to claim the Community's allegiance to the European Convention on Human Rights, but this option faced two problems. One problem was that some of the EU's member states were late in ratifying the Convention, or late in recognising the individual right of petition under the Convention, or both. Under those circumstances, it would be difficult to accept the ECHR as an anterior treaty protected by article 307 TEC and, where appropriate, allow it to be invoked by individuals under EC law where no such invocation would be possible under the Convention

---

[63] In the literature, this position is also taken by Lenaerts and de Smijter, 'The European Union as an Actor', p. 116: 'The general wording of this provision [article 103 UN] gives the UN Charter precedence over the EC Treaty, regardless of which State's rights and obligations are at stake, and that rule therefore also applies to relations between two or more EC Member States.'

[64] In *Minin*, para. 101, the CFI summarised its position as founded on 'reasons connected, in essence, with the supremacy of international law originating under the Charter of the United Nations over Community law . . .'.

[65] See Craig and de Búrca, *EC Law*, esp. ch. 8; Lawson, *Het EVRM*; Leino-Sandberg, *Particularity as Universality*.

[66] See, e.g., Case 1/58, *Stork and Cie* v. *ECSC High Authority* [1959] ECR 17.

[67] For a useful discussion of the motives of the ECJ in embracing human rights law, see Jason Coppel and Aidan O'Neill, 'The European Court of Justice: Taking Rights Seriously?', *Common Market Law Review*, 29 (1992), 669–92.

itself. Second, and infinitely more treacherous, there is the fact that, under the EC Treaty, the Court of Justice is appointed as the guardian of the legality of EC law. Accepting the authority of the European Convention, including the case-law of the European Court of Human Rights, could put that function at risk: it would run the risk of subjecting the EC to the ECHR.[68]

As a result, the Court has adopted the general formula that it shall apply human rights (or fundamental rights, as the Court's preferred term seems to be), and in doing so shall draw inspiration from the common constitutional traditions of the member states, and from international treaties on which the member states have collaborated or of which they are signatories.[69] Originally, this formula allowed the Court to do away with any specific reference to the ECHR; later, however, the Court has explicitly referred to the ECHR, as well as to other human rights instruments, in particular since the adoption of what is now article 6 TEU in the Maastricht Treaty (when it was still article F TEU).[70] The European Court of Human Rights, in turn, has thus far accepted this approach, but at a price: the ECtHR has tended to hold the EC's member states responsible for their conduct even when that conduct is a direct consequence of the member states' obligations under Community law.[71]

Having declined an invitation to hold that the European Convention is itself part and parcel of Community law,[72] provisions of the European Convention nonetheless sometimes end up before the EC courts. A fairly typical case, illustrating the Court's general approach, is *Schmidberger*.[73] Mr Schmidberger, who ran a transport company, suffered some damage related to the blockade of a mountain pass. The Austrian authorities had allowed the blockade in the name of freedom of expression and freedom of assembly. Mr Schmidberger claimed that this ended up violating the freedom of movement of goods. The Court agreed with Mr Schmidberger

---

[68] The ECJ's reluctance to subject itself to others is nicely illustrated by Opinion 1/91 *(EEA)* [1991] ECR I-6077.

[69] See, e.g., Case 4/73, *Nold* v. *Commission* [1974] ECR 491, para. 13.

[70] See, e.g., Case C-540/03, *European Parliament* v. *Council* [2006] ECR I-5769. Article 6 TEU, incidentally, specifies that the EU 'shall respect fundamental rights', in particular as guaranteed in the ECHR.

[71] See Pieter Jan Kuiyper and Esa Paasivirta, 'Further Exploring International Responsibility: The European Community and the ILC's Project on Responsibility of International Organisations', *International Organizations Law Review*, 1 (2004) 111–38, esp. p. 131. See also below, section 3 of this chapter.

[72] See Case C-299/95, *Kremzow* v. *Austria* [1997] ECR I-2629.

[73] See Case C-112/00, *Schmidberger* v. *Austria* [2003] ECR I-5659.

that the blockade was capable of restricting intra-Community trade in goods (which it referred to, in terms reminiscent of the European Convention on Human Rights and Fundamental Freedoms, as a 'fundamental freedom')[74] but found it justified in the circumstances of the case.[75]

Of particular interest in *Schmidberger* is the Court's methodology. It declines simply to proclaim that either human rights law or EC law prevails. Instead, it aims to reconcile the two. On the one hand, the fundamental freedom of movement of goods is at issue; on the other hand, there are human rights at issue, also recognised as part of EC law. There is no specific hierarchy, in the view of the Court; indeed, a direct question to this effect from the referring national court was set aside[76] and, instead, the Court found a 'need to reconcile the requirements of the protection of fundamental rights in the Community with those arising from a fundamental freedom enshrined in the Treaty.'[77]

On the rhetorical level, such an approach suggests that human rights and such things as free movement of goods are, really, on a par with each other; indeed, to some extent (and earlier cases bear this out) fundamental freedoms such as those relating to trade in goods are themselves conceptualised as human rights.[78] On such a conceptualisation, there is no longer a conflict between EC law and a different set of rules. Instead, EC law and this different set of rules are, really, the same thing: the conflict is transformed from a conflict between treaties to a conflict between rules present in the same legal system.[79] Even so, the Court could not completely avoid taking sides: it analysed *Schmidberger* employing free movement of goods as the general rule, with human rights functioning as the possible exception: human rights were 'not incompatible' with the free movement of goods.

The key paragraph in the judgment holds that protection of fundamental rights 'is a legitimate interest which, in principle, justifies a restriction of the obligations imposed by Community law, even under a fundamental freedom guaranteed by the Treaty such as the free movement of goods'.[80] Hence, the basic rule is the free movement of goods, with the exception requiring justification. As Brown puts it, the ECJ here resorted to 'classic

---

[74] *Ibid.*, para. 59.
[75] Douglas-Scott construes this as 'suggesting a priority of fundamental rights'. See Sionaidh Douglas-Scott, 'A Tale of Two Courts: Luxembourg, Strasbourg and the Growing European Human Rights *Acquis*', *Common Market Law Review*, 43 (2006), 629–65, p. 635.
[76] *Ibid.*, para. 70, and the Court's answer (or non-answer) in paras 71–3.
[77] *Ibid.*, para. 77.   [78] As discussed in Chapter 2.   [79] As also discussed in Chapter 2.
[80] See *Schmidberger*, para. 74.

Luxembourg-style jurisprudence: free movement is the guiding principle, but there may be exceptions to it'.[81]

Yet, if both human rights and free movement principles form part of Community law, and if they cannot be hierarchically ranked, there is no particular reason to employ free movement as the fundamental rule and human rights as the exception;[82] one might just as well start from the other end and posit freedom of expression as the general rule, only to ask whether in the case at hand freedom of expression could possibly justifiably have been limited by the need to safeguard the free movement of goods.[83] Put like this, the answer in *Schmidberger* would likely have remained the same, but it would have made it that much more difficult to ever find that free movement of goods could trump freedom of expression; surely, few people would in the abstract wish to suggest that freedom of expression could be stifled in the interest of free movement of goods.

In other cases, the Court has habitually stopped short of applying the Convention directly, or of even referring to it. Typically, the Court contends itself with suggesting that the Community is somehow bound to respect human rights law, but construes this as flowing from Community law itself rather than from an external obligation.[84] Indeed, an explicit request about the legality of the Community joining the Convention was dismissed: the Community lacked the competence, the Court held, to make this move; not even an implied power could be found.[85] In short, such human rights protection as is offered by the EC Court stems from EC law itself and thus can also be undone by EC law. While the latter is not

---

[81] See Christopher Brown, 'Annotation (*Schmidberger*)', *Common Market Law Review*, 40 (2003), 1499–510, p. 1507. See also Oliver and Roth, 'The Internal Market', p. 438 (freedom of expression and assembly 'were being relied on as exceptions to the free movement of goods').

[82] Indeed, in the later *Omega* case, Advocate-General Stix-Hackl endorsed a reversal of the roles. See Case C-36/02, *Omega Spielhallen- und Automatenaufstellungs-GmbH* v. *Oberbürgermeisterin der Bundesstadt Bonn* [2004] ECR I-9609, para. 53. A useful discussion of the two cases is John Morijn, 'Balancing Fundamental Rights and Common Market Freedoms in Union Law: Schmidberger and Omega in the Light of the European Constitution', *European Law Journal*, 12 (2006), 15–40.

[83] See generally Koskenniemi, 'The Effect of Rights' (arguing that the choice for rule and exception is one manifestation of the political nature of human rights).

[84] Dowrick, 'Overlapping', p. 81, expected the Court to let the EC Treaties prevail over the Convention, but that the Convention would prevail over secondary Community law. Note also that in implementing EU law, the member states should respect human rights 'as far as possible'. See Case C-540/03, *European Parliament* v. *Council* [2006] ECR I-5769, para. 105.

[85] See Opinion 2/94 (*European Convention on Human Rights*) [1996] ECR I-1759.

likely to occur (if only because domestic courts have threatened to prevent this[86]), nonetheless it does suggest, once again, that the EC is reluctant to subject itself to other norms.

The Strasbourg attitude

Since the ECJ seems to have posited the primacy of EC law over much else, including, eventually, the European Convention on Human Rights, the question arises how the European Court of Human Rights has addressed the same issue. Initially, the Strasbourg organs (Court and Commission of Human Rights – the latter no longer exists) were hesitant to say anything at all involving Community law, as exemplified by the leading decision in *Confédération Francaise Démocratique du Travail (CFDT)* v. *European Communities*.[87] CFDT could claim to be the second largest trade union in France and thus, under the ECSC Treaty, it ought to have a seat in the Consultative Committee of the ECSC. The Council, however, bypassed CFDT in 1976. CFDT contested that decision before the Court of Justice of the EC, but the Court declared the case inadmissible for CFDT's lack of standing. As a result, CFDT invoked the European Convention, citing in particular that it suffered a denial of justice and lacked an effective remedy. Moreover, it felt discriminated, as smaller and less representative trade unions from France had been granted a seat on the Consultative Committee.

The case would never reach the ECtHR, as the European Commission of Human Rights declared it inadmissible. The complaint directly against the EC failed as the EC was not a party to the Convention.[88] Hence, 'consideration of the applicant's complaint lies outside the Commission's jurisdiction *ratione personae*'.[89] The subsidiary complaint against the individual

---

[86] See, amongst many, Tuomas Ojanen, *The European Way: The Structure of National Court Obligation under EC Law* (doctoral thesis, University of Helsinki, 1998), pp. 313–9.

[87] Application No. 8030/77, decision of 10 July 1978 on admissibility, in *European Commission of Human Rights Decisions and Reports*, vol. 13 (1979) 231.

[88] Schermers suggests it might have been wiser for the Commission to declare the application inadmissible for want of recognition of the right of individual petition. The way the Commission actually phrased it might suggest that the Community is not bound by the Convention, and thus goes further perhaps than would have been necessary. See H.G. Schermers, 'Constituent Treaties of International Organisations Conflicting with Anterior Treaties', in Jan Klabbers and René Lefeber (eds.), *Essays on the Law of Treaties: A Collection of Essays in Honour of Bert Vierdag* (The Hague: Martinus Nijhoff, 1998), pp. 19–30, p. 25.

[89] *CFDT*, para. 3 of the *dispositif*. See also *M. & Co.* v. *Federal Republic of Germany*, application no. 13258/87, declared inadmissible by the Commission on 9 February 1990 (in *European*

member states of the EC also failed, partly because one of them (France) had not yet recognised the right of individual petition under the Convention, partly because, as the European Commission of Human Rights put it, taking part in decision-making in the Council does not amount to exercising state jurisdiction within the meaning of the Convention.[90] As a result, so observers noted, it would seem that the Communities received *carte blanche* from the Strasbourg organs.[91]

In later cases, and no doubt in response to the *carte blanche* critique, the Strasbourg organs (in particular the Court) refined their attitude, and at the time of writing it would seem that two basic scenarios are distinguished. First, there is the sort of case where the member states of the EU act within their own sphere of competences, even if the act is somehow related to their Union membership. The leading judgment from the ECtHR on this is *Matthews* v. *United Kingdom*. The second scenario is that where, somehow, the complaint refers back to the Community itself. This is the more complicated scenario, as in this case the question of the relationship between Community law and the Convention arises in full glory: should an EU member state give effect to its commitments under Community law when these are in conflict with the European Convention, or should it, instead, give effect to its commitments under the Convention? Here the leading ECtHR decision is *Bosphorus* v. *Ireland*.

In *Matthews*,[92] the applicant claimed a breach of article 3 of the third protocol to the Convention, which stipulates that the parties shall organise free elections 'which will ensure the free expression of the opinion of the people in the choice of the legislature'. The breach had occurred, she claimed, when elections to the European Parliament were organised without taking Gibraltar (her place of residence, and still part of the UK) into account. As a citizen of Gibraltar, in other words, she had been denied her right to participate in elections to the European Parliament.

This raised a number of issues, the most relevant of them for present purposes being the issue whether the UK could be held responsible for this

---

Commission for Human Rights Decisions and Reports, vol. 64 (1990) 138), for much the same reasons: there would be no jurisdiction over the EC, and it would have been awkward to treat every decision of the EC as a collective act of the member states for which they could be held responsible individually.

[90] *CFDT*, para. 4 of the *dispositif*. Under article 1 of the Convention, the parties guarantee respect for human rights to the extent of their jurisdiction.

[91] See, e.g., Lawson, *Het EVRM*, p. 48.

[92] *Matthews* v. *United Kingdom*, application no. 24833/94, judgment of 18 February 1999, in *European Court of Human Rights Reports of Judgments and Decisions* (1999/I) 251.

alleged violation, as the applicant suggested, or whether the blame should rest elsewhere. The Court started by looking into the legal basis of elections to the EP, and found that those bases consisted in a Council decision and an Act concluded in 1976 on elections to the EP, as well as the Maastricht treaty, which at the time constituted the most recent incarnation of the European Union. The Court held that all these instruments 'constituted international instruments which were freely entered into by the United Kingdom'.[93] The fact that, on the basis of the Maastricht Treaty, the European Parliament helped guarantee the effective democratic nature of the EU prompted the Court to even go a step further: the Maastricht Treaty, which was concluded in 1991, was regarded as a posterior treaty. In the Court's words: '... the United Kingdom's responsibility derives from its having entered into treaty commitments subsequent to the applicability of Article 3 of Protocol No. 1 to Gibraltar, namely the Maastricht Treaty taken together with its obligations under the Council Decision and the 1976 Act.'[94]

Two features of the *Matthews* decision catch the eye. The first is that the ECtHR conveniently ignored the separate identity of the EU/EC edifice, and could do so by casting the relevant instruments as international treaties of the sort that parties can enter into, rather than as Community instruments. While undeniably plausible with regard to the Maastricht Treaty and the 1976 Act, this stand is less plausible with regard to the Council decision which, after all, is a decision by an organ of an international organisation, and cannot without more be seen as something that parties can freely enter into; at least not while maintaining the idea of the international organisation having a separate identity.[95]

Second, and more interesting for present purposes, the ECtHR clearly posited the Convention as the sort of instrument that prevails over later, conflicting treaties, and therewith endorsed the *lex prior* maxim. Again, though, some conceptual wizardry was required before it could make this work, for to have the Convention prevail on the basis of the *lex prior* maxim would only be plausible upon casting the EU treaty as the later in time. As a factual matter, then, much would depend on which incarnation of the EU treaty to uphold: the original treaties go back to 1951 and 1957 (or 1952 and 1958, if the date of entry into force is regarded as decisive).

---

[93] *Ibid.*, para. 33.   [94] *Ibid.*, para. 34.
[95] Much of the law of international organisations is informed by a tension between conceiving the organisation as merely a vehicle for its member states, and conceiving it as having a separate identity. See generally Klabbers, *An Introduction*.

While the Convention is older for some EU member states, it would be newer for those who ratified late; hence, the Court had somehow to regard the date of the Maastricht Treaty (concluded in late 1991) as decisive, as this would definitely allow for regarding the Convention as the earlier in time. This also suggests, incidentally, that the Court was not thinking in terms of strict hierarchy: had it done so, there would have been no need to point to the circumstance that the Maastricht Treaty was later in time.[96]

Be this as it may, at the very least it becomes clear that where the EU's member states retain a competence (or part of it), they will be held responsible for their behaviour, even if the behaviour is, in turn, the result of some Community act. While this no doubt prevents the creation of an 'accountability' gap and is clearly defensible on that basis, it does mean that the existence of the EC qua EC is taken not entirely seriously. Things become more problematic though when the member states of the EC have no competence left. This arose in the *Bosphorus* case.

The ECtHR, in *Bosphorus*,[97] has – wisely perhaps – refused to be dragged into a power game, competing with the EC's Court of Justice.[98] The situation involved, as set out above, the implementation of UN sanctions by the EC, and the application thereof in Ireland. Bosphorus suggested eventually that its right to property had been violated by the EC's action, which prompted the ECtHR into an analysis of the relationship between the Convention and Community law.

In two earlier cases, both involving the European Space Agency, the ECtHR had suggested that it was receptive toward attempts at establishing international cooperation.[99] Joining an international organisation,

---

[96] The ECtHR confirmed as much in *Prince Hans-Adam II of Liechtenstein* v. *Germany*, application no. 42527/98, judgment of 12 July 2001, para. 47 (in *European Court of Human Rights Reports of Judgments and Decisions* (2001/VIII) 1), again holding that responsibility under the Convention continued to exist despite the conclusion of subsequent treaties.

[97] See *Bosphorus Hava Yollari Turizm ve Ticaret anonim Sirketi* v. *Ireland*, application 45036/98, judgment of 30 June 2005 (Grand Chamber).

[98] Indeed, it has been suggested that the main policy reason behind its decision in *Bosphorus* was precisely to escape a possible confrontation with the ECJ. See Annalisa Ciampi, 'L'Union Européenne et le respect des droits de l'homme dans la mise en oeuvre des sanctions devant la Cour Européenne des Droits de L'Homme', *Revue Générale de Droit International Public*, 110 (2006), 85–116, pp. 105–6.

[99] See *Waite and Kennedy* v. *Germany*, application no. 26083/94, judgment of 18 February 1999 (Grand Chamber), paras. 67–68 (in *European Court of Human Rights Reports of Judgments and Decisions* (1999/I) 393); it uses identical words in *Beer and Regan* v. *Germany*, application no. 28934/95, judgment of 18 February 1999, paras. 57–58 (unpublished).

it suggested, was not by definition irreconcilable with a party's obligations under the Convention, even if, at the face of it, the level of human rights protection in the international organisation would be less than what individual member states would have to guarantee. In short, the ECtHR recognised the need for a certain trade-off between human rights protection and, in general terms, the desirability of fostering international cooperation.[100]

It continued the same line of thought in *Bosphorus*. The ECtHR, laying down its general approach, felt that member state action in compliance with decisions taken by an international organisation is justified 'as long as the relevant organization is considered to protect fundamental rights, as regards both the substantive guarantees offered and the mechanism controlling their observance, in a manner which can be considered at least equivalent to that for which the Convention provides', and it further specified that 'equivalent' did not mean 'identical' (as this could undermine the interest in international cooperation) but rather 'comparable'.[101] If an organisation such as the EU provides equivalent protection, then this will create a presumption that a state abides by the Convention when merely implementing the organisation's decisions. There is, however, a way in which this presumption can be rebutted: this may happen if, in the particular circumstances of a case, the protection of Convention rights was 'manifestly deficient'.[102]

Putting the matter to the test in the circumstance of Bosphorus's complaint involving Ireland's application of Community law, the Court found no grounds to agree with Bosphorus. It held, somewhat generously perhaps, that there is access to justice for individuals in the EC, both directly under article 230 TEC, and indirectly via the national courts of the member states, and that in its rhetoric the Union has embraced human rights in general and the European Convention in particular. Hence, the presumption of Convention-equivalence could easily be founded.[103] And that presumption, as the ECtHR concluded in a brief paragraph, has not been rebutted.[104] As a result, the Court found that no violation of the first protocol to the Convention had occurred.[105]

---

[100] An early version of this reasoning was already contained in *M. & Co.* ('the transfer of powers to an international organisation is not incompatible with the Convention provided that within that organisation fundamental rights will receive an equivalent protection').

[101] *Bosphorus* (EctHR), para. 155.   [102] *Ibid.*, para. 156.   [103] *Ibid.*, para. 165.

[104] *Ibid.*, para. 166.

[105] *Ibid.*, para. 167. The CFI, in *Ayadi*, para. 124, referred to the ECtHR's conclusion in *Bosphorus*, seemingly accepting it as based on an in-depth investigation of the substance

There seems little reason to disagree with the ECtHR given the facts of *Bosphorus*, despite the circumstance that the sanctions did create considerable hardship for the applicant. Still, the test laid down by the ECtHR is less obvious: by creating a strong presumption and a weak possibility for rebuttal (only if protection is 'manifestly deficient'), the Court makes it difficult for individual applicants to show that mandatory Community law violates their individual human rights. That is no doubt a wise policy, from the perspective of co-existence between courts, but it does amount to paving the way for EU law.[106] On the basis of the *Bosphorus* doctrine, few claims involving EU legislation will ever be successful, not so much because the EU would always respect human rights, but rather because the test may be on the strict side.[107] As a joint concurring opinion puts it, this 'would be tantamount to consenting tacitly to substitution, in the field of Community law, of Convention standards by a Community standard which might be inspired by Convention standards but whose equivalence with the latter would no longer be subject to authorized scrutiny'.[108]

Human rights, on this reading, are not absolute: they must be weighed against the desirability of international cooperation and, what is more, the latter is thought to weigh at least as much, and possibly more, than human rights protection. If *Bosphorus* sets the tone (and it certainly looks like doing so at the time of writing), then the ECtHR and the ECJ are singing in harmony:[109] both have a tendency to place EU law above human rights protection. There is, as a matter of political choice, clearly nothing wrong with this, but it does seem a bit at odds with the ECtHR's pronouncements about the Convention being a constitutional document.

of the case rather than the marginal testing of the presumption of 'equivalent protection' within the EC.

[106] Wildhaber provides a positive spin: in deciding *Bosphorus*, the Court 'acknowledged not only the indispensable role of inter-State cooperation within the framework of international organisations in general, but also the legitimacy and specificity of the European Union integration project, including in respect of its implications for the protection of fundamental rights.' See Wildhaber, 'The European Convention', p. 230.

[107] So also Ciampi, 'L'Union Européenne', esp. p. 100 ('Il est donc difficile d'imaginer des circonstances dans lesquelles la presumption de compatibilité avec la Convention pourrait être renversée').

[108] See *Bosphorus* (EctHR), Rozakis, Tulkens, Traja, Botoucharova, Zagrebelsky and Garlicki, JJ, concurring, at 51. In a similar vein also Ress, J, concurring.

[109] For a discussion in terms of harmony between the two courts, see also Allan Rosas, 'With a Little Help from My Friends: International Case-Law as a Source of Reference for the EU Courts', *The Global Community Yearbook of International Law and Jurisprudence*, 5 (2006), 203–230, esp. pp. 215–6.

Escherian images

There is another aspect to the *Yusuf* and *Kadi* decisions which warrants some discussion. Those cases, like *Bosphorus*, involved not just the relationship between Community law and the Convention, but concerned also the UN Charter. Typically, the argument is that EC law incorporates human rights standards as laid down in the Convention (or, alternatively, that the EC ought to respect the Convention), and that in applying UN law, the Community should be mindful of those human rights or, in fact, grant them supremacy. Hence, by being incorporated in Community law, so the argument goes when reduced to its bare bones, the provisions of the European Convention become applicable also when it comes to implementing UN sanctions.[110]

The argument thus displays an almost Escherian quality: UN law may prevail, but while on top nonetheless has to abide by the Convention which, in turn, derives its supremacy not from itself, but from Community law which, in turn, may well be superior to UN law or, to the extent it does acknowledge the supremacy of UN law, does so voluntarily, which actually suggests it is superior after all, except for the possibility that the Convention may actually be more superior still.[111] As in Escher's drawings of staircases tumbling over and running into one another, so too the case-law of the EC courts (the CFI in particular, but this may be because it is the port of first call) seems to have neither a natural starting point nor a natural point of conclusion.[112]

The only way out, or so it would seem, is to radically dismiss one of the normative orders involved, and this is precisely what Advocate-General

---

[110] A similar idea lies at the heart of Nikolaos Lavranos, *Decisions of International Organisations in the European and Domestic Legal Orders of Selected EU Member States* (Groningen: Europa Law Publishing, 2004), arguing that decisions of international organisations can become directly effective through the intermediary of Community law. See also Nikolaos Lavranos, 'UN Sanctions and Judicial Review', *Nordic Journal of International Law*, 76 (2007), 1–17 (suggesting that Community law demands that the CFI test the compatibility of EU implementations of UN sanctions by testing against the EC Treaty and the European Convention).

[111] Even without involving the UN dimension, Douglas-Scott likewise evokes images of 'non-Euclidian geometry, Borromean knots and Moebius bands', leading to a situation of 'Kafkian [sic] complexity'. See Douglas-Scott, 'A Tale', p. 639.

[112] Note also how some feel that human rights protection is in good hands with the Community: '"as long as" the international level has not generated an equivalent standard of human rights protection, the Community legal order should be entitled to review United Nations law against its *European* constitutional standard.' See Schütze, 'Middle Ground', p. 27 (emphasis in original).

Maduro does in his courageous opinion in the *Kadi* appeal:[113] he posits a radical closing off of the European legal order, rendering it immune to influences from the outside except to the extent (as with human rights) that such influences have become part of EU law. In his reading, it may well be that there is such a thing as the UN Charter, and that there is such a thing as the Security Council, but for purposes of EU law these are irrelevant. Admittedly, the EU may incur responsibility for ignoring UN law (or rather, the member states may incur such responsibility), but that is simply too bad: damn the torpedoes. The only way out, then, is a strict, traditional dualism; but that, needless to say, offers only temporary relief, for at some point – for instance, when determining the responsibility of the EU's member states for the EU's refusal to adhere to Security Council sanctions – questions as to the relationship between the UN Charter, the EU, and the European Convention will surface again.

Conclusion

The previous chapter suggested that article 307 TEC, while ostensibly protecting anterior treaties, almost invariably ends up protecting EC law. The Court's handling of the UN Charter and the European Convention on Human Rights suggests much the same, with the possible exception of *Kadi* and *Yusuf*. Even there, though, while the Court of First Instance acknowledged (following the pleas of Commission and Council) that EC law was subservient to UN law, this subservience resulted from EC law, not UN law, and therewith, in a roundabout way, actually confirmed the supremacy of EC law.

Likewise, the case-law on the European Convention suggests that for the EC courts, EC law is decisive. To the extent that the Convention is referred to or applied, it is on the basis of EC law, in particular article 6 TEU. The Strasbourg organs, in the meantime, have done little to prevent this; instead, they seemed to have accommodated the special position of the EC, as evidenced in particular by the *Bosphorus* judgment of the ECtHR.

---

[113] See Case C-402/05 P (*Kadi* appeal).

8

Posterior treaties: conceptual issues

Introduction

The EC Treaty, as seen in the previous two chapters, in article 307 contains its own rule on what to do with treaties concluded by EC member states before they joined the EC, and the Court of Justice of the EC has had on various occasions to clarify the scope of that provision. Perhaps as a result, article 307 has also met with some treatment in the academic literature, albeit only in the form of law review articles or a few pages here and there in broader studies on EU external relations law.

By contrast, fairly little has been written about what to do with treaties concluded by or between EC member states after they have joined the EC (posterior treaties, as I shall refer to them). With the exception of some of the writings of Bruno de Witte, not much attention has been paid to posterior treaties as such; at best, the topic is treated sideways (or by extension) in the textbooks on external relations of the EC (if at all),[1] in writings on the connections between EC law and international law,[2] and in writings on differentiation in EU law.[3] And the EC Treaty itself lacks a provision on posterior treaties, something that is sometimes deplored in the scarce academic literature.[4]

---

[1] McGoldrick, in his brief survey of the external relations framework, does not mention posterior treaties, and MacLeod *et al.* merely remark that the member states retain a certain "legitimate freedom to act." See, respectively, McGoldrick, *International Relations Law* and MacLeod, Hendry and Hyett, *External Relations*, p. 234. There is the briefest of discussions in Eeckhout, *External Relations of the European Union*, pp. 334–5, and a slightly longer one in Koutrakos, *EU International Relations Law*, pp. 316–17. In both cases, the posterior treaties are discussed more or less under the heading of extended application of article 307.

[2] See, e.g., Jan Vanhamme, *Volkenrechtelijke beginselen in het Europees recht* (Groningen: Europa Publishing, 2001), pp. 278–9.

[3] See, e.g., Filip Tuytschaever, *Differentiation in European Union Law* (Oxford: Hart, 1999).

[4] Krück, for instance, advocates an expansive reading of article 307 for those situations where member states conclude bilateral agreements with third parties and where the Community competence comes to be based on implied powers or has not been exercised earlier: in short, where Community competence could not easily have been foreseen. This, he suggests, is

The aim of this chapter and the next is to clarify the legal position of posterior treaties. The next chapter will have a look at practice; the present chapter aims first and foremost to address some conceptual issues, concentrating in particular on four questions. The first of these relates to the moment in time when an anterior commitment becomes posterior. In other words: how to draw the line between something protected (however fleetingly, perhaps) under article 307 TEC, and something no longer protected.

Second, there is the difficult issue of classification: how to decide that a certain situation is one of conflicting treaties rather than, say, a modification between parties *inter se*, or an agreement replacing an earlier one, or perhaps even merely a subsequent agreement for purposes of interpretation of the earlier agreement?

The third question central to this chapter analyses the connection between the conclusion of posterior treaties, and the division of powers between the EC and its member states.[5] As we shall see, most problems arise due to the transitory nature of this division: something that the member states are still permitted to do on Monday may no longer be permitted on Tuesday, which raises the obvious question whether a treaty concluded on Monday should still be considered as having legal effects; at any rate, one might venture that the treaty partner might, on occasion, be keen on having Monday's treaty continued.[6]

The fourth and final issue is, perhaps, the most tantalising: conflicts between EC law and treaties are typically treated as treaty conflicts, even when the conflict is one between a treaty between two states on the one hand, and an EC regulation, on the other. Yet, how realistic is it still to treat regulations as, somehow, akin to treaties or emanating from treaties rather than as a source of domestic law? If the latter is more appropriate, then also the international law problem would change character: it would no longer be a treaty conflict, but instead a conflict between international law and something that comes perilously close to domestic law. And in such cases, at least international law (if not always domestic law) offers a fairly clear-cut solution, as we shall see.

---

demanded by the interest of the treaty partner. See Hans Krück, *Völkerrechtliche Verträge im Recht der Europäischen Gemeinschaften* (Berlin: Springer, 1977), p. 136.

[5] On the various ways in which powers can be conferred upon international organisations, see Dan Sarooshi, *International Organizations and their Exercise of Sovereign Powers* (Oxford: Oxford University Press, 2005).

[6] For a rare discussion of the treaty partner's position, see Panayi, 'Exploring the *Open Skies*'.

A word of caution: the following discussion does not offer any final answers to the issues raised and, in all likelihood, would be unable to do so within relatively limited confines: each could justifiably be the topic of a separate monograph. The point of the present chapter is rather to raise awareness and outline possible avenues for further reflection.

The time of conclusion

Time is an important factor in dealing with posterior treaties. Mostly, it relates – as already discussed in Chapter 6 in connection with some of the *Open Skies* cases – to the question whether an anterior treaty becomes posterior upon being amended or revised. As noted in Chapter 6, the Court has been less than generous on this point, and has consistently held, without developing much of an underlying theory, that a treaty changes its relevant date upon revision, no matter (it seems) how small the revision may be. There are, at best, only hints in the relevant case-law that the treaty concerned must pass some kind of 'centre of gravity test' first. One can imagine that merely cosmetic changes – a spelling correction, for example – do not change the nature (or the 'centre of gravity') of the treaty concerned, and thus ought not to affect the timing either, but the case-law leaves this possibility open; there are no readily applicable *dicta*.[7] There remains always, therefore, some doubt as to what exactly constitutes a substantive revision which will be substantive enough to turn the old, anterior treaty into a new posterior treaty.[8]

Still, the need for a sensible approach becomes obvious upon the realisation that what holds true for treaties concluded by the member states with third parties, may also hold true for the Community at large. Simply put, the EU established by the Maastricht Treaty, in 1991, is a different animal from the EEC originally created in 1957, as the ECtHR recognised in *Matthews*.[9]

---

[7] In Case C-466/98, *Commission* v. *United Kingdom (Open Skies)* [2002] ECR I-9427, para. 29, the Court limited its finding to the circumstances of the case before it, where the UK and the US had stipulated that their recent agreement was concluded 'for the purpose of replacing' the earlier one. This allowed the Court to conclude that it gave rise to 'new rights and obligations', not merely the continuation of existing rights and obligations.

[8] Pauwelyn takes this doubt to the extreme when discussing the notion of what he calls 'living treaties', which continuously evolve and develop through accession, interpretation, amendment and other, related activities. See Pauwelyn, *Conflict of Norms*, pp. 378–80. Taken seriously, this reduces itself to the position that all treaties are 'living' treaties.

[9] As discussed in Chapter 7.

What this would mean, in law, remains somewhat unclear. Clearly, it is not a serious argument to claim that all existing powers the EC has gathered over the years come to an end when a new treaty version replaces an older one, only to be replaced by identical, and possibly more extensive, powers. In other words, to suggest a succession in law between EEC and EC, EC and EU, EU and Constitutional EU, is not very persuasive; and even if it were, it is by no means certain that legal powers would not succeed accordingly as well.[10]

However, it also seems unlikely to suggest that nothing of legal relevance happens whenever the EC reincarnates. At the very least, there seems to be no plausible reason to suggest that a treaty concluded by a member state with a third party becomes a 'new' instrument upon amendment, whereas the EU treaty itself does not become a 'new' instrument when amended. This would suggest, once more, that the EU Treaty be treated differently from other treaties; yet this begs the question.

Of course, with anterior treaties (as discussed in Chapter 6), there is no particular problem: the text of article 307 TEC provides a definition of sorts, referring to treaties concluded before the entry into force of the EC Treaty or before a member state's accession, as appropriate. There is, however, no corresponding clause (and so no definition either) in the context of posterior treaties. Thus, while a posterior treaty is not protected by article 307, the question does arise that if member state X engages in treaty relations with a third party on Monday, yet on the basis of the development of EU law it would no longer be allowed to have such a treaty on Tuesday, why precisely it is the developed version of EC law that is thought to apply, rather than the original position that member state X found itself in.

As noted, the Court has so far ducked such questions – understandably perhaps, and justifiably in the sense that there has not been any direct need to address them. Arguably, cases such as *Open Skies* concerned amendments that by themselves could be considered as substantive to the extent that they changed the nature of the commitment. Even so, some guidance from the Court could be useful to let the member states know how far things can be taken.

Classifying the problem

One of the preliminary issues to be decided before things can progress is how to characterise the situation that may arise. The Vienna Convention

---

[10] For a discussion of succession of organisations, see Klabbers, *An Introduction*, ch. 15.

on the Law of Treaties distinguishes at least four different situations. First, and most important, there is a regular conflict of the type according to which either A and B have an agreement, and then conclude a new one between themselves (this is the easy scenario), or when A has entered into conflicting obligations with B and C. If this sort of situation is regarded as one of conflicting norms, then article 30 VCLT would apply, in particular paragraphs 3 and 4. The same holds true with respect to multilateral variations (e.g., agreements between A, B, C, D and E, versus agreements between B, C, D, E and F).

Second, the Vienna Convention envisages the amendment of a treaty between all of its parties (article 40) or, more difficult, a modification between some parties *inter se* (article 41). Third, the Vienna Convention also recognises that agreements may be concluded in order to abrogate, terminate or replace earlier agreements (article 59). And fourth, the Convention accepts the conclusion of 'subsequent agreements' for purposes of interpretation of an earlier and, it may be presumed, more central, treaty (article 31). To all this may be added a fifth, left unaddressed in the Vienna Convention: there may be a situation where some or all parties to a treaty conclude an ostensibly non-legally binding instrument which, somehow, conflicts with an earlier binding treaty. While there are no precise rules on how to solve such problems,[11] it is clear that if such instruments are nonetheless expected to somehow have the effect of influencing behaviour (despite being non-legally binding), then some conflict may well arise.

An example of how the Union can be confronted with a successive treaties problem (and the ensuing difficulties of classification) is when the member states decide, *inter se*, to adapt the terms of a convention binding all of them and others. Such an example arose in the late 1990s, when the then Spanish Prime Minister, Aznar, proposed the inclusion of a provision to the effect that the member states would, in their *inter se* relations, not grant refugee status to nationals of other member states. The proposal did not make it into the Amsterdam Treaty, but resulted in a protocol, the so-called Spanish Protocol,[12] which, according to some authoritative observers, is to be considered as a legally binding instrument.[13]

---

[11] Elsewhere, I have argued that the absence of such rules suggests that the faculty of withholding agreements from the workings of law altogether may be more imagined than real. See Klabbers, *The Concept of Treaty*, esp. pp. 135–40.

[12] Formally the Protocol on Asylum for Nationals of Member States of the European Union, annexed to the Treaty establishing the European Community in 1997. See OJ 1997, C 340.

[13] See Gregor Noll, *Negotiating Asylum: The EU Acquis, Extraterritorial Protection and the Common Market of Deflection* (The Hague: Martinus Nijhoff, 2000), pp. 224–7.

On one interpretation, the Spanish Protocol would be in conflict with the Refugee Convention of 1951 and its 1967 Protocol: nationality of the refugee applicant should in no way be decisive. Yet, under the Spanish Protocol, it is in part the nationality of the applicant which helps decide the issue, unless there is a special set of circumstances at work (e.g., if the state of origin has declared an emergency under the European Convention on Human Rights, or if in the EU a procedure for human rights violations has started).

I am not aware of the Spanish Protocol ever having come before a court, be it the EC Court or a court in a member state, but it is perhaps interesting to speculate what might happen. A number of possible interpretations would arise. Under the first, the Spanish Protocol would simply be regarded as an instrument of primary Community law, and as such trump all other concerns bar, perhaps, another primary EC law document – no further questions asked. In the absence of any conflicting document of EU law, the Court would simply apply, and uphold, the Spanish Protocol.

A more subtle argument would resort to article 307 TEC, and go as follows. Granted, so the argument would start, the EC member states are bound by the Refugee Convention. However, it may not constitute an anterior treaty for all of them, especially not if the 1967 Refugee Protocol is factored in (for this might turn it into a posterior agreement, at least for the Community's original member states), and even so, anterior agreements only protect, under most of the cases, the rights of the other contracting parties. This then is premised on a conception of treaties as creating reciprocal rights and duties between states; the Refugee Convention, however, is not such an agreement, but is rather what Sir Gerald Fitzmaurice used to refer to as an integral agreement, creating rights and possibly also obligations for individuals rather than states.[14] Since individuals are not protected by article 307, the Spanish Protocol prevails; end of story.

That is a plausible argument, but also rather unsatisfactory: it makes too much of a literal reading of the case-law, to the detriment of the legal position of the individual, whereas it is precisely the purpose of the Refugee Convention to protect individuals. Consequently, one could imagine a more thoughtful version of the same argument, referring to parts of the case-law where the Court has held not so much that article 307 protects the

---

[14] See in particular Fitzmaurice, 'Third Report', pp. 27–8.

position of third states, but rather, more generically, third parties.[15] This argument would make it possible to have the Refugee Convention prevail as an anterior treaty, unless, on the facts, it would not be anterior, for example, when some of the EU members would have ratified the Refugee Convention after they joined the EU, and on a reading which would not necessarily have to include the 1967 Refugee Protocol. In the end, then, under this interpretation, the Refugee Convention could prevail and, of practical relevance, could prevail not by virtue of international law, but by virtue of EU law itself. The Spanish Protocol would arguably still be valid law, but would remain without application. There are, however, other possibilities still, based on general international law. Two of those warrant discussion.

Under article 30 of the Vienna Convention, arguably, the Spanish Protocol would simply be the *lex posterior* (if a Protocol such as this can be considered as *lex* to begin with; if not, then it would seem that it can be ignored when incompatible with a legal instrument, but that, in turn, would seem to defy the intentions behind the Spanish Protocol) and therewith be fully applicable in relations between the member states of the EU; in relation with other states, the Refugee Convention would continue to apply. That, of course, was exactly in line with Aznar's proposal: to de-activate the Refugee Convention in *inter se* relations while keeping it active in relations with third parties.

Even so, this particular line of thought could be regarded as disingenuous: it would take the sting out of the Refugee Convention's application in Europe, and would be based on the highly debatable proposition that the political situation in the EU's member states would be such as to render it implausible that people would ever have to flee for political reasons.

This then leads to another argument, invoking not article 30 of the Vienna Convention, but rather article 41 of that Convention. Under article 41, the proposal would probably not have been acceptable: it would quite possibly amount to a modification between some of its parties of

---

[15] See in particular Case 812/79, *Attorney General* v. *Burgoa* [1980] ECR 2787. In para. 11, the Court held that article 307 TEC should be read as meaning 'that the application of the Treaty does not affect either the duty to observe the rights of non-member countries under an agreement concluded with a Member State prior to the entry into force of the Treaty . . . or the observance by that Member State of its obligations under the agreement'. The latter passage opens the door for a broader reading of article 307, and this broader reading finds some support in the decisions in Case C-62/98, *Commission* v. *Portugal* [2000] ECR I-5171, and Case C-84/98, *Commission* v. *Portugal* [2000] ECR I-5215. For a discussion along these lines, see Klabbers, 'Moribund on the Fourth of July?'.

the Refugee Convention, in conflict with the object and purpose thereof (if it can be accepted that object and purpose of the Refugee Convention is to protect refugees without regard for their nationality, which seems reasonable enough[16]), and therewith be impermissible.[17]

While it is clear that the Spanish Protocol is not meant to terminate the Refugee Convention (nor could it), it might still be possible to regard it as a 'subsequent agreement' for purposes of interpretation of the Refugee Convention. On this reading, the idea would be that the text of the Refugee Convention remains unaffected as such, but would come to be understood in relations between EU members *inter se* as being inapplicable. To the extent that this interpretation would prevail, it would, arguably, take the place of the Refugee Convention. The one counter-argument would seem to be that, under article 31, it is plausible to suggest that *inter se* agreements are excluded: the text speaks of subsequent agreements between the parties to the original treaty, suggesting that all parties ought to be included, not just some of them. Then again, if remaining parties to the Refugee Convention were to accept, explicitly or, more likely, tacitly, the Spanish Protocol as a subsequent agreement, then arguably the requirement of comprising all parties is sufficiently met.

As the example suggests, figuring out the precise status of successive treaties can be a complicated task and can lead to radically diverging results. Applying only EU law, it is possible to find the agreement both permissible and impermissible, depending on whether the Refugee Convention is construed as anterior or not, and depending on the proper interpretation of the case-law. And under the Vienna Convention, the same two possibilities are arguable in a plausible manner: either permissible under article 30 (and perhaps under article 31 as well), or impermissible under article 41.[18]

---

[16] See the discussion on the definition of 'refugee' in Guy Goodwin-Gill, *The Refugee in International Law* (Oxford: Clarendon Press, 1983), pp. 12–13. Note that internally displaced persons are not regarded as refugees in the meaning of the Refugee Convention, but surely it would be a stretch to regard Community refugees within the Community as internally displaced: such would only be plausible on the basis of a conception of the Community as a state, or at least a state-like entity (see, however, section 4 of this chapter for an argument to that effect).

[17] Note, moreover, that under article 63, paragraph 1 TEC, any Community policy on asylum must be in accordance with the 1951 Refugee Convention and the 1967 Refugee Protocol.

[18] It would seem less plausible, though some do, to treat the Spanish Protocol as an impermissible reservation to the Refugee Convention; this would require both formal submission of the reservation (which is usually only possible when expressing consent to be bound or before, but not after having been a party for many years) and giving the treaty partners the

Part of the problem, then, is that there is no way to determine *a priori* which rules to apply (article 30, on conflict? Or article 31, on interpretation? Or article 41, addressing modification?), nor even which set of rules to apply: EU law, or international law? The case-law of the EU Court suggests that it will usually be quite content to apply EC law alone,[19] but to this the international lawyer can argue, with some cogency, that the EU cannot isolate itself from international law completely.

Relevant for present purposes, then, is that the precise qualification of an issue (how to determine the 'field constitution' of an issue[20]) may be of some importance: is the agreement to be qualified as a later treaty? Or as a modification *inter se*? And who gets to decide this?[21] Under EC law, it is clear that the Court of Justice would consider itself the final arbiter on this sort of issues – it could hardly be otherwise.[22] But again, as already noted, Community law (and thus the EC Court) cannot decide with finality on matters involving international law and affecting the rights of third parties. The opposite would entail that the Community would consider itself above the law.

Powers and institutional law

The third issue is arguably the most intricate. In its classic *Kramer* decision,[23] the Court held that until such time as the Community started to exercise its powers, the member states would be free to keep on exercising their own (residual) powers. *In casu*, the Community had obtained, by means of the Act of Accession of Ireland, Denmark and the UK, an exclusive power to set up a common fisheries policy, including external action. External action relating to the conservation of marine resources was not

---

possibility to object. For such a reservations approach, see Lenaerts and de Smijter, 'The European Union as an Actor', esp. pp. 116–7.

[19] See, e.g., Klabbers, 'International Law in Community Law'.

[20] See Duncan Kennedy, *A Critique of Adjudication {Fin de Siècle}* (Cambridge, MA: Harvard University Press, 1997), pp. 140–1.

[21] It is of course possible, if not always desirable perhaps, that the member states conclude treaties together which do not relate to earlier treaties involving third parties, e.g. to give effect to assignments contained in the EC treaties themselves (such as the erstwhile EEX-Treaty). As these do not create problems of successive treaties, I will leave them undiscussed. For a useful discussion, see de Witte, 'Internationale verdragen tussen lidstaten van de Europese Unie', esp. pp. 94–101.

[22] See, e.g., Case C-415/93, *Union Royale Belge des Sociétés de Football Association ASBL and others* v. *Jean-Marc Bosman and others* [1995] ECR I-4921.

[23] Joined Cases 3, 4 and 6/76, *Kramer* [1976] ECR 1305.

immediately forthcoming, however, which led to the question whether catch quota adopted by the Netherlands, in implementation of an international obligation, were compatible with EC law. The Court famously held that any authority the member states might have was to be transitional, and was to last only until the Community would fully exercise its functions in the matter.[24]

In other words, there might be situations where the member states may seem free to act, but are not, in that their actions (including the conclusion of agreements *inter se* or with third parties) can only take place by the acquiescence of the Community; they act on 'borrowed time', so to speak. Such a situation arose in *Arbelaiz-Emazabel*.[25] Mr Arbelaiz-Emazabel, a Spanish fisherman, was caught fishing in French waters in 1977, without the licence required by Community Regulation 2160/77. He claimed (and a lower court agreed) that he was entitled to do so on the basis of a French-Spanish exchange of notes concluded in 1967, a document that was itself based on the 1964 London Fisheries Convention. The EC Court, however, disagreed, holding that whatever rights France and Spain possessed until the adoption of a Community regime were only of an interim nature, since the power to adopt conservation measures had been transferred to the Community. The conclusion of a bilateral exchange of notes, therefore, was useful while it lasted, but subordinate to Community legislation.

The Court's task was made somewhat easier by the existence of a few special circumstances. Thus, the London Fisheries Convention itself recognised the possibility of supervening EC legislation,[26] and Spain seemed to have accepted the position that its rights under the London Fisheries Convention and the 1967 Exchange of Notes would not persist during the negotiating of a fisheries agreement between the Community and Spain (at the time not yet a member state).[27] Moreover, the Court observed that the rights to fish as such were left untouched; the only thing Community law demanded was that the fishermen respect catch quotas (just like Community fishermen) and obtain a licence, and that in itself was justified since it would be practically impossible to control fishing by non-Community nationals in any other way.[28]

---

[24] *Ibid.*, paras. 39–41.
[25] Case 181/80, *Procureur Général* v. *Arbelaiz-Emazabel* [1981] ECR 2961.
[26] *Ibid.*, paras. 12–13.
[27] *Ibid.*, para. 18. See also paras. 27–28, in which the Court observes that Spain actively participated in the administration of Community's new regime, e.g. by issuing licences.
[28] *Ibid.*, para. 25.

The most interesting issue for present purposes to arise from *Arbelaiz-Emazabel* is the assumption of power on the part of the Community, and this in itself raises two related problems. First, there is the problem of timing: when exactly can the Community be deemed to have obtained a power? Second, there is the problem of drawing lines: what exactly belongs to the Community's power, and what is still left to the member states? And how to make this determination?

It is, of course, as a matter of principle perfectly reasonable to allow the Community to act within the sphere of its own powers; indeed, many would agree that the very point of international organisations (including the Community) is to act on the basis, and within the limits, of the powers conferred upon them by their member states.[29]

More problematic perhaps, but still easily justifiable, is the presumption of power during an interim period. One may argue (and the Court has in fact argued) that in the period between the granting of a power to the Community and the actual exercise thereof, the field must nonetheless be regarded as occupied by the Community. After all, to allow the member states to act without limits after having delegated a power to the Community would run the risk of undermining that very power. It is no coincidence that the law of treaties recognises the existence of an interim obligation to cover the periods between signing, ratifying and entry into force of a treaty;[30] by analogy, as soon as a power has been conferred upon the Community, it seems reasonable to suggest that the member states are no longer completely free to act on the topic encompassed by that power.[31] And it seems equally reasonable to allow the member states to continue employing activities, subject to Community approval.

---

[29] See generally Klabbers, *An Introduction.*

[30] This is codified in article 18 of the Vienna Convention, and has been relied upon also within EC law itself, both when it comes to treaties concluded by the EU (see Case T-115/94, *Opel Austria GmbH* v. *Council,* [1997] ECR II-39) and when it comes to the effects of EC instruments before their entry into force: see Case C-129/96, *Inter-Environnement Wallonie ASBL* v. *Région Wallonne* [1997] ECR I-7411, para. 45. The Commission relied on the same argument in the Dutch *Open Skies* case, suggesting that the Netherlands could not conclude a bilateral agreement incompatible with a regulation pending entry into force of that Regulation. The Court did not (and did not have to) address the issue. See Case C-523/04, *Commission* v. *Netherlands,* para. 60 (judgment of 24 April 2007).

[31] The same reasoning has also been applied by the Court pending the full use of the Common Commercial Policy. See already Case 41/76, *Suzanne Criel, née Donckerwolcke and Henri Schou* v. *Procureur de la République au Tribunal de Grande Instance de Lille and Directeur-Général des Douanes* [1976] ECR 1934.

For such a system to work, however, one thing is imperative, and that is that it is clear to all concerned that a power conferral concerns an exclusive power, or at least a general power which can be divided into various specific powers, some of which must be exclusive. For it is only on such a scenario that one can meaningfully claim that the member states become subservient to the Community. In *Arbelaiz-Emazabel*, arguably, that condition was met (or rather, met as fully as possible[32]): it is generally accepted that the Community, on the basis of articles 100 and 102 of the 1972 Act of Accession, acquired the exclusive competence to deal with fisheries and conservation of marine biological resources.

It would be less self-evident, though, when a power is shared between the Community and its member states, or where the treaty speaks in terms of the Community's powers being 'complementary' to powers of the member states.[33] In such a scenario, the precise scope of Community powers can only be determined by Community action; it would be difficult to justify blaming the member states for doing something that, they feel, is at least partly justifiable on the basis of their own powers.

This brings us to the second issue arising, in this connection, from *Arbelaiz-Emazabel*: it raises the question what exactly the scope of powers of the Community is. As noted, the Court's position in *Arbelaiz-Emazabel* itself was defendable, both on the basis of Spain's actions and on the basis of the fairly uncontroversial nature of the Community's competence over fisheries and marine conservation.

However, in other cases, things were decidedly less clear-cut, and a prime example would be the *Open Skies* cases. The bilateral agreements concluded by a number of member states with the US were fairly complicated agreements, dealing with a variety of issues, ranging from aviation security to adoption of a computerised reservations system, and from licensing to fares. The Court eventually held that on some (but not all) of these issues, the Community had acquired an exclusive external competence, meaning that on some of these topics the member states would not be allowed to take any action any more. Yet, the Court did not reach that conclusion without some re-routings.

---

[32] I will return to this below, outlining the unsatisfactory nature of analysing powers as communicating barrels.
[33] See, e.g., article 164 TEC (on research policy) and article 177 TEC (development policy power). For an analysis in constitutional-theoretical terms, see Robert Schütze, 'Co-operative Federalism Constitutionalised: The Emergence of Complementary Competences in the EC Legal Order', *European Law Review*, 31 (2006), 167–84.

For one thing, there was evident discord within the Community itself about whether the Community would have such an external power and, if so, on what basis. The Commission, as early as 1992, had claimed that the Community's external competence would derive from article 133 TEC (which grants the Community an exclusive competence in the field on international commerce and trade in goods), but this was, at the time, rejected by the Council.[34] Later on, the Council suggested that instead, a (non-exclusive) Community external aviation policy could be based on article 84 TEC (which provides for some action in the field of transport, based on a Council decision), something the Court rejected in *Open Skies*.[35] Indeed, in 1993 the Council suggested that member states 'retain their full powers in relations with third countries in the aviation sector, subject to measures already adopted or to be adopted by the Council in that domain'.[36]

Before the Court, the Commission employed two different arguments. It argued, first, that the Community's external competence derived from the Court's earlier finding in *Opinion 1/76*.[37] In this opinion, the Court had held that an external power may exist if it is the case that an internal power (conferred expressly) can only be used effectively if accompanied by external action.[38] In *Open Skies*, however, this was not the case: *Open Skies* 'does not disclose a situation in which internal competence could effectively be exercised only at the same time as external competence'.[39]

The Court would, however, find that the Community had an exclusive external competence within the meaning of its classic *ERTA* decision and relying on the adoption of Regulation 2409/92:[40] if the Community has taken measures internally, the member states are pre-empted from taking

---

[34] See, by way of example, Case C-469/98, *Commission v. Finland (Open Skies)*, [2002] ECR I-9627, paras. 17–18.

[35] *Ibid.*, paras. 55–56: the circumstance that Community action would only be possible on the basis of an explicit Council decision under article 84 entailed that this article itself could not be considered a grant of an external competence.

[36] *Ibid.*, para. 18.

[37] *Ibid.*, esp. para. 45. This refers to Opinion 1/76 *(Laying-up Fund)*, [1977] ECR 741.

[38] It is perhaps useful to note, with Gaja, that acceptance of this doctrine by the member states is by no means certain. See Giorgio Gaja, 'Trends in Judicial Activism and Judicial Self-Restraint Relating to Community Interests', in Enzo Cannizzaro (ed.), *The European Union as an Actor in International Relations* (The Hague: Kluwer, 2002), pp. 117–34, p. 122.

[39] See *Open Skies* (Finland), para. 62.

[40] See Case 22/70, *Commission v. Council (ERTA)* [1971] ECR 263, paras. 80, 100.

external measures which may affect those internal measures or distort their scope. This the Court now held to be the case in *Open Skies*: some of the provisions of the Open Skies agreements would involve stepping on the Community's toes, even if the member state concerned had made sure that either there would be no conflict with Community law, or in case of conflict Community law would prevail: the member state's failure 'to fulfil its obligations lies in the fact that it was not authorised to enter into such a commitment on its own, even if the substance of that commitment does not conflict with Community law.'[41] In the end, this would violate article 10 TEC (formerly article 5), which lays down the very general notion of Community solidarity ('*Gemeinschaftstreue*', in good German): member states are to refrain from measures which might jeopardise the attainment of the objectives of the EC Treaty.[42]

Thus, throughout the *Open Skies* saga, at least four bases for the existence of an exclusive Community competence were invoked by the Commission: two regular treaty provisions (first article 133 TEC, later article 84 TEC), the *1/76* doctrine, and the *ERTA* doctrine. This alone suggests that the situation is far from clear. That impression is strengthened by the Court's finding that it was only on some points that the bilateral agreement with the US went against a Community competence – on other points captured within the same bilateral agreement, no Community competence was affected.[43] The fact that widespread litigation was required to identify Community competence, moreover, once again suggests that things are far from clear.

This can lead to several possible conclusions. One is that when the divisions of power are far from clear, a mixed agreement (an agreement entered into both by the EC and its member states) might be the most practicable solution.[44] But that presupposes as a minimum that it is clear that the power division is unclear. Where (as was arguably the case in *Open Skies*) the member states are convinced, in fairly large numbers, that the

---

[41] See *Open Skies* (Finland), para 101.

[42] *Ibid.*, para. 112. The Court also held that concluding the agreement violated two regulations; this raises issues which will be discussed below.

[43] Eeckhout sensibly suggests that much of the case-law on external powers can be understood by distinguishing between the existence of a power, and its substantive scope. The Court, he suggested, has been quick to find a power to exist, but has always been careful to sketch the substantive limits of such a power. See Eeckhout, *External Relations*, ch. 3.

[44] The leading study is Joni Heliskoski, *Mixed Agreements as a Technique for Organizing the International Relations of the European Community and its Member States* (The Hague: Kluwer, 2001).

power to conclude external aviation agreements has not been transferred to the EC, it might be difficult to get them to accept the wisdom of mixity. Additionally, there is the drawback that a mixed agreement, almost by definition, signifies the existence of shared competences. While there are useful policy reasons to suggest that mixed agreements ought also to be concluded when the Community has exclusive powers and thus, technically, could go it alone (in particular, the member states' involvement will add to the political acceptance of the agreement concerned, and might facilitate its implementation), it would seem that mixed agreements are typically used in cases of non-exclusive powers.[45]

Alternatively, of course, it might be simplest to let the Community handle anything in case the power division is unclear, and this seems to be the course adopted by both Commission and Court. There are advantages to such an approach. For one thing, a unified EC representation might be in the position to demand greater or better concessions from partners than the individual member states are capable of, and it prevents the worst effects of nebulous power divisions from arising by simply ignoring it. The drawback, however, is that it steps on the toes of the prerogatives of domestic political communities and their institutions: as long as a power has not been delegated or transferred, there is no *a priori* reason to suppose that it has come to rest on the would-be recipient.[46]

This lack of clarity about the division of competences is, of course, nothing new: it has been a constant feature of the external relations law of the EC since the early 1970s and is at the heart of the classic judicial decisions and opinions, from the *ERTA* case onwards. Tuytschaever summarises the general position well:

> It is of course difficult, if not impossible, to determine the Member States' room for manoeuvre in the abstract. Whether or not an envisaged agreement with one or more third countries is of a kind to affect or to alter the

---

[45] Heliskoski subtly suggests that the term 'shared competence' or 'shared power' here is somewhat out of place: it is not the power that is shared; rather it is the exercise by EC and member states of their own respective powers that is shared. *Ibid.*, p. 48.

[46] The member states had recognised as much in the Treaty establishing a Constitution for Europe, which stipulated in no uncertain terms that unless a transfer had taken place, powers were assumed to have rested with the member states. Article I-11, paragraph 2, reads: 'Under the principle of conferral, the Union shall act within the limits of the competences conferred upon it by the Member States in the Constitution to attain the objectives set out in the Constitution. Competences not conferred upon the Union in the Constitution remain with the Member States.' This is retained in the 2007 Reform Treaty, in the new article 3(a) TEC.

scope of existing Community rules will have to be assessed on the basis of the merits of each case.[47]

Tuytschaever's words point to a more general issue: to what extent is it feasible, or useful, or realistic, to employ a 'power perspective' when discussing and analysing the division of tasks (it is difficult to avoid writing the word 'powers' here) between international organisations and their member states? At least with respect to the European Community, an argument can be made that doing so is not, or no longer perhaps, very useful.

That argument starts from the recognition that, in some cases, it may be possible for a member state to act squarely within the scope of its own powers, and yet end up in conflict with Community law. The possibility was first recognised, so it seems, in the early 1990s, when in enforcing aspects of its abortion legislation (surely as such unaffected by Community law), the Irish government saw itself confronted with the possibility that in doing so it might impede the freedom to provide services within the Community.[48] Thus, acting within its own power, Ireland would nonetheless end up undermining a Community power.[49] Preventing individuals from advertising the possibility of having a legal abortion abroad could possibly,[50] so it turned out, interfere with the free movement of services.

This suggests that powers are not communicating barrels: while both member state and EC act within their powers, nonetheless a collision or interference can take place. In other – and possibly more familiar – words, a division of powers between two distinct entities is not a zero-sum game. Yet this is how powers are usually conceived: whatever A bestows upon B comes to rest upon B and will either stay there or flow back,[51] but the assumption, widely held, is that they will not interfere with each other.[52]

---

[47] See Tuytschaever, *Differentiation*, p. 172.

[48] See Case C-159/90, *Society for the Protection of Unborn Children Ireland Ltd* v. *Stephen Grogan and others* [1991] ECR I-4685.

[49] Probably the first to have recognised this is Gráinne de Búrca, 'Fundamental Human Rights and the Reach of EC Law', *Oxford Journal of Legal Studies*, 13 (1993), 283–319. I have explored this with respect to external relations in Jan Klabbers, 'Restraints on the Treaty-Making Powers of Member States Deriving from EU Law: Towards a Framework for Analysis', in Cannizzaro (ed.), The EU as an Actor, pp. 151–75.

[50] The Court never had to reach that conclusion: as the 'advertisements' were provided without remuneration, they fell outside the scope of EC law.

[51] The latter is rare, but not impossible. See, e.g., Daniela Obradovic, 'Repatriation of Powers in the European Community', *Common Market Law Review*, 34 (1997), 59–88.

[52] Compare, e.g., Sarooshi, *International Organizations*.

There are, however, a few problems with such a conception. First, as already alluded to above, it might be next to impossible to actually identify the division of powers. This difficulty may result from a more general legislative uncertainty (it may be problematic to figure out whether a power to do X does or does not encompass a power to do Y[53]) but, more fundamentally, it may also result from a problem with perspectives.

In more concrete terms (and as practice abundantly suggests), a general power to do something need not necessarily include all sorts of specific powers on all individual aspects. A general power to conclude international aviation agreements, to resort to the *Open Skies* scenario, may or may not encompass a specific power to address computerised reservations systems; it may or may not encompass a specific power to discuss landing rights; it may or may not encompass a specific power to regulate aircraft security. In other words: the general power to conclude external aviation agreements by no means necessarily includes certain specific powers: what looks from a distance like a power resting upon the Community may, upon closer scrutiny, turn out to rest with the member states – and *vice versa*.

The conclusion then must be that analysing things in terms of a general division of powers is, in the Community context, at best a useful starting point, but not likely to be conclusive without more. Community law has of course fully realised as much, but has some problems coming to terms with the paucity of the power perspective. One answer which has had some success has been the invention of mixed agreements, celebrated by Joseph Weiler as constituting the EU's 'near-unique contribution to true federalism'.[54] Another answer, less successful, has been the attempt to borrow the notion of pre-emption from federalism theory.[55] This has proven less successful because a doctrine of pre-emption actually presupposes the existence of some federal type of system; it presupposes a closed and working federalism where the exercise of powers does not get

---

[53] This drives the implied powers doctrine, in its narrow version: a power to do one thing might necessarily imply the power to complete a preliminary or related step. For a discussion, see Klabbers, *An Introduction*, pp. 67–73.

[54] See Joseph H. H. Weiler, 'The External Legal Relations of Non-Unitary Actors: Mixity and the Federal Principle', as reproduced in his *The Constitution of Europe* (Cambridge: Cambridge University Press, 1999), pp. 130–87, p. 130.

[55] On the doctrine of pre-emption in Community law generally, see Eugene Daniel Cross, 'Pre-emption of Member-State Law in the European Economic Community: A Framework for Analysis', *Common Market Law Review*, 29 (1992), 447–72; Jan H. Jans, 'National Legislative Autonomy? The Procedural Constraints of European Law', *Legal Issues of European Integration*, 25 (1998/I), 25–58.

suspended in mid-air.[56] In addition, some might suggest that the notion of subsidiarity has a role to play here (the result being greater latitude for the member states) but, as Davies has persuasively argued, subsidiarity only works when there is clarity about the division of competences: it is less helpful when the question arises how exactly powers have been, or should be, divided.[57]

Either way, both mixity and pre-emption still work on the basis of a division of powers being a zero-sum game; yet, as *Open Skies* makes abundantly clear, the model of the zero-sum game is itself not persuasive, and it might be more sound to adopt a different, broader, perspective.[58] In addition to borrowing the notion of subsidiarity from the way Christianity has organised itself, the main solution the member states have thought of is to stipulate quite explicitly in the EC Treaty, since Maastricht in particular, that Community powers are shared with those of the member states, or that the powers of EC and member states are complementary to one another.[59]

While this is neither the time nor the place to develop an alternative way of studying the activities of the EU and the relations between the EU and its member states,[60] this discussion is of relevance in the present context because it suggests that, with posterior treaties, the problems identified in *Open Skies* (and earlier in *Arbelaiz-Emazabel*) are bound to occur time and again: there is no possibility of ever achieving an airtight division of powers between Community and member states allowing both

---

[56] In the words of George Bermann, pre-emption 'is a quintessential federalism issue', not suitable within an 'international law paradigm'. See George A. Bermann, 'Taking Sub-sidiarity Seriously: Federalism in the European Community and the United States', 94 *Columbia Law Review*, 94 (1994), 331–456, p. 358.

[57] See Gareth Davies, 'Subsidiarity: The Wrong Idea, in the Wrong Place, at the Wrong Time', *Common Market Law Review*, 43 (2006), 63–84: 'Subsidiarity's weakness is that it assumes the primacy of the central goal, and allows no mechanism for questioning whether or not it is desirable, in the light of other interests, to fully pursue this' (p. 78).

[58] In 'Restraints' I have elaborated a 'restraints' perspective, which suggests that it is not merely the absence of a power which may inhibit actors from acting.

[59] For an overview with respect to external relations (and it is in this field that the prob-lem manifests itself most clearly), see Marise Cremona, 'External Relations and External Competence: The Emergence of an Integrated Policy', in Paul Craig and Gráinne de Búrca (eds.), *The Evolution of EU Law* (Oxford: Oxford University Press, 1999), pp. 137–75. See also Schütze, 'Co-operative Federalism'.

[60] Davies, 'Subsidiarity', suggests a role for 'true proportionality', i.e. a proportionality that recognises the legitimate interests of member states, resulting in the possibility of saying that involvement of the Community in a policy area is simply 'too much'. Schütze, 'Co-operative Federalism', notes the existence of so-called 'negative powers'.

actors to know in advance whether or not a certain envisaged action falls within their competences or, more importantly perhaps, does not infringe someone else's prerogatives.

It is perhaps no coincidence that, in the relevant cases, a prominent role is played by the surprisingly under-analysed and under-theorised notion of *Gemeinschaftstreue*: Community solidarity, which plays, in the words of one commentator, a significant role in creating general duties on national authorities of member states: most of these general duties are said to follow from this notion.[61] Under article 10 TEC (formerly article 5) member states shall take measures to ensure fulfilment of obligations under the treaty, shall facilitate the achievement of the Community's tasks, and abstain from measures which can jeopardise the attainment of the Community's objectives.[62] That is an extremely useful and relevant provision, but cannot amount to a granting of carte blanche power. To paraphrase the ICJ on the related notion of good faith: good faith alone cannot create obligations where otherwise none would exist.[63]

The point, then, is how to draw the borderline between finding a Community treaty-making power on the basis of article 10 alone (which would not seem plausible) and finding that a treaty concluded between member states or between a member state and a third party, while acting within the scope of their powers, nonetheless violates Community law by somehow interfering with the proper exercise of Community powers. That borderline may well be impossible to draw, and perhaps it is useful to point out that in the relevant cases, the Court could also always bolster its conclusion by pointing to the violation of secondary Community law. But that, in turn, raises another issue: if a treaty concluded by a member state with a third party conflicts with secondary Community law, can the conflict meaningfully be classified as a treaty conflict? Or should it rather be seen, more classically, as a conflict between international law and domestic law?

---

[61] See John Temple Lang, 'The Duties of National Authorities under Community Constitutional Law', *European Law Review*, 23 (1998), 109–31, p. 111.

[62] For an early overview and taxonomy, see John Temple Lang, 'Community Constitutional Law: Article 5 EEC Treaty', *Common Market Law Review*, 27 (1990), 645–81.

[63] See *Border and Transborder Armed Action* (Nicaragua v. Honduras), [1988] *ICJ Reports* 69, para. 94. Likewise, Lang (generally favouring a broad application of *Gemeinschaftstreue*, or so it seems), is compelled to note that article 10 cannot be used 'to create new kinds of obligations for Member States'. See Lang, 'Article 5', p. 647. But see Due, who argues that the ECJ has used article 10 TEC as the basis for finding new member state obligations and Community powers. See Ole Due, 'Article 5 du traité CEE: Une disposition de caractère fédéral?', *Collected Courses of the Academy of European Law*, 2 (1991/II), 17–35.

A domestic law paradigm?

This is the fourth issue to be discussed when it comes to posterior treaties. So far, the general position has been to treat posterior treaties, when they conflict with Community law, as entailing a violation by a member state of its obligations under Community law. As a result, the member state in question is urged, under Community law, to rectify the situation.

This way of looking at things is premised on an important dual assumption: first, it assumes that any conflict between EC law and a posterior treaty is regarded as a treaty conflict; and, second, it assumes that, as allowed (if not exactly prescribed) by the law of treaties, in case of conflict EC law prevails.[64] The member state has to bring its international commitments into line with Community law; Community law does not give way, with posterior treaties, to the international commitment entered into, in all innocence, by the member state.

The question then arises whether, and in what circumstances, this dual assumption is tenable, and here it may be useful to make a distinction between primary Community law (the rules of the EC Treaty and its related instruments), and secondary law (the 'legislation' made by the EC in the form of regulations, directives and the like).

It would seem perfectly reasonable to treat a conflict between a posterior treaty and a rule of primary Community law as a treaty conflict, for that is, after all, what it is: a conflict between article X of treaty Y, and article A of treaty B. One of those treaties just happens to be the EC Treaty. From the perspective of international law, this basic situation is not different from that involving any other treaty, with the possible exception of the UN Charter (due to article 103 UN).

Things may be different, though, if the conflict is between article X of treaty Y, concluded by one the EC member states with a non-member, and article A of Community Regulation B. The question here is whether the regulation at issue should be regarded as being inextricably connected to the EC Treaty, to such an extent that one can still meaningfully speak of a treaty conflict, or whether it would be more realistic to view the regulation not as a treaty emanation, but rather as a piece of domestic legislation.

---

[64] Boulois notes that one of the few possibilities for the EC to do away with posterior treaties concluded by member states with third parties would be by invoking the procedural rule relating to a violation of domestic (in this case: European) treaty-making procedures, as laid down in article 46 of the Vienna Convention. He adds, with a sense of irony, that in such a case Community law would derive its prevalence from international law. See Boulois, 'Le droit des Communautés Européennes', p. 71.

Again, two perspectives vie for prominence. Under the classic international organisations model, EC instruments are indeed best regarded as emanations from the original EC Treaty: a regulation gives rise to obligations under the EC Treaty, albeit in an indirect manner. Those obligations derive, ultimately, from the effect the EC Treaty attaches to Regulations, and thus, one could plausibly argue, they are extensions of the EC Treaty. Without the EC Treaty, there would be no regulations; without the EC Treaty, regulations would be devoid of any legal effect. In much the same way, a Security Council resolution gives rise to obligations under the UN Charter, and a decision by the WTO's Ministerial Conference is thought to give rise to obligations under the WTO Agreement: the resulting obligations emanate from the organisation's constituent document, and form part of the legal order established by that constituent document.[65]

Importantly, though, the effects of such resolutions or decisions taken within the UN or the WTO remains limited, without more, to the legal order of the organisation: there are no effects, without more, in the domestic legal orders of the member states. In order for effects to arise in the legal orders of the member states, the member states must separately recognise such resolutions or decisions as being part of their domestic order, either by constitutionally providing for their direct effect or, on a case-by-case basis, through acts transforming them into domestic law.[66]

This is, so it would seem, an accurate description of the way decisions of most international organisations gain their effects; it is, however, gainsaid by Community law. Since the early 1960s, the Community prides itself on being a 'new legal order', 'the subjects of which comprise not only Member States but also their nationals', as the Court put it in its classic *Van Gend & Loos* decision.[67] Community law is pictured as imposing obligations and granting rights to individuals '[i]ndependently of the legislation of Member States';[68] its legal effects in the legal orders of the member states follow from Community law itself and do not, as in

---

[65] In this sense, e.g., H. G. Schermers and Niels M. Blokker, *International Institutional Law*, 4th edn (The Hague: Martinus Nijhoff, 2003), p. 720.

[66] Lavranos suggests that for member states of the EU, direct applicability in domestic law of decisions by international organisations may follow from transformation through Community law. Thus, a decision of the Security Council, say, may become directly applicable in the EU's member states upon having been transposed into a Community Regulation. See Nikolaos Lavranos, *Decisions of International Organizations in the European and Domestic Legal Orders of Selected EU Member States* (Groningen: Europa Law Publishing, 2004).

[67] See Case 26/62, *Van Gend & Loos* v. *Netherlands Fiscal Administration* [1963] ECR 1.

[68] *Ibid.*

the classical scenario, depend on domestic legal provisions concerning the way international law enters domestic law. Indeed, often enough the Community prides itself on being different from regular international organisations, and being unique within the setting of international law (perhaps even so unique as to no longer qualify as part of international law). And many observers tend to think of the direct effect that Community law exercises by virtue of itself as one of the defining constitutional hallmarks of the Community.[69]

The very defining feature of a regulation, moreover, is that it shall be 'directly applicable in all Member States',[70] with the underlying idea being that the legal effect of a regulation shall be exactly the same in all member states. Settled case-law suggests that this goes so far as not allowing domestic legislative or implementing bodies to tamper with the terms of a regulation.[71] For purposes of the legal orders of the member states, in other words, a regulation is to be regarded as domestic law, having the same (or even higher[72]) status as other domestic law. The only difference relates to the source of the obligation: it springs from a non-domestic source rather than a purely domestic one.[73]

On this line of reasoning, then, it is plausible to regard a conflict between a posterior treaty and a regulation no longer as a treaty conflict, but rather as a conflict between international and domestic law. The regulation, after all, is indistinguishable from other pieces of domestic legislation. But doing so will also imply that the situation will be subject to a different regime: on the above line of reasoning, the rules on treaty conflict are not applicable. Instead, the conflict between a posterior treaty and a regulation would be governed by the rule that a state or a party 'may not invoke the provisions of its internal law as justification for its failure to perform a treaty'.[74]

---

[69] See, classically, Eric Stein, 'Lawyers, Judges, and the Making of a Transnational Constitution', *American Journal of International Law*, 75 (1981), 1–27.

[70] See article 249 TEC (formerly article 189).

[71] See, e.g., case 50/76, *Amsterdam Bulb* v. *Produktschap voor Siergewassen* [1997] ECR 137, para. 7.

[72] See Case 6/64, *Flaminio Costa* v. *ENEL* [1964] ECR 585.

[73] Blokker notes that regulations are 'fundamentally different from the traditional types of decisions of international organizations', and adds that they may still require practical implementation by domestic authorities. Then again, the same can be said about much domestic law. See Niels M. Blokker, 'Decisions of International Organizations: The Case of the European Union', *Netherlands Yearbook of International Law*, 30 (1999), 3–44, p. 19.

[74] As laid down in article 27 of the Vienna Convention on the Law of Treaties. The 1986 Convention (on treaties concluded with or between international organisations) adds,

It is, perhaps, no accident that much of the literature on the effects of WTO law in the Community legal order takes this route: a claim that a regulation has been enacted in violation of WTO law is presented as a claim involving the effects of one legal system in another, rather than as a treaty conflict (or a conflict between two distinct legal orders, if you will). And this presupposes that, at least for this purpose, the EC legal order is viewed as akin to a domestic legal order.[75]

Much of this depends, of course, on whether one views the EC legal system as akin to a domestic legal order. The German lawyer Krück, writing thirty years ago on the position of treaties in the community legal order, happily did so. Drawing an analogy between the EC and a federal state, he reached the conclusion that under international law, the federal authorities have an obligation to enable the component parts to fulfill their (outstanding) obligations under international law: 'Deshalb verlangt das Völkerrecht vom Bundesstaat, sich Verfassungsrechtlich die Möglichkeit zur Sicherstellung der Erfüllung der völkerrechtlichen Verpflichtungen, die seine Gliedstaaten eingegangen sind, zu sichern'.[76]

One might, of course, add the rider that this can only apply to obligations entered into by the component units (member states) in accordance with the constitutional requirements of the *Bundesstaat*, within their own proper powers, but that is precisely the point: when the component units act within their competences, international law demands, *dixit* Krück, that the federal authorities enable the component units to uphold their commitments. The Community, however, applies this only with respect to anterior treaties, and even then strictly curtailed: as already noted, under article 307, member states have an obligation to eliminate incompatibilities, and the Court has been less than generous in upholding even anterior agreements – never mind posterior agreements.

Either way though, even those who do not (yet?) wish to see the Community as akin to a domestic legal order, would do well to realise that here an intriguing paradox can set in: the more the Community insists on being a single legal order, the closer it will resemble the domestic legal

---

moreover, that an organisation 'may not invoke the rules of the organization as justification for its failure to perform a treaty.' Note that in preparing the 1986 Vienna Convention, the ILC all but ignored the question of how best to view decisions of international organisations. See UN Doc. A/37/10, Report of the International Law Commission on the Work of its Thirty-Fourth Session, reprinted in *Yearbook of the International Law Commission* (1982), vol. II, part. 2.

[75] One example among many is Hilf and Schorkopf, 'WTO und EG'.

[76] See Krück, *Völkerrechtliche Verträge*, p. 120.

order, and the less leeway it will enjoy under international law. For if and when the analogy to a domestic legal order becomes meaningful to draw, the unique position (and therewith much of its liberties) of the Community will dissipate. The only way out would be to acknowledge that Community law has characteristics of its own no longer making it plausible to treat it either as a form of international law or a form of domestic law. Many would happily subscribe to such a position (and indeed, it is this that is often meant when the Community is described as *sui generis*), but few have developed concepts to capture the Community in its own right.[77]

Conclusion

As previously noted, the idea behind the present chapter was not so much to find answers to the issues raised: all of them could easily occupy an entire monograph. I did have the feeling, though, that it might be useful to raise the issues and provide a preliminary, tentative discussion, as they keep coming back somewhat underneath the surface.

Very particular conclusions are therefore not to be expected, but perhaps some tentative conclusions may be stipulated. First, it would seem that the Court has been very strict on the timing issue: an amendment is presumed to be a new agreement. One would expect the Court to keep the door open for those cases where an amendment is merely of a technical nature, and indeed the case-law leaves this possibility open, but the overall message is that any substantive change turns the amendment into a new agreement.

Second, while classification of the problem as a problem of conflicting treaties, or a modification between parties *inter se*, or even as something else, gives rise to theoretical puzzles, in practice it does not appear to be all that problematic. Common sense usually dictates how a situation should be classified, and does so without giving rise to much controversy. Then again, this may simply mean that there is a strong paradigm in place according to which in most circumstances, the article 30 scenario seems to be the most appropriate.

---

[77] A partial exception is the notion of meta-constitutionalism developed by Neil Walker to capture the sort of conceptual apparatus needed to make sense of Community law. See Neil Walker, 'Flexibility within a Metaconstitutional Frame: Reflections on the Future of Legal Authority in Europe', in Gráinne de Búrca and Joanne Scott (eds.), *Constitutional Change in the EU: Between Uniformity and Flexibility?* (Oxford: Hart, 2000), pp. 9–30.

Such a strong paradigm would also seem to be in place on the powers issue: many take it for granted that treaty conflict should be looked at from the perspective of EC law, rather than the perspective of member state powers or the position of treaty partners under international law. Perhaps the present discussion can contribute to a growing awareness of the hold of this perspective, and a growing awareness that there might be other possible, and perhaps plausible, perspectives.

The same holds, *mutatis mutandis*, with respect to the fourth issue discussed above: it may be unorthodox to treat secondary Community law as part of domestic law, but surely, to treat secondary Community law as itself part of the EC treaty for purposes of treaty conflicts is unsatisfactory. Perhaps this may provide some inspiration for further conceptual work on decisions of international organisations.

9

Posterior treaties: practice

Introduction

The previous chapter discussed conceptual issues related to posterior treaties concluded by the member states of the European Community. The present chapter broadens the field somewhat by focusing on posterior treaties in (selected) practice. I will discuss predominantly treaties entered into by member states, but also, to some extent, the practice of the Community or Union itself. The justification for including the latter is, simply, that the general picture which emerged from the Court's case-law on Article 307 TEC, discussed in Chapter 6, continues to be confirmed: the *acquis communautaire* shall be protected, no matter what. Individual member states use various techniques for doing so (most well known is the so-called disconnection clause), but the Community itself also uses techniques to safeguard the sanctity of Community law when concluding treaties with third parties. Moreover, in some cases, of course, external agreements are concluded as mixed agreements, involving both the Community and its member states. Given those circumstances, it would be difficult to justify a complete exclusion of the practice of the Community (as distinct from its member states).

This chapter will be structured as follows. I will begin with a discussion of a methodological nature, followed by a brief discussion of Nordic cooperation in light of its compatibility with EC law. Subsequently, I shall discuss agreements concluded between member states *inter se*; this discussion will contain elements of state practice (and thus be very practical), but it will also remain somewhat hypothetical as far as legal analysis goes, in that it appears that there are few decisions by either of the EC courts on point. This section will be followed by a more concrete (i.e., less hypothetical) discussion of agreements concluded between member states and third parties. Subsequently, a section will be devoted to practical techniques developed by the member states and the Community (indeed, by the member states as urged by the Community) in order to protect

Community law from outside influences. Finally, the chapter will once again become more hypothetical (though not devoid of practical significance) when it discusses the possibility of external action not so much through new agreements, but as modifying, between the Community's member states, an existing treaty.

A (brief) methodological note

Much of this chapter is derived from two distinct sources. First, to the extent that I discuss the practice of Finland, it is based on the Finnish Treaty Series (*Suomen Sopimussarja*).[1] The main reason for focusing on Finnish practice is mainly pragmatic: the Finnish Treaty Series is available on-line,[2] as opposed to, for example, the Dutch *Tractatenblad*, of which only an index is available on-line.[3] There are, of course, other pragmatic concerns as well: I thought it would be useful, for example, to have a look at the treaty practice of a state whose language I speak; hence, Greece, Slovakia, Lithuania and quite a few others did not make the cut.

Substantively, I am not aware of any member state's treaty practice having been analysed in a systematic manner concerning the possible regulation of possible conflicts with EU law, with the exception of Dutch practice, which has been reviewed in two fine pieces written by Bruno de Witte.[4] Even so, Dutch practice played merely an illustrative role in those two pieces: the lead part was reserved for an analysis of the position of agreements concluded by member states under EC law.

What makes Finland potentially an interesting case is that it is still a relatively new member state: it joined in 1995, together with Sweden and Austria, so it may be hypothesized that it has mostly got used to EU membership (unlike, perhaps, the twelve that joined in 2005 and 2007), but not quite as used as the original member states or those who joined during the 1970s and 1980s. To put the point differently, most, perhaps

---

[1] The Finnish Treaty Series habitually publishes the text of a treaty, as well as the relevant instruments through which it enters into Finland's domestic legal order: typically either a law or a decree. Some texts are not published though; this typically holds with respect to technical treaties setting up common projects. These are available for viewing at the Foreign Ministry. For a discussion of Finland's handling of treaties, see Jan Klabbers, 'Coming in from the Cold? Treaties in Finland's Legal Order', in Timo Koivurova (ed.), *Kansainvälistyvä Oikeus: Juhlakirja Professori Kari Hakapää* (Rovaniemi: University of Lapland, 2005), pp. 143–52.

[2] Available at www.finlex.fi/sopimukset/sopimussarja.

[3] Available at www.minbuza.nl/verdragen/en/zoek verdragen.

[4] See de Witte, 'Old-fashioned Flexibility' and de Witte, 'Internationale verdragen'.

all government officials in the Netherlands, or Belgium, or Italy, have grown up during the EU's existence. By contrast, the Finns, and probably the Swedes and Austrians as well, are still working on internalising their membership: it is not entirely novel anymore, but has not yet become second nature either.

The Finnish practice covered is the practice starting in January 2002 and running until the end of 2006, thus covering a full five-year period. That is not to say that all treaties covered were concluded during that period, or all treaties concluded during that period are covered: some treaties were concluded in the 1990s but only entered into force during the period under review; some may have been concluded during the 2002–06 period, but are awaiting ratification or entry into force.

Covering a five-year period seems perfectly justifiable, as long as the aim is not to provide a complete overview (in which case I should have started with 1995) but rather a more or less representative overview: a cross-section, if you will. My aim in this chapter (its first part) is not to investigate Finland's treaty practice *tout court*; my aim, more modest, is to see whether and how treaties concluded by Finland take Finland's membership of the EU into account. In doing so, moreover, I will concentrate mainly on bilateral treaties, divided over two groups: bilateral treaties with other EU members (*inter se* agreements), and bilateral treaties with third parties.[5] Multilateral treaties would appear to be less interesting, in that typically, Finland will not be the only EU member state engaged in multilateral treaty X, Y or Z. Typically, such treaties will encompass at least a handful of EU member states; consequently, there is every chance that the position of that treaty vis-à-vis EU law has been dealt with in some detail, and quite possibly following instructions or suggestions emanating from the EU Commission. Indeed, the practice within the Council of Europe would seem to bear this out. Within the Council of Europe, many treaties involving most or all EU member states contain a so-called disconnection clause, of which the Commission has been the greatest sponsor – and advocate.

The second part of this chapter will shift the focus to treaties concluded by the EC (or, more sporadically, the EU) itself, and the techniques used therein to safeguard the position of Community (respectively Union) law. This part will be based on a systematic analysis of the Community practice as published in the *Official Journal* during the years 2005 and

---

[5] The observant reader will note that some treaty partners figure in both categories. This is the result, of course, of them changing their status from third party to member state, and applies most of all to Estonia.

2006: again, what matters is not to provide an exhaustive overview of the treaty practice, but rather to provide a cross section of the various techniques used to safeguard the Community law *acquis*.[6]

To both sections applies, that I have left out of consideration treaties having to do with the EU and its membership itself: thus, there is no discussion of the accession agreements with Bulgaria and Romania, for example, although these fall within the period of review, and neither will there be a discussion of agreements adapting Finland to the accession of new members. I will also leave undiscussed the few occasions where, following the accession of a new member state, Finland denounced an existing agreement.[7] The text of the announcements of these denunci-ations does not specify any reasons, so it can only be speculated that accession was the cause.[8]

Nordic cooperation

The five Nordic countries have, since the 1950s, engaged in all sorts of forms of legal cooperation mainly under the auspices of the Nordic Council;[9] before that, they were joined in various other manners, with Finland having been part of Sweden for a long time, Norway and Denmark having been a single state, and Iceland having been part of Denmark. In short, the relations between the five have been intense for centuries, and to the extent that local lawyers look abroad, they tend to look first of all to other Nordic countries.[10]

---

[6] It follows Jan Klabbers, 'Safeguarding the Organizational *Acquis*: The EU's External Prac-tice', *International Organizations Law Review*, 4 (2007), 57–89.

[7] Note also that under article 104 of the Act of Accession, Finland itself was under an obligation to denounce some treaties upon accession: the EFTA agreement and free trade agreements with the Baltic states were mentioned specifically in what was clearly not meant to be an exhaustive list. Article 96, moreover, effectively substituted the Community for Finland in fisheries agreements with third countries. The Act of Accession can be found in *Official Journal* C 241, 29 August 1994.

[8] Finland denounced an agreement with Poland on saving energy and environmental pro-tection in 2005 (*Suomen Sopimussarja*, 2005, nos. 103–104), following Poland's accession, and finalised the denunciation of an agreement with Austria on trainee exchange (*Suomen Sopimussarja* 2003, no. 50). This denunciation had already been agreed upon in 1995, again suggesting that it may have had something to do with both states' accession to the EU at the beginning of that year.

[9] For background, see Frantz Wendt, *The Nordic Council and Co-operation in Scandinavia* (Copenhagen: Munksgaard, 1959).

[10] As Wendt explains in possibly somewhat overblown language: 'Since the dawn of history, the Nordic peoples have had identical concepts of right and wrong, and practically the same legal principles.' *Ibid.*, p. 11.

Yet it would seem that Nordic cooperation and EC law are, in practice, more than a little compatible. For one thing, much Nordic cooperation and harmonisation takes place on issues that have not yet been encompassed by Community law, ranging from criminal law to the prevention of double taxation and ranging from educational cooperation to harmonisation of private law, and to some extent on fairly mundane matters.[11] To the extent, moreover, that there might be overlap between Nordic and Community activities (both, for example, have developed schemes for student exchange), these activities tend to be compatible with one another: they do not result in irreconcilable conflicts.

It is also the case that Nordic cooperation sometimes is used to give fuller effect to Community law. An example is the 1992 Nordic Convention on Social Security, which further elaborates the principles and spirit of a Community Regulation on social security (no. 1408/71): such conventions between member states are explicitly envisaged by that regulation. The 1992 Nordic Convention came before the ECJ in *Rundgren*, but played no role whatsoever in the Court's decision-making process. The Court merely confirmed that one of the important provisions of the Convention (a reciprocal waiver of reimbursement of costs for social benefits paid by one member state to people residing in another) had no bearing on the interpretation of Regulation 1408/71.[12]

Likewise, a Nordic Convention for the prevention of double taxation played no role in the *Nikula* case, dealing with the question of whether a pension from a different member state should be included for purposes of determining an individual's taxable income. Again, the Court relied fully on applicable Community law, in particular, again, Regulation 1408/71.[13]

To be sure, the Act of Accession regulating the accession of Finland, Sweden and Austria to the Community does make the formal point of rendering the fruits of Nordic cooperation subservient to Community law. But it is perhaps telling for the lack of urgency envisaged that the clause on the primacy of Community law is not laid down in the Accession Treaty itself, but in a joint declaration made by the EC member states plus the three acceding states. Joint Declaration No. 28 provides, in somewhat laconic terms, that the member states of the EU 'record' that Sweden

---

[11] An example of a Nordic treaty is the agreement by which Iceland acceded to an earlier agreement establishing a Nordic Tax Research Council. See *Suomen Sopimussarja* (2002) no. 121.

[12] See Case C-389/99, *Sulo Rundgren* [2001] ECR I-3731, esp. para. 64.

[13] See Case C-50/05, *Maija T.I. Nikula* [2006] ECR I-7029.

and Finland 'intend to continue, in full compliance with Community law and the other provisions of the Treaty on European Union, Nordic Cooperation amongst themselves as well as with other countries and territories.'[14]

Inter se agreements

Article 307 does not cover *inter se* agreements concluded between the member states, whether anterior or ulterior. Yet, such agreements are still concluded with some regularity, and on a wide range of topics. Obviously, if the conclusion of such a topic does not touch upon Community prerogatives, there is no particular problem: member states are free to act in any way they wish on topics not covered by Community law, and as long as they do not violate substantive EC law in the process. The question then is, though, what exactly is covered by Community law?[15] As we have seen in the previous chapter and will again see below, it is disturbingly easy to touch upon EC law, even while exercising a domestic prerogative.[16]

  Case-law which is strictly on point is, as far as I am aware, not available, with the possible exception of cases addressing treaties to avoid double taxation:[17] to the extent that case-law has been available, it has invariably dealt with anterior treaties, not treaties concluded after the member states concerned had joined the EU.[18] That circumstance suggests that the member states are well aware that there may be limits to what they can do *inter se*; indeed, it is no coincidence that the Schengen Agreement, arguably the example coming closest to interfering with Community law, explicitly related to Community law. As De Witte puts it, the Schengen regime was

---

[14] See *Official Journal*, C 241, 29 August 1994, joint declaration no. 28. The Joint Declaration also mentions Norway but Norway never acceded.

[15] And, additionally, how to tell the difference between a Community act and an agreement between all member states? On this, see the somewhat disturbing decision in Joined Cases C-181/91 and C-248/91, *European Parliament* v. *Council and Commission (Emergency aid)* [1993] ECR I-3685, in which the Court was very quick to dismiss law-making formalities.

[16] Elsewhere, I have argued that a focus on distribution of powers alone is insufficient. See Klabbers, 'Restraints on the Treaty-Making Powers'.

[17] These will be discussed below. It is worth noting that double taxation treaties are not the most illuminating examples of treaties concluded between member states *inter se* in that their conclusion is warranted by article 293 TEC.

[18] The closest analogue would be case 235/87, *Annunziata Matteucci* v. *Communauté française of Belgium and others* [1988] ECR 5589. Here, at issue was a bilateral treaty concluded between Belgium and Germany in 1956. See the discussion in Chapter 6.

an attempt to reach Community goals by setting aside a reluctant Great Britain.[19] The preambles to the two Schengen agreements clarify the connection with Community law, and article 134 of the 1990 Convention stipulated that the provisions of Schengen II 'shall apply only insofar as they are compatible with Community law.'[20] Already fairly early on there were high-level discussions on the integration of Schengen in Community law.[21]

It is different with the Western European Union, which was originally set up as a defensive agreement between the EC member states (plus the UK), but without any ambitions of becoming integrated into Community law. Indeed, at roughly the same time the WEU was created, a proposed European Defence Community between the Six was defeated by a no-vote in the French parliament, signifying that the two ought not to be conflated.[22]

More generally, a number of different groups of agreements can be distinguished, and much of the classification depends on the approach chosen. Thus, De Witte distinguishes between treaties between member states *inter se* and treaties with third parties.[23] Alternatively, one can think in terms of substance, or powers, and thus distinguish treaties on criminal assistance from boundary treaties, treaties on road traffic from agreements on environmental protection, etc. The approach in this chapter combines elements of both, but most of all uses two basic distinctions: the overarching one is between agreements concluded by member states, and those to which the Community is party, complemented by a distinction between *inter se* agreements and agreements with third parties as concluded by member states. The reason for doing so rests with the main purpose of this study: my aim is not to provide comprehensive overviews

---

[19] See De Witte, 'Internationale verdragen', p. 110.
[20] The first Schengen agreement on gradual abolition of border checks was concluded in 1985 between Belgium, France, Luxembourg, Germany and the Netherlands; the second, elaborating on the first and encompassing the same states, in 1990. They are reproduced in 30 *International Legal Materials* (1991) 68 and 84, respectively.
[21] See Tuytschaever, *Differentiation*, p. 41.
[22] On the connections between EU and WEU, see Ramses A. Wessel, 'The EU as Black Widow: Devouring the WEU to Give Birth to a European Security and Defence Policy', in Vincent Kronenberger (ed.), *The EU and the International Legal Order: Discord or Harmony?* (The Hague: TMC Asser Press, 2001), pp. 405–34.
[23] See De Witte, 'Internationale verdragen'. *Inter se* agreements are further divided into revision treaties, parallel treaties (further subdivided into implementing agreements, complementary agreements, and autonomous agreements) and partial treaties, while treaties with third parties may be member state agreements or mixed agreements.

or fine-grained taxonomies, but simply to figure out what happens with posterior treaties.

It is perhaps useful to point out at the outset that some posterior treaties between member states are envisaged (albeit not in so many words) in the EC Treaty itself.[24] Article 293 authorises member states 'to enter into negotiations with each other with a view to securing for the benefits of their nationals' a number of substantive goals, and it stands to reason that the main instruments envisaged would be *inter se* agreements. These goals include the non-discriminatory protection of persons and rights, mutual recognition of firms, simplification of formalities concerning the recognition and enforcement of judgments and awards[25] and, perhaps most of all, the avoidance of double taxation.

Double taxation agreements are regularly concluded between member states *inter se*, and are generally not regarded, apparently, as being difficult to reconcile with Community law, partly no doubt because of the authorisation contained in article 293 TEC.[26] Indeed, the ECJ has held that that the elimination of double taxation still falls with the scope of powers of the member states, in the absence of any harmonisation at the EU level,[27] and has, moreover, theorised that the reciprocal nature of treaties for the elimination of double taxation with third parties precludes a finding of discrimination on the basis of nationality.[28]

Still, the acceptance of double taxation agreements may also, in part, reside in the circumstance that harmonisation or unification of tax law is politically sensitive. Any attempt by the Commission to prevent member states from concluding double taxation agreements or any attempt to fight their legality under Community law might be seen (and will

---

[24] Additionally, it is also possible for the Community legislator to stipulate that a Community instrument will come to replace earlier treaties concluded between member states; this is under consideration, e.g., with respect to a Regulation on the Law applicable to Contractual Obligations. See EU Commission Document COM (2005) 650 final, of 15 December 2005, Article 23. I am indebted to Fabrizio Marrella for bringing this to my attention.

[25] The Brussels Convention on Jurisdiction and the Enforcement of Judgments has been held, by virtue of EC law, to overrule conflicting national law. See Case 288/82, *Ferdinand Duijnstee* v. *Lodewijk Goderbauer* [1983] ECR 3663, esp. paras. 12–14.

[26] Despite the circumstance that they are typically concluded bilaterally, whereas the accepted interpretation of article 293 would seem to be that it refers to all member states together, at least according to de Witte. See de Witte, 'Old-fashioned Flexibility', p. 43.

[27] See Case C-336/96, *Gilly* v. *Directeur des Services Fiscaux du Bas-Rhin* [1998] ECR I-2793, para. 30.

[28] See Case C-376/03, *D* v. *Inspecteur van de Belastingdienst/Particulieren/Ondernemingen Buitenland te Heerlen* [2005] ECR I-5821.

be seen) as an intrusion of a strong member state prerogative: taxation symbolises solidarity between citizens and bonds of allegiance between states and their citizens and residents.[29] Moreover, double taxation treaties serve an EU-friendly purpose: eliminating obstacles to free movement.[30] A convention between all member states *inter se* to avoid double taxation would not be out of place, and has indeed been advocated.[31] With that in mind, bilateral double taxation agreements are conceptualised as paving the way for a Community-wide exercise, and are thus acceptable for that reason alone.

The practice of a member state such as Finland is that it concludes a fairly limited number of bilateral agreements with other member states of the EU and, more interestingly, most of these are in one way or another intended to implement EU law or otherwise related to the EU. A first category includes agreements intended to provide further details to an obligation incorporated in EU law, and the one example found in the period under review is an agreement between Finland and Estonia, concluded on 4 September 2006, on the Reciprocal Holding of Crude Oil and Petroleum Products.[32] As its preamble suggests, this agreement serves to implement Directive 98/93, which envisages the creation of oil stocks within member state territories for the account of companies located in another member state. The directive explicitly calls upon the member states to conclude further agreements to this effect.

Most eye-catching is a second category, consisting of a number of agreements intended to fill a void left by EU law. A main example is the group of agreements concluded with territories falling outside the scope of the EU's fiscal territory, to address and harmonise taxation of savings. It includes agreements with Jersey, Guernsey, the Isle of Man and two with the Netherlands concerning the Netherlands Antilles and Aruba, respectively.[33] Likewise, a string of agreements was concluded with Great Britain concerning Anguilla, the British Virgin Islands, the Cayman Islands, Montserrat and the Turks and Caicos Islands; these also deal with taxation of savings and follow EC Directive 2003/48.[34] Quite possibly, something similar applies to an agreement with the Netherlands on behalf of the Netherlands Antilles and some other entities, concerning

---

[29] It is precisely to foster a sense of 'Europeanness' that sometimes a European tax is proposed. An example is Chaltiel, *Naissance*, p. 129.

[30] De Witte makes the same point in 'Old-fashioned Flexibility', p. 50, but also adds that different bilateral tax agreements may raise concerns about discrimination on the basis of nationality.

[31] See de Witte, 'Internationale verdragen', p. 97.   [32] *Suomen Sopimussarja*, 2006, no. 104.

[33] *Suomen Sopimussarja*, 2005, nos. 46–55.   [34] *Suomen Sopimussarja*, 2005, nos. 56–65.

savings.[35] By the same token, an agreement with Estonia on social security is meant, specifically, to cover individuals falling outside the ambit of EC Regulation 1408/71,[36] as is an agreement with Luxembourg.[37]

A third category consists of a single treaty concluded on the basis of article 34 TEU: an agreement concluded with all member states of the EU (thus no longer bilateral in nature) and dealing with justice and police cooperation. These agreements are foreseen in the EU treaty itself: they derive their legal basis from the EU treaty.[38]

Quite curious is the conclusion by Finland of two treaties, with Germany and France respectively, on protection of classified information.[39] These apply to classified information in the broadest sense of the term (relating to defence and foreign policy, but also industrial information), and the curiosity resides in the circumstance that similar treaties are concluded by the EU itself with non-member states.[40] Still, the two bilateral treaties make no reference whatsoever to the EU, or to the position of Community law; and neither does an exchange of notes with Sweden updating an earlier agreement on television reception.[41]

The Finnish practice provides some tacit support for what seems to be the basic principle regarding *inter se* agreements: in their relations *inter se*, member states should respect their obligations under Community law, in much the same way as they should when acting unilaterally.[42] The bigger question, of course, is whether the matter is to be governed by Community law (and its supremacy and *Gemeinschaftstreue*) to begin with: the elimination and avoidance of double taxation is so far left to the member states. Still, as the TEC remains silent on the fate of later *inter se* agreements, one could simply urge that it is not solely a matter of EU law, but that international law too enters the picture.

Two alternative scenarios present themselves, in addition to the position that EC law prevails. On the first, more obvious one, the conflict is construed as one between two treaties: the EC Treaty on the one hand, the

---

[35] The text whereof is not made public; the governmental decree implementing it in Finnish law is published in *Suomen Sopimussarja*, 2005, no. 77.

[36] *Suomen Sopimussarja*, 2006, no. 78.   [37] *Suomen Sopimussarja*, 2002, no. 13.

[38] *Suomen Sopimussarja*, 2004, no. 57.

[39] *Suomen Sopimussarja*, 2004, no. 97 (with Germany) and 2005, no. 67 (with France).

[40] An example is the Agreement between the Republic of Croatia and the European Union on security procedures for the exchange of classified information, *Official Journal* L 116/74, 29 April 2006.

[41] *Suomen Sopimussarja*, 2003, no. 45.

[42] The same follows from de Witte's treatment of *inter se* agreements as modalities of flexibility: such a conception also renders them subservient to general Community law. See De Witte, 'Old-fashioned Flexibility'.

bilateral *inter se* agreement on the other. If there is a genuine conflict, they must relate to the same subject matter, and article 30 VCLT would have the result that to the extent of the incompatibilities, the EC treaty applies in relations between the two member states concluding the *inter se* agreement and all others, but that between themselves they can apply their bilateral agreement. This would, of course, create a highly undesirable situation.

The second scenario is more intricate and, in a sense, treats EU law more seriously by not regarding the TEC as simply a treaty among treaties but as giving rise to obligations of a domestic law nature. On this reading, EC law forms part of the national legal orders of its member states, fully incorporated as it is. That seems plausible, of course: as discussed in the previous chapter, regulations (and decisions as well, albeit not in quite the same manner) are by definition to be treated as such, whereas also many of the more relevant Treaty provisions have been deemed directly effective and are thus, for all practical purposes, part of the domestic legal orders.

The picture then changes, and quite dramatically, for on this reading, member states concluding a posterior *inter se* agreement are not concluding a treaty in conflict with an earlier treaty, but rather in conflict with their domestic laws. Domestic law (whose source, in this case, just happens to be EC law) suggests that a certain practice must be permitted: their later treaty disagrees. In such a situation, it is not article 30 or article 41 of the Vienna Convention which applies, but rather article 27: domestic law is no excuse for non-compliance. In other words, the later treaty prevails, with the curious (and paradoxical) result that taking EU law as something more than a treaty would have the result of rendering it inapplicable. Perhaps in order to pre-empt this sort of conclusions, in *Matteucci* the Court left no doubt where it would stand on the issue. Confronted with the argument that the treaty at issue (on cultural cooperation) fell within a sphere where Community law does not apply, the Court proclaimed the supremacy of Community law: '... the application of Community law cannot be precluded on the ground that it would affect the implementation of a cultural agreement between two Member States.'[43]

The still bigger question, and one that has to remain unsolved, is whether a conflict between a treaty and domestic law should be governed by international law or by domestic law. The Vienna Convention suggests

[43] See *Matteucci*, para. 14.

that international law should govern this sort of conflict, but can do so only on the basis of the Kelsenian point that international law is superior to domestic law because it alone is capable of holding law together.[44] Those who do not share this point of departure may also come to have difficulties with the conclusion, and instead hold that in case of conflict between the domestic and international legal orders, the domestic ones should prevail, or perhaps, by way of compromise, hold the position that the later norm in time should prevail regardless of whether it finds its source in domestic or international law.[45]

Much of this appears to be an academic problem though, as practice does not reveal all that many *inter se* agreements being concluded, and even less which might cause problems. Bruno de Witte, in a thoughtful piece written a few years ago, found the Dutch practice to be unproblematic;[46] and the above perusal of the Finnish Treaty Series over the last couple of years also reveals little that is worrying.

Posterior treaties with third parties

The more inherently problematic scenario is that of successive treaties with third parties, as, for example, happened in the *Open Skies* cases. A serious argument can be made that under EC law itself, in case of conflict EC law would prevail. This would follow from such considerations as the *ERTA* case-law (disavowing the possibility that EC law be affected by an agreement concluded with a third party), as well as the notion of *Gemeinschaftstreue* of article 10 TEC, and seems perfectly in line with the ambitions of the EC to have an uniform system of EU law, where the EU's citizens are subject to the same rules no matter where they are or reside within the EU.

Yet, this is no argument as far as general international law is concerned. Similar considerations arise as with respect to agreements *inter se*. One option, at least with secondary EC law, is to regard it as domestic law, and thereby declare it subservient to any treaties with third parties. Another option is to apply article 30 Vienna Convention; given that the third party is not a member of the EC, the fourth paragraph of that article enters the

---

[44] See Kelsen, *Introduction to the Problems*, p. 71.
[45] A fine, if lengthy, discussion of the relationship between domestic and international law is Veijo Heiskanen, *International Legal Topics* (Helsinki: Finnish Lawyers' Publishing Co., 1992), pp. 1–199.
[46] See de Witte, 'Internationale verdragen'.

picture; it provides, in essence, for application of the later treaty between the parties to that later treaty.

The net result then is, of course, that the member state might end up violating EU law in the process of honouring a later international commitment. Under international law, there is nothing particularly problematic about that, but it is understandable enough that EU law would not appreciate that situation. Still, under international law, there is fairly little that the EU could invoke against it; article 27 VCLT provides that international law prevails over domestic law, and article 46 Vienna Convention stipulates that violation of domestic treaty-making rules (e.g., when a member state acts under a power reserved for the EU) is no excuse either, in most circumstances.[47] Perhaps as a result, the Court has done its best to downplay the relevance of international law in this sort of matters.

The most pertinent case thus far is quite possibly the British *Open Skies* case.[48] This revolved around a UK-US air traffic agreement concluded in 1995, well after the UK had joined the EC. The UK tried to convince the Court that it was really merely amending an earlier agreement, and thus protected by article 307 TEC. The Court, however, did not fall for it, and decided not to apply article 307.

That opened the door, or so the Court thought, for a substantive analysis: if article 307 TEC does not apply, then the agreement is without protection. In other words: the Court simply presumed the supremacy of EC law, testing the agreement against article 43 TEC (on establishment) and finding it wanting. At no point did the Court consider the possibility that international law might have something else to say. Instead, it affirmed that '[e]ven if a matter falls within the power of the Member States, the fact remains that the latter must exercise that power consistently with Community law.'[49]

While Advocate-General Tizzano's approach was arguably somewhat more subtle, nonetheless he too seemed to work on the premise that if article 307 does not apply, then EC law reigns supreme.[50] Perhaps here the parties themselves are to blame, as none of them seems to have thought of invoking the possibility of international law trumping Community law,

---

[47] For the record, the corresponding articles in the 1986 Convention do not change this picture.

[48] Case C-466/98, *Commission* v. *United Kingdom* [2002] ECR I-9427.   [49] *Ibid.*, para. 41.

[50] See in particular para. 115 of his opinion. His subtlety resides in his argument that the conclusion of a bilateral agreement as such does not violate Community law unless the Community's power was exclusive.

and if that is true, then perhaps not too much ought to be read into the British *Open Skies* case, or the other *Open Skies* cases for that matter.

That said, some passages of the *Open Skies* cases seem to have been written for public consumption. Thus, in the Finnish case (by way of example), the Court makes a point of underlining (or recovering, perhaps) the doctrine of pre-emption: a Community regulation created an exclusive power for the Community to deal with aspects of air transport, and the fact that Finland aspired to preserve the relevant regulation was, so the Court held, utterly irrelevant: Finland's failure to fulfil its obligations under EC law 'lies in the fact that it was not authorised to enter into such a commitment on its own, even if the substance of that commitment does not conflict with Community law.'[51] It would seem, then, that the *Open Skies* decisions were in part designed to deter member states from going solo.[52] And practice suggests, as with *inter se* agreements, that the member states have been listening rather carefully.

There may be one major exception, and that is the class of social security conventions. These have typically been applied by the ECJ with the individual interest in mind, rather than on the basis of any dogma about treaty conflict.[53] Thus, in *Grana-Novoa*, the Court held that two bilateral social security treaties (one between Germany and Spain, and one between Germany and Switzerland) could not displace the provisions of a Community Regulation.[54] Under the regulation, Ms Grana-Novoa was entitled to an invalidity pension; the combined effect of the two agreements would have left her without such a pension. By contrast, an Italian-Swiss agreement was relied on so as to prevent nationality discrimination of a French worker in *Gottardo*.[55]

---

[51] Case C-469/98, *Commission* v. *Finland* [2002] ECR I-9627, para 102.

[52] Note also the blunt rendition of the import of the second paragraph of article 307: 'Member States are prevented not only from contracting new international commitments but also from maintaining such commitments in force if they infringe Community law.' See *ibid.*, para. 39. What is missing here is that article 307 does not create an immediate obligation of result, and cannot be taken to suggest that treaties be terminated even in cases where international law would make such difficult to achieve. In the same vein, see Vanhamme, *Volkenrechtelijke*, p. 264 (noting that article 307, para. 2 creates an obligation to make an effort, not an obligation of result).

[53] Such conventions are envisaged, and explicitly allowed, in the relevant regulation (no. 1408/71), which also displaces earlier conventions between member states.

[54] See Case C-23/92, *Maria Grana-Novoa* v. *Landesversicherungsanstalt Hessen* [1993] ECR 4505, esp. para. 22.

[55] See Case C-55/00, *Elide Gottardo* v. *Istituto Nazionale della Previdenza Sociale* (INPS) [2002] ECR I-413.

Still, the practice of Finland by and large illustrates the general point that member states should not engage in solo operations too lightly. During the five-year period under review, a number of agreements were concluded (or entered into force), falling broadly into five or six categories: Finland concluded a large number of bilateral investment treaties, a large number of double taxation agreements, a couple of air services agreements, a handful of road traffic agreements, a number of agreements with the Russian Federation dealing with border crossings and similar issues, and finally a fairly large (relative to the total number) miscellaneous category.

The bilateral investment treaties (BIT) all provide for what might be termed a 'common market exception'. An example is to be found in the BIT with Macedonia:

> The provisions of this Agreement shall not be construed so as to oblige one Contracting Party to extend to the investors or investments by investors of the other Contracting Party the benefit of any treatment, preference or privilege by virtue of: (a) any existing or future free trade area, customs union, common market, economic union or similar economic integration agreement to which one of the Contracting Parties is or may become a party.[56]

With minor variations, such a clause recurs in literally all BITs contained in the Finnish Treaty Series in the period under review.[57] Sometimes it is provided for in a general article on treatment of investments, sometimes it figures in a general exceptions provision (and for some reason the more recent BITs list it under the heading 'exemptions'[58]), but the main point is that the clause is included in all BITs.

It is unclear what the precise status of such a provision is. Obviously, at first sight it would seem to isolate the BIT from the possible effects of any existing common market scheme; yet, also at first sight, another clause also found in all BITs studied might seem to undo this. This other

---

[56] *Suomen Sopimussarja*, 2002, no. 21, article 5.

[57] See the agreements with Croatia (*Suomen Sopimussarja*, 2002, no. 92, art. 4), Tanzania (2002, no. 94, art. 4), El Salvador (2003, no. 11, art. 4), Morocco (2003, no. 28, art. 3), India (2003, no. 30, art. 4), Qatar (2003, no. 36, article 4), Tunisia (2003, no. 52, art. 7), Iran (2004, no 82, art. 4), Uruguay (2004, no. 84, art. 4), the Kyrgyz Republic (2004, no. 163, art. 4), Azerbaijan (2005, no. 2, art. 5), Egypt (2005, no. 11, art. 4), Namibia (2005, no. 42, art. 5), Mozambique (2005, no. 93, art. 4), Ukraine (2005, no. 102, art. 4) and Guatemala (2006, no 108, art. 4).

[58] The general term 'exemption' is used in the BITs with Egypt, Namibia, Mozambique, Ukraine and Guatemala: see previous note for the references.

clause may well be termed a most-favoured-nation clause, holding as follows:

> If the provisions of law of either Contracting Party or obligations under international law existing at present or established hereafter between the Contracting Parties in addition to this Agreement contain a regulation, whether general or specific, entitling investments made by investors of the other Contracting Party to a treatment more favourable than is provided for by this Agreement, such provisions shall, to the extent that they are more favourable to the investor, prevail over this Agreement.[59]

Speculating, it would seem that this could mean that if EU law would grant investors a more favourable treatment than the BIT, than the working of the EU provision should be extended to cover also the treaty partners of Finland, unless such would be automatically excluded by the earlier common market clause. As a matter of treaty systematics, it is useful to note that in all cases, the common market exception is included early on in the treaty, which might indicate its relative weight vis-à-vis the most-favoured-nation clause. Moreover, it would seem that in order to expand the working of Community law through an MFN clause in a bilateral agreement, some form of consent of the other EU members would be required. Hence the better view would be that the common market exception prevails, and the MFN clause does not apply to possible benefits of investors under Community law.

If the 'common market exception' isolates the BIT from Community law, it does not automatically mean that the member state was entitled or empowered to conclude the BIT in question; and the 'common market exception' cannot, if the case-law of the ECJ on anterior treaties and in *Open Skies* is anything to go by, protect the member states from allegations of violating their Community law obligations by concluding the BITs in the first place. Indeed, at the time of writing several member states have been indicted by the Commission for concluding such BITs.[60]

---

[59] The wording is again taken from the BIT with Macedonia (*Suomen Sopimussarja*, 2002, no. 21, art. 14). It recurs though, with minor variations, in all BITs under review, usually under the heading 'Application of Other Rules'.

[60] Three cases involving the conclusion of BITs are pending at the time of writing (January 2008): Case C-205/06, *Commission* v. *Austria* (by order of 17 October 2006, Lithuania, Finland, Germany and Hungary have been allowed to intervene); Case C-249/06, *Commission* v. *Sweden*, and Case C-118/07, *Commission* v. *Finland*.

The other sizeable group of bilateral agreements concluded by Finland with non-EU members comprises double taxation agreements.[61] These contain no reference whatsoever to EU law, the common market, or the Community *acquis*, and would generally seem to be considered as falling outside the scope of Community powers, but with the caveat that in exercising their powers related to taxation, the member states 'nevertheless may not disregard Community rules.' Where the obligations under Community law do not affect the treaty partners (e.g., by extending tax advantages to others than residents of the contracting party, so as to prevent nationality discrimination), bilateral treaties to avoid double taxation have been left untouched by the Court.[62]

Neither do most of the agreements concluded with neighbouring Russia on border crossings and border crossing posts refer to EU law (for obvious reasons), with one notable exception: an agreement for moving a border crossing refers to the EU in its preamble, but mainly, so it seems, due to the circumstance that the project is financed by the EU.[63]

Various road traffic agreements concluded by Finland with third parties contain a general deference clause, to the effect that the agreement at issue shall not affect the rights or obligations the contracting parties may have under other international agreements – no special reference is made with respect to the EU, though.[64] The one exception is the road traffic agreement with Croatia, which contains no such clause.[65] In addition, those treaties typically make specific reference to other international bodies, most notably the UN Economic Commission for Europe, and contain a reference to ADR standards.

---

[61] This includes an agreement with Switzerland amending an existing double taxation agreement: *Suomen Sopimussarja*, 2006, no. 92. Regular agreements were concluded with Macedonia (*Suomen Sopimussarja*, 2002, no. 23), Russia (2002, no. 110), Singapore (2002, no. 115), the Kyrgyz Republic (2004, no. 14), Slovenia (2004, no. 70) and Azerbaijan (2006, no. 94).

[62] See Case C-307/97, *Compagnie de Saint Gobain, Zweigniederlassung Deutschland* v. *Finanzamt Aachen-Innenstadt*, [1999] ECR I-6161, esp. paras. 57–9.

[63] *Suomen Sopimussarja*, 2004, no. 161.

[64] The typical formulation in Finnish reads: 'Tämä sopimus ei vaikuta muista sopimuspuolten tekemistä kansainvälistä sopimuksista, joiden osapuolet ne ovat, johtuviin oikeusiin ja velvollisuuksiin.' This clause is taken from article 13 of the road traffic agreement with Lithuania (*Suomen Sopimussarja*, 2004, no. 87). Similar provisions can be found in similar agreements with Moldova (2004, no. 114, art. 16), Slovenia (2004, no. 116, art. 1), Uzbekistan (2004, no. 118, art. 21), and Kazakhstan (2004, no. 120, art. 21).

[65] *Suomen Sopimussarja*, 2005, no. 17.

During the period under review, Finland has concluded two agreements to either amend or implement earlier air services agreements. The first of these was concluded with Singapore in the form of an exchange of notes, and concerned implementation of an existing agreement.[66] It contains no reference to EU law or the *acquis*. The same applies to an agreement with China, also in the form of an exchange of notes, to amend an existing air services agreement: again, no EU reference.[67]

The various agreements on criminal cooperation concluded during the period under review also do not contain any specific reference to the EU. The criminal cooperation treaty with Poland provides that it does not affect rights or obligations under other agreements, nor shall it preclude further cooperation under other treaties, but this falls somewhat short of being a specific EU clause.[68] Likewise, the criminal cooperation treaties with Turkey and Hungary contain a general deference clause, as well as a preambular reference to the existence of other treaties, but nothing specific concerning the EU.[69]

With other agreements, a specific EU reference was never to be expected. Thus, agreements on the possible employment position of the family members of diplomats do not concern the EU in any way.[70] Nor would one expect an agreement on education to refer to the EU *acquis* in any way,[71] and *mutatis mutandis*, the same would apply to an agreement with Russia on the debts of the former Soviet Union,[72] and the lengthy agreement with Russia on railway traffic.[73] An agreement with Estonia on the reduction of greenhouse gases is explicitly concluded against the background of the Kyoto Protocol, but contains no EU savings clause.[74]

Some agreements were concluded to give effect to obligations arising under EC law. This concerns in particular an agreement with Estonia

---

[66] *Suomen Sopimussarja*, 2002, no. 900.   [67] *Suomen Sopimussarja*, 2003, no. 32.

[68] *Suomen Sopimussarja*, 2003, no. 70, article 13.

[69] *Suomen Sopimussarja*, 2004, no. 139, article 11 (Turkey) and 2003, no. 66, article 10 (Hungary).

[70] Two treaties on this topic were concluded, one with Hungary (*Suomen Sopimussarja*, 2003, no. 20) and one with Chile (2005, no. 85).

[71] Such an agreement was concluded with the Palestinian Authority (*Suomen Sopimussarja*, 2005, no. 95). Interestingly, however, it contains a very explicit conditionality clause, not unlike the clauses included in the EU's external agreements and insisting on respect for democracy, human rights, the rule of law and the market economy. For a discussion of EU conditionality, see Päivi Leino-Sandberg, 'European Universalism? The EU and Human Rights Conditionality', *Yearbook of European Law*, 24 (2005), 329–83.

[72] *Suomen Sopimussarja*, 2003, no. 49.   [73] *Suomen Sopimussarja*, 2006, no. 49.

[74] *Suomen Sopimussarja*, 2004, no. 23.

on transboundary environmental impact assessment (which refers to EC legislation relevant to the 1991 Espoo Convention).[75] One agreement with Norway (on exchange of goods in times of crisis and war) aims to give effect to an obligation arising under the European Economic Area agreement,[76] and two agreements (on visas with Estonia and Latvia, respectively) were necessary to bring existing agreements into line with Finland's accession to the Schengen regime.[77]

Arguably, the only really specific EU savings clause included in the treaties concluded by Finland with third states during the period under review is contained in an agreement with China on economic, industrial and technical cooperation.[78] Article 7 of this treaty provides:

> This Agreement shall apply without prejudice to the international obliga-
> tions of both Contracting Parties. The provisions of the Agreement may
> not be invoked or interpreted in such a way to invalidate or otherwise affect
> the obligations imposed by the Treaties on which the European Union is
> founded or by agreements between the People's Republic of China and the
> European Community.

The rationale behind this provision is, no doubt, to guarantee that in case of conflict between Finland's obligations under EU law and those under the agreement with China, EU law shall prevail; yet, whether it would satisfy the strict approach of the EC Court (if it should ever get there) appears doubtful in light of the *Open Skies* cases. Here, it will be remembered, various member states had included similar clauses in their bilateral agreements, but this failed to pacify the Court: what mattered, so the Court stipulated, was not the prevention of actual conflict alone, but also the prevention of a potential conflict. The member states were pre-empted, by Community law, from concluding air services agreements with third states, regardless of the safeguards they built in.

The remarkable thing, ultimately, about the *Open Skies* cases is the circumstance that international law was not even mentioned, let alone taken seriously. At no point is there any awareness on the part of the Court that a treaty between, say, Finland and the US, or the UK and the US, is actually supposed to be binding on those states by virtue of international law, even if concluded in violation of domestic (or internal) treaty-making norms. As a result, there is also no awareness that the

---

[75] *Suomen Sopimussarja*, 2002, no. 51.   [76] *Suomen Sopimussarja*, 2006, no. 55.
[77] *Suomen Sopimussarja*, 2002, no. 11 (Estonia), and no. 81 (Latvia).
[78] *Suomen Sopimussarja*, 2005, no. 71.

question is not so much whether Finland, or the UK, was allowed, as a matter of Community law, to conclude such a treaty, but rather whether such a treaty, once concluded, would have to give way to the earlier TEC, or whether, instead, it would prevail over the TEC as *lex posterior*.

This may, to some extent, have been a function of the parties' arguments, but even so, the parties' arguments are most likely coloured by their expectations of the sort of argument the Court will take into consideration. And the Court has a history of submitting international law to Community law. This is apparent from the string of cases on the possible direct effect of WTO law in the Community legal order;[79] it is even more apparent from the cases involving the effects of foundational international instruments. As discussed in Chapter 7 above, the Court has consistently refused to directly apply resolutions adopted by the Security Council; instead, when giving them effect, it typically relies on the manner in which those were reflected in a Community regulation, applying the regulation to the case in hand in the hope that the regulation would be a faithful rendition of the Security Council resolution.[80] And more recent decisions, such as *Yusuf* and *Kadi*, more receptive to UN law at first sight, turn out be highly ambivalent. This neglect of international law has, of course, one substantive advantage: the world created by the Court of Justice is a world where treaty conflict is non-existent. To paraphrase Binder, the European Court of Justice 'conjures up a world without treaty conflict',[81] as any possible conflict is eradicated simply by assuming the supremacy of Community law, even in circumstances where an appeal to international law might lead to a different result.[82] The drawback then will be the reverse: the Court's policy is that of the ostrich, aiming to avoid problems by sticking its head in the sand and pretending they do not exist.

The disconnection clause

The most well-known example of a treaty provision included in multilateral agreements involving the EC's member states (sometimes also

---

[79] See generally Klabbers, 'International Law in Community Law'.
[80] See generally Chapter 7.
[81] See Binder, *Treaty Conflict and Political Contradiction*, p. 33.
[82] Petersmann's claim then that article 307 (ex article 234) reflects the principle of European integration within the framework of international law (*Grundsatz der völkerrechtskonformen Integration*) appears to be something of an overstatement. See Petersmann, 'Artikel 234', p. 5728.

involving the EC itself as a treaty partner) is the so-called 'disconnection clause' (*'clause de deconnexion'*), which is to be found mostly in treaties concluded under auspices of the Council of Europe.[83] Typically, the disconnection clause provides something to the effect that, between themselves, parties to a treaty which are also members of the EC shall continue to apply EC law. The treaty concerned then shall be applied by EC members only in their relations with parties that have remained outside the EC, but not between EC members *inter se.*

Usually, the disconnection clause finds its way into a regular treaty provision. This is the case, for instance, in what is possibly the first treaty in which it is contained, the 1988 Convention on Mutual Administrative Assistance on Tax Matters. Article 27 of that convention provides: "Notwithstanding the rules of the present Convention, those Parties which are members of the European Economic Community shall apply in their mutual relations the common rules in force in that Community.'[84] Sometimes the clause is inserted as a preambular consideration, as with, for example, the 1989 Protocol to the Convention on Insider Trading. This simply, but effectively, considers 'that between States members of the European Economic Community the application of Community law should be reserved'.[85]

While neither of these agreements count the Community itself as a party, nothing prevents the disconnection clause from also being present in mixed agreements, as is made clear already by means of article 27, paragraph 1 of the 1989 European Convention on Transfrontier Television.[86] In fact, one could argue that the Transfrontier Television Convention takes disconnection a step further: it does not so much leave the Convention inapplicable between Community members in case of conflict, but starts from the other end, so to speak: it provides that Community member states shall, between themselves, continue to apply Community law 'and shall not therefore apply the rules arising from this Convention except insofar as there is no Community rule governing the particular subject concerned.'

---

[83] A useful general discussion is Constantin P. Economidès and Alexandros G. Kolliopoulos, 'La clause de deconnexion en faveur du droit communautaire: une pratique critiquable', *Revue Générale de Droit International Public*, 110 (2006), 273–302. See also, briefly, Régis Brillat, 'La participation de la Communauté Européenne aux conventions du Conseil de l'Europe', 37 *Annuaire Francais de Droit International*, 37 (1991), 819–32, esp. pp. 828–9.

[84] *European Treaty Series*, no. 127.   [85] *European Treaty Series*, no. 133.

[86] *European Treaty Series*, no. 132.

The disconnection clause has come under some fire in the literature recently,[87] the general gist of the critique being that somehow it is not right for the Community and its member states to carve out a special position for Community law. To do so would violate the equality of states, risk a further fragmenting of the international legal order, and is difficult to reconcile with what is perceived as the generally and traditionally open attitude of the Community to international law.

Part of the critique stems from the precise way the clause operates. As Economidès and Kolliopoulos underline, the disconnection clause, typically, is a general clause, which does not specify which precise provisions of Community law are to be protected from the workings of an agreement involving third parties; it is, therefore, a fairly blunt instrument. Second, the typical disconnection clause works automatically: it needs no further act or declaration to activate it.[88] And third, the typical disconnection clause is unconditional and, so to speak, absolute: it is not interested in reconciling Community law and an external agreement; instead, it is interested in making Community law prevail.[89]

In response to charges such as these, the Commission's defence of the disconnection clause focuses on its beneficial effects not on the international legal order, but on the European legal order. The disconnection clause, so the Commission habitually writes when asked to explain or defend it, promotes legal certainty and clarity. It helps to prevent the fragmentation of EC law, and the segmentation of the internal market. Third, it helps to remind the member states of the importance of EC law; and fourth (summarising the other arguments, essentially), the disconnection clause safeguards the primacy of EC law.[90]

---

[87] See especially Economidès and Kolliopoulos, 'La clause'.

[88] Exceptionally, some become activated upon notification to the depository, such as the 1995 UNIDROIT Convention on Stolen or Illegally Exported Cultural Property. As reported in *ibid.*, p. 277. The UNIDROIT Convention on Agency in the International Sale of Goods contains a general deference clause (article 23), whereas the 1970 UNIDROIT International Convention on Travel Contracts does not single out Community law, but does have a so-called 'federal clause'. The 2001 UNIDROIT Convention on International Interests in Mobile Equipment allows for participation by a regional economic integration organisation, but demands statements as to the division of competences between such organisations and their member states (article 48).

[89] *Ibid.*, p. 275.

[90] The arguments are taken from Commission Document SEC (2001) 315 of 19 February 2001, available at www.statewatch.org/news/2001/mar/18comm315.htm (last visited 29 October 2006). This particular document related to the Council of Europe's Draft Convention on Cybercrime; the arguments, however, are regularly invoked in explanatory reports to Council of Europe Draft Conventions.

Obviously, by pointing to the benefits for Community law of use of the disconnection clause, the Commission's reasoning fails to respond to concerns about its effects on the international legal order at large.[91] Still, on the technical legal level, there is nothing much wrong with the disconnection clause. After all, it is included in a variety of treaties with the consent of the treaty partners; as long as this is the case, in the decentralised and horizontal international legal order, there is not much to criticise: states are presumed to know what they consent to, and can simply refuse to consent to the disconnection clause.[92] It is, indeed, no coincidence that the most ardent critics of the disconnection clause have to resort to systemic arguments (risk of increased fragmentation, undermining legal equality) rather than any concrete and enforceable legal norm.

And yet, it is surely also no coincidence that the main (or only) venue for the disconnection clause is the Council of Europe setting, in which the EC, with its twenty-seven member states, plays an important role. A general Council of Europe agreement without participation by the twenty-seven member states of the EC would remain toothless; if a treaty is to have any impact at all, the EC's member states must be included, and this in turn entails that, for all practical purposes, the EC is in a position if not actually to dictate the terms of the treaty concerned, then at least to carve out a special position for EC law.

The argument has been made that the validity of the disconnection clause may also hinge on its compatibility with a treaty's object and purpose, by analogy with the regime relating to *inter se* modifications of treaty regimes as laid down in article 41 of the Vienna Convention on the Law of Treaties.[93] The reason for this would be that, owing to the dynamic nature of Community law, what may be an acceptable 'reservation' on Monday may turn out to be more problematic on Friday: Community law changes all the time, so the 'object and purpose' test would seem to guarantee that Community law does not change so as to undermine the broader treaty. Indeed, some instruments make reference to the object and purpose of the external agreement; an example is the 2005 Convention on the Prevention of Terrorism, which refers to application of EC law by

---

[91] As Olivier Tell, a French judge experienced in the field of private international law, puts it bluntly, the disconnection clause represents 'a surer means to guarantee the interests of the Community' than resort to the Vienna Convention's conflict provisions. See Olivier Tell, *La "Disconnecting Clause"/Disconnection Clause* (unpublished seminar paper, 2001, on file with the author), at p. 4.

[92] So also, generally, Koskenniemi, *Fragmentation*, p. 151: 'The validity of a disconnection clause flows from party consent.'

[93] See *ibid.*, pp. 150–1.

EC member states 'without prejudice to the object and purpose of the present Convention and without prejudice to its full application with the other Parties.'[94]

That is a laudable attempt to limit the Community's room for manoeuvre, but whether it will actually work seems doubtful. For one thing, the 'object and purpose' test is notoriously difficult to apply in its own right.[95] Second, should push come to shove, the situation will be that the parties to a convention will be hopelessly divided on whether or not Community law undermines the object and purpose of this external agreement: the twenty-seven members of the Community, it may safely be predicted, will resist the attempt to classify Community law as disruptive of the treaty's object and purpose, while the remaining parties may be more keen. In the end, then, some compromise may have to be reached, and it is not unlikely that the relative power of the Community within the Council of Europe may prove decisive.

At the time of writing, the disconnection clause has not, as such, come before the Court of Justice. It has made an appearance in only one decision, and then only tangentially. In Opinion 01/03 (*Lugano Convention*), the central question is whether the Community had the exclusive power to join the Lugano Convention. The inclusion of a disconnection clause in such a convention, so the Court found, provides an indication that Community law may be affected by the Convention at hand (which in turn would suggest that the Community at least has some powers on the topic), but this is where the Court stopped.[96]

Community agreements

If member states work, in concluding agreements, to preserve Community law and shield the *acquis communautaire*, so does the Community itself. The most common clause utilised by the EC is what might be

---

[94] *Council of Europe Treaty Series*, no. 190, article 26, paragraph 3. Other examples are listed in Economidès and Kolliopoulos, 'La clause', p. 277, note 6.

[95] See Jan Klabbers, 'Some Problems Regarding the Object and Purpose of Treaties', *Finnish Yearbook of International Law*, 8 (1997), 138–60; see also Isabelle Buffard and Karl Zemanek, 'The "Object and Purpose" of a Treaty: An Enigma?', *Austrian Review of International and European Law*, 3 (1998), 311–43.

[96] Opinion 01/03 (*Lugano Convention*) [2006] ECR I-1145, paras. 130, 154–5. It is perhaps useful to point out that in this case (indeed, perhaps relating to private international law treaties more generally, which mostly delimit jurisdiction rather than regulate substantive matters), the Commission had argued that the inclusion of a disconnection clause had not been necessary, and could not be considered probative with regard to the existence of Community powers.

called a 'conditioned territorial application clause'. Typically, this specifies that, in relations with treaty partners, the treaty shall be applied, for the Community, under the conditions set out in Community law. That is a fairly innocuous-sounding statement, but still manages to disconnect Community law from the workings of such a treaty. A typical example is drawn from an audiovisual agreement concluded between the EC and Switzerland, providing that the agreement in question 'shall apply to the territories in which the Treaty establishing the European Community is applicable, under the conditions laid down in that Treaty, and to the territory of Switzerland.'[97]

Contrary to the standard disconnection clause, the conditioned territorial application clause is used predominantly in treaties concluded by the EC itself (rather than its member states). And it is used a lot, in treaties with partners spanning the globe, and covering a wide variety of topics: from taxation agreements to fisheries cooperation agreements, from trade agreements to agreements on participation in international institutions. The clause makes an appearance in fairly informal bilateral agreements, but also in highly formalised and politically significant agreements such as partnership agreements and association agreements.[98]

A second clause, mostly used by the Union, is an interesting, more forward-looking variation, found predominantly in treaties addressing issues outside the area of competences included in the first pillar: hence, found in particular in agreements on immigration, justice or security issues.[99] A good example is to be found in the 2003 EU–US Extradition Agreement, which provides that it 'shall not preclude the conclusion, after its entry into force, of bilateral Agreements between a Member State and the United States of America consistent with this Agreement.'[100] The import of the clause, it would seem, is to establish a Community-wide regime by means of a treaty with a third party, and subsequently allow

---

[97] See Agreement between the European Community and the Swiss Confederation in the Audiovisual Field, establishing the terms and conditions for the participation of the Swiss Confederation in the Community programmes MEDIA Plus and MEDIA Training, in *Official Journal*, 28 March 2006, L 90/23, Article 11.

[98] See generally, with copious references, Klabbers, 'Safeguarding'.

[99] An example of the latter is the Agreement between the European Union and Ukraine on Security Procedures for the Exchange of Classified Information, in *Official Journal*, 5 May 2005, L 172/86.

[100] In *Official Journal*, 19 July 2003, L 181/27. For general commentary, see Theodore Georgopoulos, 'What Kind of Treaty-making Power for the EU? Constitutional Problems Related to the Conclusion of the EU–US Agreements on Extradition and Mutual Legal Assistance', *European Law Review*, 30 (2005), 190–208.

only for member state agreements with that third country which are compatible with the Community-wide regime. Likewise, some treaties contain a clause not just pre-empting the member states from concluding certain agreements, but also the Community itself, and again such treaties relate predominantly to security issues.[101]

Other clauses are less often used, and perhaps more straightforward. Thus, on occasion an agreement concluded by the Community or the Union may simply provide that it is not intended to derogate from existing legal instruments.[102] Sometimes the Community decides to attach a declaration to an agreement upholding EC law.[103] And on at least one occasion the Community has used an external agreement to introduce other external standards into EC law, and make it difficult to envisage a departure from those standards by the Community or its member states (and its treaty partner, for that matter).[104]

Conclusion

While the techniques are varied, the message is clear: Community law must be upheld; neither the EC itself (or the EU, for that matter) nor its individual member states are allowed to depart from EC law by means of concluding external agreements. Indeed, it is generally acknowledged, at least since the 1971 *ERTA* case, that the existence of external powers for the EC serves not so much to facilitate the reaching of the EC's goals in any abstract matter, but rather serves to protect the *acquis communautaire*. In *ERTA* the EC Court already observed that 'any steps taken outside the

---

[101] There are, for example, several agreements on security procedures for the exchange of classified information, for instance with Croatia (*Official Journal*, 29 April 2006, L 116/74) and the Former Yugoslav Republic of Macedonia (*Official Journal*, 13 April 2005, L 94/39). Additionally, such a clause can be found in an agreement between the EU and NATO on Security of Information, in *Official Journal*, 27 March 2003, L 80/36.

[102] See the EU-US Agreement on the Processing and Transfer of Passenger Name Record (PNR) Data by Air Carriers to the United States Department of Homeland Security, in *Official Journal*, 27 October 2006, L 298/29.

[103] See the Protocol on the Implementation of the 1991 Alpine Convention in the Field of Mountain Farming, in *Official Journal*, 30 September 2006, L 271/63.

[104] In a fisheries agreement between the EC and Ivory Coast, it is stipulated that the legal situation concerning seamen aboard EC vessels shall be governed by the ILO Declaration on Fundamental Principles and Rights at Work, and that Ivory Coast seamen's wage conditions shall not be below ILO standards. See *Official Journal*, 22 March 2005, L 76/5, Article 9. For a useful discussion of the ILO Declaration, see Philip Alston, '"Core Labour Standards" and the Transformation of the International Labour Rights regime', *European Journal of International Law*, 15 (2004), 457–521.

framework of the Community institutions would be incompatible with the unity of the Common Market and the uniform application of Community law.'[105] More recently, in Opinion 01/03 (*Lugano Convention*) the Court put it even more clearly. With respect to exclusive powers to act externally, the Court observed that the 'purpose of the exclusive competence of the Community is primarily to preserve the effectiveness of Community law and the proper functioning of the systems established by its rules'.[106]

In the end, then, when confronted with the choice between international law and Community law, the Community, inspired by the Commission and with the firm backing of the Court, unwaveringly opts for Community law. It does so when anterior treaties are concerned, rendering the protection offered by article 307 TEC more nominal than real; and it does so with posterior agreements as well.

As a political choice among political choices, the EC is, of course, fully entitled to do so. Still, on occasion the choice for having Community law prevail is a rather parochial one, which would not be tolerated if coming from a state. Surely, not even the United States could insist on fencing off its domestic law from international law without being subjected to severe critiques. It is ironic then that Europe, so often depicted as supportive of international law, fares little better when the chips are down.

There is, moreover, a second irony or paradox. Part of the goodwill the EU enjoys undoubtedly stems from its being seen as an experiment in cosmopolitanism: to many, especially outside the EU perhaps, the EU represents a model experiment in international cooperation.[107] Yet, the closer the EU begins to resemble a 'regular' state, the less it will be allowed to tap into this reservoir of goodwill: the more like a 'regular' state it becomes, the more it will be treated as one, with all the international legal implications this may entail.

---

[105] See Case 22/70, *Commission* v. *Council (ERTA)* [1971] ECR 273, para. 31.
[106] See Opinion 01/03 (*Lugano Convention*), para. 131.
[107] See, e.g., John Dryzek, *Deliberative Global Politics* (Cambridge: Polity, 2006), p. 135.

10

Conclusions

The first major conclusion to be drawn from this study is that the law of treaties has little to offer when it comes to solving the really difficult cases of treaty conflict. That should not come as a surprising conclusion: in their own way, other studies have made much the same point, culminating in the fairly generally accepted proposition that, at the end of the day, the principle of political decision applies: when confronted with conflicting treaty obligations, a state must simply pick and choose which one to honour, and compensate the party which loses out.

What this study offers, however, in relation to the principle of political decision, is two things. First, it suggests reasons why the law has to fall back on the principle of political decision: with every treaty being *res inter alios acta*, international law cannot, while remaining true to its horizontal nature, facilitate any choice; and with the Vienna Convention focusing on the treaty as instrument rather than as obligation, a choice based on substantive values (e.g., human rights treaties shall prevail over all other treaties) is also out of reach. Secondly, this study also makes the point that perhaps this is not something to despair at, but rather something to celebrate: the open-ended nature of the treaty conflict provisions of the Vienna Convention facilitates the search for a fair and just settlement in each and every individual case. Instead of mechanistically applying a single one-size-fits-all rule (which, of course, only fits in the sense that cheap suits off the rack can be said to fit), the principle of political decision opens up space for political discussion and debate, for the involvement of civil society in international relations, and for the balancing of all that is relevant to the dispute concerned. The endorsement by some of a more active role for article 31, paragraph 3(c), holding that when interpreting a treaty all of any rule of international law applicable between the parties may – and perhaps should – be taken into account, points in the same direction.[1]

---

[1] See, e.g., Koskenniemi, *Fragmentation*, esp. part F; McLachlan, 'Systemic Integration'.

It is, as always, possible to think of counter-arguments. Thus, histor-ically, a broad approach is hardly dictated by the intent underlying the provision; although in fairness it is not excluded either: the provision is the somewhat contorted version resulting from the attempt by the drafters to deal with the vexed problem of intertemporal law.[2] Practically, moreover, there may be no end to the rules of law actually applicable between par-ties: in particular between neighbouring states, dozens of treaties may be applicable. While not all of these will address the issue at hand, obviously much will depend on how the issue at hand is framed – and by whom.[3] Still, an open-ended principle such as the principle of political decision is much to be preferred over any single rule.

Indeed, the third part of this study suggests that the approach adopted by the ECJ (put bluntly: apply the rule that EC law prevails) may not always lead to satisfactory results.[4] It may come to affect individuals negatively (as in the various Spanish Fishermen cases) and, moreover, tends to subject all values to the value of the internal market. This is most obviously the case with human rights which, as *Schmidberger* suggests, are afterthoughts to the process of market integration; at best, they may come to justify exceptions to the free movement of goods.

As the third part also suggests, the reputation of article 307 as being the friend of public international law is, shall we say, a mite exaggerated: the case law of the Court has proved to be less than generous (far less than generous) in upholding anterior treaties. At best – but even this is rare – an anterior treaty may result in the temporary de-activation or suspension of bits and pieces of Community law, as Schütze puts it,[5] but, even so, the ECJ has been highly creative in defining anterior treaties away (think again of those Spanish fishermen), and has relied predominantly on a test which

---

[2] See generally Klabbers, 'Reluctant *Grundnormen*'.

[3] It is partly for the same reason – the open-ended nature of the notion of *travaux préparatoires* – that the Vienna Convention, in article 32, minimises recourse to the *travaux*. See generally Jan Klabbers, 'International Legal Histories: The Declining Importance of *Travaux Préparatoires* in Treaty Interpretation?', *Netherlands International Law Review*, 50 (2003) 267–88.

[4] More generally, it has been observed that the case-law of the EC courts involving the law of treaties is not always above criticism. See Pieter Jan Kuiyper, 'The Court and the Tribunal of the EC and the Vienna Convention on the Law of Treaties 1969', *Legal Issues of European Integration*, 25 (1998/I), 1–23; Jan Klabbers, 'Re-inventing the Law of Treaties: The Contribution of the EC Courts', *Netherlands Yearbook of International Law*, 30 (1999), 45–74.

[5] See Schütze, 'EC Law and International Agreements'.

may work with some treaties but encounters problems with treaties concluded for the general interest. Typically, since *Commission* v. *Italy*,[6] the dominant construction has been to divide treaties (including multilateral treaties) into bundles of rights and obligations; but that is a construction ill-suited for the analysis of, say, human rights treaties, or environmental protection treaties. The case-law has on occasion opened the possibility for a more subtle approach (*Burgoa*;[7] the Advocate-General's suggestions in *Henn and Darby*[8]), but such an approach remains far from settled.

In addition, the EC Treaty lacks a rule on what to do with posterior treaties, which has led to the predictable result that these are, typically, seen as problematic from the point of view of the EC courts, even if those treaties are concluded by member states exercising their own proper powers. This owes much to the reach (or expansion) of the notion of *Gemeinschaftstreue*, laid down in article 10 TEC and functioning as something of a *deus ex machina*, coming to the EU's rescue whenever an analysis in terms of exercising powers might otherwise necessitate the acceptance of posterior treaties.

One option then might be for the EU to insert a clause outlining the fate of treaties concluded after entry into force of the EC Treaty itself or the dates of accession, so as to avoid misunderstandings and create a clearer legal picture. This, however, does not appear terribly realistic at present – not when there is a Reform Treaty waiting to be ratified (which does not introduce such a provision). Moreover, it would politically be awkward to open up the Reform Treaty; and even if it were decided to do so, it seems safe to assume that the fate of posterior treaties is not considered to be of great political urgency.

Alternatively, as has recently been suggested, there might be merit in the idea of amending the Vienna Convention, so as to take due account of the interests of the EC and, perhaps, try to get the Vienna Convention to place EU law beyond general international law.[9] This too, however, would be politically awkward: surely, there is no good reason why other states should be willing to create a privileged position for the EU if even the EU itself cannot be bothered. As it is, article 5 of the Vienna Convention does

---

[6] See Case 10/61, *Commission* v. *Italy* [1961] ECR 1.
[7] See Case 812/79, *Attorney General* v. *Burgoa* [1980] ECR 2787.
[8] See Case 34/79, *Regina* v. *Henn and Darby* [1979] ECR 3795.
[9] The argument is made in Delano Verwey, *The European Community, the European Union and the International Law of Treaties* (The Hague: TMC Asser Press, 2004).

create the possibility for the EU; the circumstance that the EU does not make much use of it can hardly be blamed on others, nor can those others be expected to pull the chestnuts out of the fire on the EU's behalf.

In the end, then, it would seem that the most viable alternative is to put all sorts of clauses in treaties relating to the relative positions of both the EU and its member states, and that seems indeed to be increasingly what is going on, as the previous chapter has discussed. In more ways than one, the Community and its member states do their utmost to safeguard the position of Community law. The one risk here is a political risk: surely, at times the insistence of the Community on the inclusion of disconnection clauses and their ilk may upset potential treaty partners. While legally there is little wrong with such clauses (as long as treaty partners accept them), politically it might be wise to show some restraint every now and then.

Lord McNair could write in 1961 that 'conflict between treaties or incompatibility of treaties with one another is a complicated matter and it cannot be said that clear guidance has yet come from judicial or arbitral sources'.[10] For his part, Sir Ian Sinclair felt compelled to note, writing in 1984, that the Convention rules on successive treaties may best be regarded as 'residuary in character, so that the negotiators of treaties are left reasonably free to determine for themselves the relationship between the text which they are seeking to draw up and previous, or future, treaties, in the same field'.[11] Both these statements still stand, both as a general matter and in light of the reluctance of the European Court even to acknowledge the possible existence of a possible conflict. With that in mind, it would perhaps be advisable were legislative or constitutional authorities to step in to formulate a flexible rule which does justice to both the Community's interests and to those of third parties. For, lest we forget, those third parties may be the ones losing out due to the Community's insistence on the prevalence of Community law.[12]

Such considerations as legal certainty would make it advisable to some-how determine a position. This would also be nicely in tune with what some of the EU's highest-ranking public officials identify as the EU's legalism. Thus, Christiaan Timmermans, a former deputy director at the Commission's legal service and presently a judge at the Court of Justice,

[10] See McNair, *The Law of Treaties*, p. 219.   [11] See Sinclair, *The Vienna Convention*, p. 98.
[12] A rule to address posterior treaties has occasionally been advocated in the literature. See, e.g., Churchill and Foster, 'Prior Treaty Obligations', p. 523; Petersmann, 'Artikel 234', pp. 5731–2; Krück, *Völkerrechtliche*, p. 136.

holds the EU to have adopted a general 'rule-oriented approach'; indeed, even 'by simply being there', the EU contributes to the development of international law.[13]

While in other settings the principle of political decision allows for the introduction of political debate on the wisdom of having one set of norms prevail over another, within the EU it would seem that the principle does not apply: there is but a single rule, and according to that rule EU law shall prevail. That is to some extent understandable, and perhaps the inevitable result of being able to adopt only one prism at a time; and sometimes it might even be the case that friend and foe alike may agree on the wisdom, or political desirability, of having EC law prevail over anything else – a case in point is constituted by UN sanctions regimes which, as discussed in Chapter 7, are not big on things such as human rights protection, in particular due process rights. Perhaps in such a scenario the only decent thing to do is what Advocate-General Maduro proposes: close EC law (including human rights protection) off from UN law, regardless of the consequences this may have on the international plane.

But what may be advisable in individual cases is perhaps less acceptable as a general proposition: surely, the EC cannot close itself off from international law all the time and in all situations. Article 307 would seem to have been inspired either by a desire to protect the integrity of international law (EC law itself, lest it be forgotten, is an offspring of international law) or, at the very least, by the wisdom of balancing EC law and international law. Yet, the evidence presented above suggests that the EC courts, and the Commission, have over the years become less interested in balancing than might legitimately have been expected. That may help protect European integration in the short run, but is bound to give rise to some resentment along the road on the part of the treaty partners of the EU's member states – and quite possibly on the part of those member states as well.

[13] See Timmermans, 'The EU and Public International Law', p. 194 (emphasis omitted).

BIBLIOGRAPHY

Ahmed, Tawhida and Israel de Jesús Butler, 'The European Union and Human Rights: An International Law Perspective', *European Journal of International Law*, 17 (2006), 771–801

Alexy, Robert, *Theorie der Grundrechte* (Frankfurt am Main: Suhrkamp, 1994, first published 1985)

Alkema, Evert A., 'The Enigmatic No-Pretext Clause: Article 60 of the European Convention on Human Rights', in Jan Klabbers and René Lefeber (eds.), *Essays on the Law of Treaties: A Collection of Essays in Honour of Bert Vierdag* (The Hague: Martinus Nijhoff, 1998), pp. 41–56

Alston, Philip, '"Core Labour Standards" and the Transformation of the International Labour Rights Regime', *European Journal of International Law*, 15 (2004), 457–521

'Resisting the Merger and Acquisition of Human Rights by Trade Law: A Reply to Petersmann', *European Journal of International Law*, 13 (2002), 815–44

Alvarez, José E., *International Organizations as Law-makers* (Oxford: Oxford University Press, 2005)

'The WTO as Linkage Machine', *American Journal of International Law*, 96 (2002), 146–58

Atiyah, Patrick, review of Charles Fried, *Contract as Promise, Harvard Law Review* 95 (1981), 509–28

Aufricht, Hans, 'Supersession of Treaties in International Law', *Cornell Law Quarterly*, 37 (1951–52), 655–700

Aust, Anthony, *Handbook of International Law* (Cambridge: Cambridge University Press, 2005)

Modern Treaty Law and Practice (Cambridge: Cambridge University Press, 2000)

'The Theory and Practice of Informal International Instruments', *International and Comparative Law Quarterly*, 35 (1986), 787–812

Azoulai, Loïc, 'The *Acquis* of the European Union and International Organisations', *European Law Journal*, 11 (2005), 196–231

Barnett, Michael and Martha Finnemore, *Rules for the World: International Organizations in Global Politics* (Ithaca, NY: Cornell University Press, 2004)

Beitz, Charles R., *Political Theory and International Relations* (Princeton, NJ: Princeton University Press, 1999, first published 1979)

Berlin, Isaiah, *Four Essays on Liberty* (Oxford: Oxford University Press, 1969)

Bermann, George A., 'Taking Subsidiarity Seriously: Federalism in the European Community and the United States', *Columbia Law Review*, 94 (1994), 331–456

Bernhardt, Rudolf, 'Article 103', in Bruno Simma *et al.* (eds.), *The Charter of the United Nations: A Commentary*, 2nd edn (Oxford: Oxford University Press, 2002), pp. 1292–302

Binder, Guyora, *Treaty Conflict and Political Contradiction: The Dialectic of Duplicity* (New York: Praeger, 1988)

Bladel, Ineke van, 'The Iron Rhine Arbitration Case: On the Right Legal Track?', *Hague Justice Journal*, 1 (2006), 5–21

Bleckmann, Albert, 'Zur Wandlung der Strukturen der Völkerrechtsverträge – Theorie des multipolaren Vertrages', *Archiv des Völkerrechts*, 34 (1996), 218–36

Blokker, Niels M., 'Decisions of International Organizations: The Case of the European Union', *Netherlands Yearbook of International Law*, 30 (1999), 3–44

Borgen, Christopher J., 'Resolving Treaty Conflicts', *George Washington International Law Review*, 37 (2005), 573–648

Boulois, Jean, 'Le droit des Communautés Européennes dans ses rapports avec le droit international général', *Recueil des Cours*, 235 (1992/IV), 9–80

Boyle, Alan and Christine Chinkin, *The Making of International Law* (Oxford: Oxford University Press, 2007)

Breitenmoser, Stephan and Gunter E. Wilms, 'Human Rights v. Extradition: The *Soering* Case', *Michigan Journal of International Law*, 11 (1989–90), 845–86

Brierly, James L., 'The Codification of International Law', *Michigan Law Review*, 47 (1948), 2–10

Brillat, Régis, 'La participation de la Communauté Européenne aux conventions du Conseil de l'Europe', *Annuaire Francais de Droit International*, 37 (1991), 819–32

Brölmann, Catherine, *The Institutional Veil in Public International Law: International Organizations and the Law of Treaties* (Oxford: Hart, 2007)

Brown, Christopher, 'Annotation (Schmidberger)', *Common Market Law Review*, 40 (2003), 1499–510

Brownlie, Ian, *Principles of Public International Law*, 4th edn (Oxford: Clarendon Press, 1990)

'The Calling of the International Lawyer: Sir Humphrey Waldock and his Work', *British Yearbook of International Law*, 54 (1983), 7–74

Buffard, Isabelle and Karl Zemanek, 'The "Object and Purpose" of a Treaty: An Enigma?', *Austrian Review of International and European Law*, 3 (1998), 311–43

Búrca, Gráinne de, 'Fundamental Human Rights and the Reach of EC Law', *Oxford Journal of Legal Studies*, 13 (1993), 283–319

Burke-White, William W., 'International Legal Pluralism', *Michigan Journal of International Law*, 25 (2004), 963–79

Burley, Anne-Marie and Walter Mattli, 'Europe before the Court: A Political Theory of Legal Integration', *International Organization*, 47 (1993), 41–76

Burton, Steven J., *Judging in Good Faith* (Cambridge: Cambridge University Press, 1992)

Capotorti, Francesco, 'Cours général de droit international public', *Recueil des Cours*, 248 (1971/III), 9–343

  'L'Extinction et la suspension des traités', *Recueil des Cours*, 134 (1971/III), 417–587

Carlson, Scott N., 'The Montreal Protocol's Environmental Subsidies and GATT: A Needed Reconciliation', *Texas International Law Journal*, 29 (1994), 211–30

Chaltiel, Florence, *Naissance du peuple européenne* (Paris: Odile Jacob, 2006)

Chinkin, Christine, *Third Parties in International Law* (Oxford: Oxford University Press, 1993)

Churchill, Robin R. and Nigel G. Foster, 'European Community Law and Prior Treaty Obligations of Member States: The Spanish Fishermen's Case', *International and Comparative Law Quarterly*, 36 (1987), 504–24

Ciampi, Annalisa, 'L'Union Européenne et le respect des droits de l'homme dans la mise en oeuvre des sanctions devant la Cour Européenne des Droits de l'Homme', *Revue Générale de Droit International Public*, 110 (2006), 85–116

Coppel, Jason and Aidan O'Neill, 'The European Court of Justice: Taking Rights Seriously?', *Common Market Law Review*, 29 (1992), 669–92

Craig, Paul and Gráinne de Búrca, *EC Law: Text, Cases and Materials* 3rd edn (Oxford: Oxford University Press, 2003)

Cramér, Per, 'Recent Swedish Experiences with Targeted UN Sanctions: The Erosion of Trust in the Security Council', in Erika de Wet and André Nollkaemper (eds.), *Review of the Security Council by Member States* (Antwerp: Intersentia, 2003), pp. 85–104

Craven, Matthew, 'Legal Differentiation and the Concept of the Human Rights Treaty in International Law', *European Journal of International Law*, 11 (2000), 489–519

  'Unity, Diversity and the Fragmentation of International Law', *Finnish Yearbook of International Law*, 14 (2003), 3–34

Cremona, Marise, 'External Relations and External Competence: The Emergence of an Integrated Policy', in Paul Craig and Gráinne de Búrca (eds.), *The Evolution of EU Law* (Oxford University Press, 1999), pp. 137–75

Crisp, Roger and Michael Slote (eds.), *Virtue Ethics* (Oxford: Oxford University Press, 1997)

Cross, Eugene Daniel, 'Pre-emption of Member State Law in the European Economic Community: A Framework for Analysis', *Common Market Law Review*, 29 (1992), 447–72

Czaplinski, W. and G. Danilenko, 'Conflict of Norms in International Law', *Netherlands Yearbook of International Law*, 22 (1991), 3–42

Davies, Gareth, 'Subsidiarity: The Wrong Idea, in the Wrong Place, at the Wrong Time', *Common Market Law Review*, 43 (2006), 63–84

Denys, Christine, *Impliciete bevoegdheden in de Europese Economische Gemeenschap* (Antwerp: MAKLU, 1990)

Douglas-Scott, Sionaidh, 'A Tale of Two Courts: Luxembourg, Strasbourg and the Growing Human Rights *Acquis*', *Common Market Law Review*, 43 (2006), 629–65

Dowrick, F. E., 'Overlapping International and European Laws', *International & Comparative Law Quarterly*, 31 (1982), 59–98

Dryzek, John, *Deliberative Global Politics* (Cambridge: Polity, 2006)

Due, Ole, 'Article 5 du traité CEE: Une disposition de caractère fédéral?', *Collected Courses of the Academy of European Law*, 2 (1991/II), 17–35

Dunoff, Jeffrey L., 'Constitutional Conceits: The WTO's 'Constitution' and the Discipline of International Law', *European Journal of International Law*, 17 (2006), 647–75

Dworkin, Ronald, *Law's Empire* (London: Fontana, 1986)
  Taking Rights Seriously (Cambridge, MA: Harvard University Press, 1977)

Dyzenhaus, David, *Legality and Legitimacy: Carl Schmitt, Hans Kelsen and Hermann Heller in Weimar* (Oxford: Oxford University Press, 1997)

Economidès, Constantin P. and Alexandros G. Kolliopoulos, 'La clause de deconnexion en faveur du droit communautaire: une pratique critiquable', *Revue Générale de Droit International Public*, 110 (2006), 273–302

Eeckhout, Piet, *External Relations of the European Union: Legal and Constitutional Foundations* (Oxford: Oxford University Press, 2004)

Ely, John Hart, *Democracy and Distrust: A Theory of Judicial Review* (Cambridge, MA: Harvard University Press, 1980)

Evans, Malcolm (ed.), *Blackstone's International Law Documents*, 7th edn (Oxford: Oxford University Press, 2005)

Eyffinger, A. C. and B. P. Vermeulen (eds. and trans.), *Hugo de Groot: Denken over oorlong en vrede* (Baarn: Ambo, 1991)

Farrall, Jeremy Matam, *United Nations Sanctions and the Rule of Law* (Cambridge: Cambridge University Press, 2007)

Fassbender, Bardo, 'The United Nations Charter as Constitution of the International Community', *Columbia Journal of Transnational Law*, 36 (1998), 529–619

Fischer-Lescano, Andreas and Gunther Teubner, 'Regime-Collisions: The Vain Search for Legal Unity in the Fragmentation of Global Law', *Michigan Journal of International Law* (2004), 999–1046
  Regime-Kollisionen: Zur Fragmentierung des Globalen Rechts (Frankfurt am Main: Suhrkamp, 2006)

Fish, Stanley, *Doing What Comes Naturally: Change, Rhetoric, and the Practice of Theory in Literary and Legal Studies* (Oxford: Clarendon Press, 1989)

Fitzmaurice, Sir Gerald, 'The General Principles of International Law Considered from the Standpoint of the Rule of Law', *Recueil des Cours*, 92 (1957/II), 1–227

'Fourth Report on the Law of Treaties', *Yearbook of the International Law Commission* (1959/II), 37–81

'Third Report on the Law of Treaties', *Yearbook of the International Law Commission* (1958/II), 20–46

'Report on the Law of Treaties', *Yearbook of the International Law Commission* (1956/II), 104–28

Fitzmaurice, Malgosia and Olufemi Elias, *Contemporary Issues in the Law of Treaties* (Utrecht: Eleven, 2005)

Foot, Philippa, *Natural Goodness* (Oxford: Oxford University Press, 2001)

Footer, Mary E. and Christoph Beat Graber, 'Trade Liberalization and Cultural Policy', *Journal of International Economic Law*, 3 (2000), 115–44

Franklin, Christian N. K., 'Flexibility vs. Legal Certainty: Article 307 EC and Other Issues in the Aftermath of the Open Skies Cases', *European Foreign Affairs Review*, 10 (2005), 79–115

Fuller, Lon L., *Legal Fictions* (Palo Alto, CA: Stanford University Press, 1967)

'Positivism and Fidelity to Law – A Reply to Professor Hart', *Harvard Law Review*, 71 (1958), 630–72

The Morality of Law, rev. edn (New Haven, CT: Yale University Press, 1969)

Gaja, Giorgio, 'Trends in Judicial Activism and Judicial Self-Restraint Relating to Community Interests', in Enzo Cannizzaro (ed.), *The European Union as an Actor in International Relations* (The Hague: Kluwer, 2002), pp. 117–34

Gardner, Richard N., *Sterling-Dollar Diplomacy in Current Perspective: The Origins and Prospects of Our International Economic Order*, 2nd edn (New York: Columbia University Press, 1980)

Georgopoulos, Theodore, 'What Kind of Treaty-making Power for the EU? Constitutional Problems Related to the Conclusion of the EU-US Agreements on Extradition and Mutual Legal Assistance', *European Law Review*, 30 (2005), 190–208

Goodwin-Gill, Guy, *The Refugee in International Law* (Oxford: Clarendon Press, 1983)

Gray, John, *Two Faces of Liberalism* (New York: New Press, 2000)

Grimes, Julie M., 'Conflicts between EC Law and International Treaty Obligations: A Case Study of the German Telecommunications Dispute', *Harvard International Law Journal*, 35 (1994), 535–64

Grotius, Hugo, *Denken over oorlog en vrede* (Baarn: Ambo, 1991, A. C. Eyffinger and B. P. Vermeulen, eds.)

On the Law of War and Peace (Oxford: Clarendon Press, 1925, Kelsey trans., first published 1625)

Guzman, Andrew, 'Global Governance and the WTO', *Harvard International Law Journal*, 45 (2004), 303–51

Hart, H. L. A., 'Positivism and the Separation of Law and Morals', *Harvard Law Review*, 71 (1958), 593–629

The Concept of Law (Oxford: Clarendon Press, 1961)

Hartley, Trevor C., 'International Law and the Law of the European Union – A Reassessment', *British Yearbook of International Law*, 72 (2001), 1–35

The Foundations of European Community Law, 6th edn (Oxford: Oxford University Press, 2007)

Heffernan, Liz and Conor McAuliffe, 'External Relations in the Air Transport Sector: The Court of Justice and the Open Skies Agreements', *European Law Review*, 28 (2003), 601–19

Heiskanen, Veijo, *International Legal Topics* (Helsinki: Finnish Lawyers' Publishing Company, 1992)

Heliskoski, Joni, *Mixed Agreements as a Technique for Organizing the International Relations of the European Community and its Member States* (The Hague: Kluwer, 2001)

Higgins, Rosalyn, *Problems and Process: International Law and How We Use it* (Oxford: Clarendon Press, 1994)

Hilf, Meinhard and Frank Schorkopf, 'WTO und EG: Rechtskonflikte vor den EuGH?', *EuropaRecht*, 35 (2000), 74–91

Hoffmeister, Frank, 'Annotation' (*Open Skies* cases), *American Journal of International Law*, 98 (2004), 567–72

Holdgaard, Rass, 'Principles of Reception of International Law in Community Law', *Yearbook of European Law*, 25 (2006), 263–314

Howse, Robert, 'Human Rights in the WTO: Whose Rights, What Humanity? Comment on Petersmann', *European Journal of International Law*, 13 (2002), 651–9

Hudson, Manley O., 'The Thirteenth Year of the Permanent Court of International Justice', *American Journal of International Law*, 29 (1935), 1–24

Ignatieff, Michael, *Isaiah Berlin: A Life* (London: Verso, 2000, first published 1998)

Jans, Jan H., 'National Legislative Autonomy? The Procedural Constraints of European Law', *Legal Issues of European Integration*, 25 (1998/I), 25–58

Jawara, Fatoumata and Aileen Kwa, *Behind the Scenes at the WTO. The Real World of International Trade Negotiations: The Lessons of Cancun*, updated edn (London: Zed Books, 2004)

Jenks, C. Wilfred, 'The Conflict of Law-making Treaties', *British Yearbook of International Law*, 30 (1953), 401–53

Jennings, Robert Y., 'Gerald Gray Fitzmaurice', *British Yearbook of International Law*, 55 (1984), 1–64

Jones, Kent, *Who's Afraid of the WTO?* (Oxford: Oxford University Press, 2004)

Jones, Martin, 'Lies, Damned Lies and Diplomatic Assurances: The Misuse of Diplomatic Assurances in Removal Proceedings', *European Journal of Migration and Law*, 8 (2006), 9–39

Johnstone, Iain, 'Treaty Interpretation: The Authority of Interpretive Communities', *Michigan Journal of International Law*, 12(1991) 371–419

Josephs, Hilary K., 'Upstairs, Trade Law; Downstairs, Labor Law', *George Washington International Law Review*, 33 (2000–01), 849–72

Kapteyn, P. J. G., 'The Role of the ECJ in Implementing Security Council Resolutions', in Erika de Wet and André Nollkaemper (eds.), *Review of the Security Council by Member States* (Antwerp: Intersentia, 2003) pp. 57–62

Karl, Wolfram, 'Treaties, Conflicts between', *Encyclopedia of Public International Law*, IV (2000), 935–41

Kelsen, Hans, 'Conflicts between Obligations under the Charter of the United Nations and Obligations under Other International Agreements: An Analysis of Article 103 of the Charter', *University of Pittsburgh Law Review*, 10 (1948–49), 284–294

  Introduction to the Problems of Legal Theory (Oxford: Clarendon Press, 1992, trans., Litschewski, Paulson and Paulson, first published 1934)

Kennedy, David, 'A New World Order: Yesterday, Today, and Tomorrow', *Transnational Law and Contemporary Problems*, 4 (1994), 1–47

  International Legal Structures (Baden-Baden: Nomos, 1987)

Kennedy, Duncan, *A Critique of Adjudication {Fin de Siecle}* (Cambridge, MA: Harvard University Press, 1997)

Kershaw, Ian, *Hitler 1889–1936: Hubris* (London: Penguin, 1998)

Klabbers, Jan, *An Introduction to International Institutional Law* (Cambridge: Cambridge University Press, 2002)

  'Coming in from the Cold? Treaties in Finland's Legal Order', in Timo Koivurova (ed.), *Kansainvälistyvä Oikeus: Juhlakirja Professori Kari Hakapää* (Rovaniemi: University of Lapland, 2005), pp. 143–52

  'How to Defeat a Treaty's Object and Purpose Pending Entry into Force: Toward Manifest Intent', *Vanderbilt Journal of Transnational Law*, 34 (2001), 283–331

  'International Law in Community Law: The Law and Politics of Direct Effect', *Yearbook of European Law*, 21 (2002), 263–98

    'International Legal Histories: The Declining Importance of *Travaux Préparatoires* in Treaty Interpretation?', *Netherlands International Law Review*, 50 (2003), 267–88

  'Moribund on the Fourth of July? The Court of Justice on Prior Agreements of the Member States', *European Law Review*, 26 (2001) 187–97

  'On Human Rights Treaties, Contractual Conceptions and Reservations', in Ineta Ziemele (ed.), *Reservations to Human Rights Treaties and the Vienna Convention Regime: Conflict, Harmony or Reconciliation* (Leiden: Martinus Nijhoff, 2004), pp. 149–82

'Possible Islands of Predictability: The Legal Thought of Hannah Arendt', *Leiden Journal of International Law*, 20 (2007), 1–23

'Rebel with a Cause? Terrorists and Humanitarian Law', *European Journal of International Law*, 14 (2003), 299–321

'Re-inventing the Law of Treaties: The Contribution of the EC Courts', *Netherlands Yearbook of International Law*, 30 (1999), 45–74

'Reluctant *Grundnormen*: Articles 31(3)(c) and 42 of the Vienna Convention on the Law of Treaties and the Fragmentation of International Law', in Matthew Craven, Malgosia Fitzmaurice and Maria Vogiatzi (eds.), *Time, History and International Law* (Leiden: Martinus Nijhoff, 2007), pp. 141–61

'Restraints on the Treaty-making Powers of Member States Deriving from EU Law: Towards a Framework for Analysis', in Enzo Cannizzaro (ed.), *The European Union as an Actor in International Relations* (The Hague: Kluwer, 2002), pp. 151–75

'Safeguarding the Organizational *Acquis*: The EU's External Practice', *International Organizations Law Review* 4 (2007), 57–89

'Some Problems Regarding the Object and Purpose of Treaties', *Finnish Yearbook of International Law*, 8 (1997), 138–60

'The Commodification of International Law', in Emmanuelle Jouannet and Hélène Ruiz-Fabri (eds.), *International Law: Do We Need It?* (Oxford: Hart, forthcoming)

The Concept of Treaty in International Law (The Hague: Kluwer, 1996)

'The Relative Autonomy of International Law, or The Forgotten Politics of Interdisciplinarity', *Journal of International Law and International Relations*, 1 (2004–05), 35–48

'The Scope of International Law: *Erga Omnes* Obligations and the Turn to Morality', in Matti Tupamäki (ed.), *Liber Amicorum Bengt Broms* (Helsinki: Finnish ILA Branch, 1999), pp. 149–79

and René Lefeber (eds.), *Essays on the Law of Treaties: A Collection of Essays in Honour of Bert Vierdag* (The Hague: Martinus Nijhoff, 1998)

Kluyver C. A. (ed.), *Documents on the League of Nations* (Leiden: Sijthoff, 1920)

Koskenniemi, Martti, *Fragmentation of International Law: Difficulties Arising from the Diversification and Expansion of International Law. Report of the Study Group of the International Law Commission* (Helsinki: Erik Castrén Institute, 2007)

From Apology to Utopia: The Structure of International Legal Argument (Helsinki: Finnish Lawyers' Publishing Co., 1989)

'Hersch Lauterpacht (1897–1960)', in Jack Beatson and Reinhard Zimmermann (eds.), *Jurists Uprooted: German-speaking Émigré Lawyers in Twentieth-century Britain* (Oxford: Oxford University Press, 2004), pp. 601–61

'Hierarchy in International Law: A Sketch', *European Journal of International Law*, 8 (1997), 566–82

'International Law: Constitutionalism, Managerialism and the Ethos of Legal Education', *European Journal of Legal Studies*, 1 (2007), no page numbers given

'The Effect of Rights on Political Culture', in Philip Alston (ed.), *The EU and Human Rights* (Oxford: Oxford University Press, 1999), pp. 99–116

'The Fate of Public International Law: Between Technique and Politics', *Modern Law Review*, 70 (2007), 1–30

and Päivi Leino, 'Fragmentation of International Law? Post-modern Anxieties', *Leiden Journal of International Law*, 15 (2002), 553–79

Koutrakos, Panos, *EU International Relations Law* (Oxford: Hart, 2006)

'Is Article 297 EC a "Reserve of Sovereignty"?', *Common Market Law Review*, 37 (2000), 1339–62

Krück, Hans, *Völkerrechtliche Verträge im Recht der Europäischen Gemeinschaften* (Berlin: Springer, 1977)

Kuyper, Pieter Jan, 'Implementation of Binding Security Council Resolutions by the EC/EU', in Erika de Wet and André Nollkaemper (eds.), *Review of the Security Council by Member States* (Antwerp: Intersentia, 2003)

'The Court and the Tribunal of the EC and the Vienna Convention on the Law of Treaties 1969', *Legal Issues of European Integration*, 25 (1998/I), 1–23

'The European Communities and the Code of Conduct for Liner Conferences: Some Problems on the Borderline between General International Law and Community Law', *Netherlands Yearbook of International Law*, 12 (1981), 73–112

and Esa Paasivirta, 'Further Exploring International Responsibility: The European Community and the ILC's Project on Responsibility of International Organizations', *International Organizations Law Review*, 1 (2004), 111–38

Lacey, Nicola, *A Life of H. L. A. Hart: The Nightmare and the Noble Dream* (Oxford Oxford: University Press, 2004)

Lang, John Temple, 'Community Constitutional Law: Article 5 EEC Treaty', *Common Market Law Review*, 27 (1990), 645–81

'The Duties of National Authorities under Community Constitutional Law', *European Law Review*, 23 (1998), 109–31

Lauterpacht, Hersch, 'Contracts to Break a Contract', in Hersch Lauterpacht, *International Law: Collected Papers. Volume 4: The Law of Peace* (Cambridge: Cambridge University Press, 1978, E. Lauterpacht (ed.); originally published 1936), pp. 340–75

'The Chinn Case', *British Yearbook of International Law*, 16 (1935), 164–6

'The Covenant as the "Higher Law"', *British Yearbook of International Law*, 17 (1936), 54–65

'Report on the Law of Treaties', *Yearbook of the International Law Commission*, (1953/II), 90–166

'Second Report on the Law of Treaties', *Yearbook of the International Law Commission*, (1954/II), 123–39

Lauwaars, Richard H., 'The Interrelationship between United Nations Law and the Law of Other International Organizations', *Michigan Law Review*, 82 (1983–84), 1604–19

Lavranos, Nikolaos, *Decisions of International Organizations in the European and Domestic Legal Orders of Selected EU Member States* (Groningen: Europa Law Publishing, 2004)

'UN Sanctions and Judicial Review', *Nordic Journal of International Law*, 76 (2006), 1–17

Lawson, Rick, *Het EVRM en de Europese Gemeenschappen* (Deventer: Kluwer, 1999)

Leino-Sandberg, Päivi, 'European Universalism? The EU and Human Rights Conditionality', *24 Yearbook of European Law* (2005), 329–383

Particularity as Universality: The Politics of Human Rights in the European Union (Helsinki: Erik Castrén Institute, 2005)

Lenaerts, Koen and Piet van Nuffel, *Constitutional Law of the European Union* (London: Sweet & Maxwell, 1999)

and Eddy de Smijter, 'The European Union as an Actor under International Law', *Yearbook of European Law*, 19 (1999–2000), 95–138

Lepper, Steven J., '*Short v. The Kingdom of the Netherlands*: Is it Time to Renegotiate the NATO Status of Forces Agreement?', *Vanderbilt Journal of Transnational Law*, 24 (1991), 867–943

Lesaffer, Randall, 'The Medieval Canon Law of Contract and Early Modern Treaty Law', *Journal on the History of International Law*, 2 (2000), 178–98

Lilla, Mark, Ronald Dworkin and Robert B. Silvers (eds.), *The Legacy of Isaiah Berlin* (New York: New York Review of Books, 2001)

Lim, Hoe, 'Trade and Human Rights: What's at Issue?', *Journal of World Trade*, 35 (2001), 275–300

Lindroos, Anja, 'Addressing Norm Conflicts in a Fragmented Legal System: The Doctrine of *Lex Specialis*,' *Nordic Journal of International Law*, 74 (2005), 27–66

Lindroos, Anja and Michael Mehling, 'Dispelling the Chimera of "Self-contained Regimes": International Law and the WTO: European Journal of International Law, 16 (2005), 857–77

Lowe, Vaughan, 'Overlapping Jurisdiction in International Tribunals', *Australian Yearbook of International Law*, 20 (1999), 191–204

Lucy, William, review of Stephen J. Burton, *Judging in Good Faith, Cambridge Law Journal*, 52 (1993), 323–7

Maas, Geesteranus, G. W. 'Recht en praktijk in het verdragenrecht', in E. W. Vierdag and G. W. Maas Geesteranus, *Spanningen tussen recht en praktijk in het verdragenrecht* (Deventer: Kluwer, 1989, Mededelingen Nederlandse Vereniging voor Internationaal Recht No. 99), pp. 89–122

Machiavelli, Niccolò, *De vorst* (Amsterdam: De Bussy, 1983, trans. Otten)

MacLeod, I., I.D. Hendry and Stephen Hyett, *The External Relations of the European Communities* (Oxford: Oxford University Press, 1996)

Manzini, Pietro, 'The Priority of Pre-existing Treaties of EC Member States within the Framework of International Law', *European Journal of International Law*, 12 (2001), 781–92

Marceau, Gabrielle, 'WTO Dispute Settlement and Human Rights', *European Journal of International Law*, 13 (2002), 753–814

Matsushita, Mitsuo, Thomas J. Schoenbaum and Petros C. Mavroidis, *The World Trade Organization: Law, Practice, and Policy* (Oxford: Oxford University Press, 2003)

McCrudden, Christopher and Anne Davies, 'A Perspective on Trade and Labor Rights', *Journal of International Economic Law*, 3 (2000), 43–62

McGinnis, John O., 'A New Agenda for International Human Rights: Economic Freedom', *Catholic University Law Review*, 48 (1998–99) 1029–34

and Mark L. Movsesian, 'The World Trade Constitution', *Harvard Law Review*, 114 (2000), 511–605

McGoldrick, Dominic, *International Relations Law of the European Union* (London: Longman, 1997)

McLachlan, Campbell, 'The Principle of Systemic Integration and Article 31(3)(c) of the Vienna Convention', *International and Comparative Law Quarterly*, 54 (2005), 279–320

McNair, Lord Arnold Duncan, *The Law of Treaties* (Oxford: Clarendon Press, 1961)

Meron, Theodor, *The Humanization of International Law* (Leiden: Martinus Nijhoff, 2005)

Merrills, John G., *Judge Sir Gerald Fitzmaurice and the Discipline of International Law* (The Hague: Kluwer, 1998)

Morijn, John, 'Balancing Fundamental Rights and Common Market Freedoms in Union Law: Schmidberger and Omega in the Light of the European Constitution', *European Law Journal*, 12 (2006), 15–40

Mus, Jan, 'Conflicts between Treaties in International Law', *Netherlands International Law Review*, 45 (1998), 208–32

Verdragsconflicten voor de Nederlandse rechter (Zwolle: Tjeenk Willink, 1996)

Noll, Gregor, *Negotiating Asylum: The EU Acquis, Extraterritorial Protection and the Common Market of Deflection* (The Hague: Martinus Nijhoff, 2000)

'Diplomatic Assurances and the Silence of Human Rights Law', *Melbourne Journal of International Law*, 7(2006), 104–6

'O' (a pseudonym), 'The Chinn Case', *British Yearbook of International Law*, 16 (1935), 162–4

Obradovic, Daniela, 'Repatriation of Powers in the European Community', *Common Market Law Review*, 34 (1997), 59–88

Ojanen, Tuomas, *The European Way: The Structure of National Court Obligation under EC Law* (doctoral thesis, University of Helsinki, 1998)

Oliver, Peter and Wulf-Henning Roth, 'The Internal Market and the Four Freedoms', *Common Market Law Review*, 41 (2004), 407–41

Ott, Andrea, 'Thirty Years of Case-law by the European Court of Justice on International Law: A Pragmatic Approach towards its Integration', in Vincent Kronenberger (ed.), *The EU and the International Legal Order: Discord or Harmony?* (The Hague: TMC Asser Press, 2001), pp. 95–140

Ovey, Clare and Robin White, *Jacobs and White: The European Convention on Human Rights*, 3rd edn (Oxford: Oxford University Press, 2002)

Panayi, Christiana, 'Exploring the *Open Skies*: EC-incompatible Treaties between Member States and Third Countries', *Yearbook of European Law*, 25 (2006), 315–62

Panhuys, van H. F., 'Conflicts between the Law of the European Communities and Other Rules of International Law', *Common Market Law Review*, 3 (1965–6), 420–49

Paolillo, Felipe, 'Convention de Vienne de 1969: Article 30: Application des traités successifs portant sur la même matière', in Olivier Corten and Pierre Klein (eds.), *Les Conventions de Vienne sur le Droit des Traités: Commentaire article par article* (Brussels: Bruylant, 2006), pp. 1247–83

Paulus, Andreas, 'Commentary to Andreas Fischer-Lescano and Gunther Teubner: The Legitimacy of International Law and the Role of the State', *Michigan Journal of International Law*, 25 (2004), 1047–58

Pauwelyn, Joost, 'Bridging Fragmentation and Unity: International Law as a Universe of Inter-connected Islands', *Michigan Journal of International Law*, 25 (2004), 903–16

   Conflict of Norms in Public International Law: How WTO Law Relates to Other Rules of International Law (Cambridge: Cambridge University Press, 2003)

Perelman, Chaim (ed.), *Les antinomies en droit* (Brussels: Bruylant, 1964)

   'Les antinomies en droit: essai de synthese', in Chaim Perelman (ed.), *Les antinomies en droit* (Brussels: Bruylant, 1964), pp. 392–404

Petersmann, Ernst-Ulrich, 'Artikel 234', in H. von der Groeben, Jochen Thiessing and Claus-Dieter Ehlermann (eds.), *Kommentar zum EWG-Vertrag*, 4th edn (Baden-Baden: Nomos, 1991), pp. 5725–53

   'Human Rights and the Law of the World Trade Organization', *Journal of World Trade*, 37 (2003), 241–81

   'Taking Human Dignity, Poverty and Empowerment of Individuals More Seriously: Rejoinder to Alston', *European Journal of International Law*, 13 (2002), 845–51

   'Time for a United Nations 'Global Compact' for Integrating Human Rights into the Law of Worldwide Organizations: Lessons from European Integration', *European Journal of International Law*, 13 (2002), 621–50

Puissochet, Jean-Pierre, 'The Court of Justice and International Action by the European Community: The Example of the Embargo Against the Former Yugoslavia', *Fordham International Law Journal*, 20 (1997), 1557–76

Reuter, Paul, *Introduction to the Law of Treaties* (London: Pinter, 1989, Mico and Haggenmacher trans.)

Rosas, Allan, 'With a Little Help from my Friends: International Case-Law as a Source of Reference for the EU Courts', *The Global Community Yearbook of International Law and Jurisprudence*, 5 (2006), 203–30

Rosenne, Shabtai, 'Bilateralism and Community Interest in the Codified Law of Treaties', in Wolfgang Friedmann, Louis Henkin and Oliver Lissitzyn (eds.), *Transnational Law in a Changing Society: Essays in Honor of Philip C. Jessup* (New York: Columbia University Press, 1972), pp. 202–27

Roucounas, Emmanuel, 'Engagements Parallèles et Contradictoires', *Recueil des Cours*, 206 (1987/VI), 9–288

Rousseau, Charles, 'De la compatibilité des normes juridiques contradictoires dans l'ordre international', *Revue Générale de Droit International Public*, 39 (1932), 133–92

Sadat-Akhavi, Seyed Ali, *Methods of Resolving Conflicts between Treaties* (Leiden: Martinus Nijhoff, n.y.)

Safrin, Sabrina, 'Treaties in Collision? The Biosafety Protocol and the World Trade Organization Agreements', *American Journal of International Law*, 96 (2002), 606–28

Salmon, Jean, 'Les antinomies en droit international public', in Chaim Perelman (ed.), *Les antinomies en droit* (Brussels: Bruylant, 1964), pp. 285–319

Sands, Philippe, *Lawless World: America and the Making and Breaking of Global Rules* (London: Allen Lane, 2005)

Sarooshi, Dan, *International Organizations and their Exercise of Sovereign Powers* (Oxford University Press, 2005)

Sasse, Christoph, 'The Common Market, between International and Municipal Law', *Yale Law Journal*, 75 (1966), 695–753

Schauer, Frederick, *Playing by the Rules: A Philosophical Examination of Rule-Based Decision-Making in Law and in Life* (Oxford: Clarendon Press, 1991)

Schepel, Harm and Rein Wesseling, 'The Legal Community: Judges, Lawyers, Officials and Clerks in the Writing of Europe', *European Law Journal*, 3 (1997), 165–88

Schermers, H. G., 'Community Law and International Law', *Common Market Law Review*, 12 (1975), 77–90

    'Constituent Treaties of International Organisations Conflicting with Anterior Treaties', in Jan Klabbers and René Lefeber (eds.), *Essays on the Law of Treaties: A Collection of Essays in Honour of Bert Vierdag* (The Hague: Martinus Nijhoff, 1998), pp. 9–30

    and Niels M. Blokker, *International Institutional Law*, 4th edn (The Hague: Martinus Nijhoff, 2003)

Schlesinger, Stephen C., *Act of Creation: The Founding of the United Nations* (Boulder, CO: Westview, 2003)

Schmitt, Carl, *The Concept of the Political* (Chicago: University of Chicago Press, 1996, first published 1932, Schwab trans.)

Schütze, Robert, 'Co-operative Federalism Constitutionalised: The Emergence of Complementary Competences in the EC Legal Order', *European Law Review*, 31 (2006), 167–84

 'EC Law and International Agreements of the Member States – An Ambivalent Relationship?', *Cambridge Yearbook of European Studies*, 9 (2006–07), 387–440

 'On 'Middle Ground': The European Community and Public International Law', *EUI Working Papers, Law*, 2007/13

Seidl-Hohenveldern, Ignaz, 'Hierarchy of Treaties', in Jan Klabbers and René Lefeber (eds.), *Essays on the Law of Treaties: A Collection of Essays in Honour of Bert Vierdag* (The Hague: Martinus Nijhoff, 1998), pp. 7–18

Shany, Yuval, 'Contract Claims vs. Treaty Claims: Mapping Conflicts between ICSID Decisions on Multisourced Investment Claims', 99 *American Journal of International Law* (2005) 835–51

 The Competing Jurisdictions of International Courts and Tribunals (Oxford: Oxford University Press, 2003)

Simma, Bruno, 'From Bilateralism to Community Interest in International Law', *Recueil des Cours*, 250 (1994/VI), 221–384

 'Reflections on Article 60 of the Vienna Convention on the Law of Treaties and its Background in General International Law', *Österreichische Zeitschrift für öffentliches Recht und Völkerrecht*, 20 (1970), 5–83

 'Self-contained Regimes', *Netherlands Yearbook of International Law*, 16(1985), 112–36

 and Dirk Pulkowski, 'Of Planets and the Universe: Self-contained Regimes in International Law', *European Journal of International Law*, 17 (2006), 483–529

Simpson, Gerry, *Great Powers and Outlaw States: Unequal Sovereigns in the International Legal Order* (Cambridge: Cambridge University Press, 2004)

Sinclair, Sir Ian, *The Vienna Convention on the Law of Treaties*, 2nd edn (Manchester: Manchester University Press, 1984)

Slaughter, Anne-Marie, *A New World Order* (Princeton, NJ: Princeton University Press, 2004)

Slot, Piet-Jan and Jacqueline Dutheil de la Rochère, 'Case-note' (*Open Skies* cases), *Common Market Law Review*, 40 (2003), 697–713

Smith, Stephen A., *Contract Theory* (Oxford: Clarendon Press, 2004)

Spiermann, Ole, *International Legal Argument in the Permanent Court of International Justice: The Rise of the International Judiciary* (Cambridge: Cambridge University Press, 2005)

Stein, Eric, 'Lawyers, Judges, and the Making of a Transnational Constitution', *American Journal of International Law*, 75 (1981), 1–27

Stein, Peter, *Roman Law in European History* (Cambridge: Cambridge University Press, 1999)

Summers, Robert S., *Lon L. Fuller* (London: Edward Arnold, 1984)

Tell, Olivier, *La 'Disconnecting Clause'/Disconnection Clause*, unpublished seminar paper, 2001 (on file with the author)

Timmermans, Christiaan, 'The EU and Public International Law', *European Foreign Affairs Review*, 4 (1999), 181–94

Tomuschat, Christian, 'Annotation' (*Kadi* and *Yusuf* cases), *Common Market Law Review*, 43 (2006), 537–51

Trachtman, Joel P., 'Institutional Linkage: Transcending "Trade and . . . "', *American Journal of International Law*, 96 (2002), 77–93

Tuori, Kaarlo, *Critical Legal Positivism* (Aldershot: Ashgate, 2002)

Tuytschaever, Filip, *Differentiation in European Union Law* (Oxford: Hart, 1999)

Ustor, Endre, 'Working Paper on the Most-Favoured-Nation Clause in the Law of Treaties', *Yearbook of the International Law Commission* (1968/II), 165–70

Vallely, Patrick J., 'Tension between the Cartagena Protocol and the WTO: The Significance of Recent WTO Developments in an Ongoing Debate', *Chicago Journal of International Law*, 5 (2004–05), 369–78

Vanhamme, Jan, *Volkenrechtelijke beginselen in het Europees recht* (Groningen: Europa Law Publishing, 2001)

de Vattel, Emeric, *The Law of Nations* (New York: AMS Press, reprint of 1863 edn, Chitty trans., first published 1758)

Vedder, Christoph and Hans-Peter Folz, 'A Survey of Principal Decisions of the European Court of Justice Pertaining to International Law in 1993', *European Journal of International Law*, 5 (1994), 448–63

Verwey, Delano, *The European Community, the European Union and the International Law of Treaties* (The Hague: TMC Asser Press, 2004)

Verzijl, J. H. W., 'La validité et la nullité des actes juridiques internationaux', *Revue de Droit International* (1935), 3–58

Vierdag, E. W., 'The Time of the Conclusion of a Multilateral Treaty: Art. 30 of the Vienna Convention on the Law of Treaties and Related Provisions', *British Yearbook of International Law*, 59 (1988), 92–111

Oorlogsverklaring (inaugural address, University of Amsterdam, 1992)

Vitta, Edoardo, *La validité des traités internationaux* (Leiden: Brill, 1940)

Vollenhoven, C. van, *De drie treden van het volkenrecht* (The Hague: Martinus Nijhoff, 1918)

Voon, Tania, 'UNESCO and the WTO: A Clash of Cultures?', *International and Comparative Law Quarterly*, 55 (2006), 635–52

Vranes, Erich, '*Lex Superior, Lex Specialis, Lex Posterior* – Zur Rechtsnatur der "Konfliktslösungsregeln"', *Zeitschrift für ausländisches öffentliches Recht und Völkerrecht*, 65 (2005), 391–405

'The Definition of "Norm Conflict" in International Law and Legal Theory', *European Journal of International Law*, 17 (2006), 395–418

Waldock, Sir, Humphrey, 'Second Report on the Law of Treaties', *Yearbook of the International Law Commission* (1963/II), 36–94

'Third Report on the Law of Treaties', in *Yearbook of the International Law Commission* (1964/II), 5–65

Walker, Neil, 'Flexibility within a Metaconstitutional Frame: Reflections on the Future of Legal Authority in Europe', in Gráinne de Búrca and Joanne Scott (eds.), *Constitutional Change in the EU: Between Uniformity and Flexibility?* (Oxford: Hart, 2000), pp. 9–30

Wallach, Lori and Patrick Woodall, *Whose Trade Organization? A Comprehensive Guide to the WTO* (New York: New Press, 2004)

Walzer, Michael, *Just and Unjust Wars*, 3rd edn (New York: Basic Books, 2000)

Warbrick, Colin, 'Coherence and the European Court of Human Rights: The Adjudicative Background to the *Soering* Case', *Michigan Journal of International Law*, 11 (1989–90), 1073–96

Watson, Geoffrey R., 'The Death of Treaty', *Ohio State Law Journal*, 55 (1994), 781–853

Weiler, J. H. H., 'Fundamental Rights and Fundamental Boundaries', in J. H. H. Weiler, *The Constitution of Europe* (Cambridge: Cambridge University Press, 1999), pp. 102–29

'The External Legal Relations of Non-Unitary Actors: Mixity and the Federal Principle', in J. H. H. Weiler, *The Constitution of Europe* (Cambridge: Cambridge University Press, 1999), pp. 130–87

and Andreas Paulus, 'The Structure of Change in International Law or Is There a Hierarchy of Norms in International Law?', *European Journal of International Law*, 8 (1997), 545–65

Wendt, Frantz, *The Nordic Council and Co-operation in Scandinavia* (Copenhagen: Munksgaard, 1959)

Wessel, Ramses, 'The EU as Black Widow: Devouring the WEU to Give Birth to a European Security and Defence Policy', in Vincent Kronenberger (ed.), *The EU and the International Legal Order: Discord or Harmony?* (The Hague: TMC Asser Press, 2001), pp. 405–34

Wet, Erika de, 'The International Constitutional Order', *International and Comparative Law Quarterly*, 55 (2006), 51–76

and André Nollkaemper (eds.), *Review of the Security Council by Member States* (Antwerp: Intersentia, 2003)

Wightman, John, *Contract: A Critical Commentary* (London: Pluto, 1996)

Wildhaber, Luzius, 'The European Convention on Human Rights and International Law', *International and Comparative Law Quarterly*, 56 (2007), 217–32

Wilting, Wilhelm Heinrich, *Vertragskonkurrenz im Völkerrecht* (Cologne: Carl Heymans Verlag, 1996)

Witte, Bruno de, 'Internationale verdragen tussen lidstaten van de Europese Unie', in Ramses Wessel and Bruno de Witte, *De plaats van de Europese Unie in het veranderende bestel van de volkenrechtelijke organisatie* (The Hague: TMC Asser Press, 2001, mededelingen van de Nederlandse Vereniging voor Internationaal Recht no. 123), pp. 79–131

'Old-fashioned Flexibility: International Agreements between Member States of the European Union', in Gráinne de Búrca and Joanne Scott (eds.), *Constitutional Change in the EU: From Uniformity to Flexibility?* (Oxford: Hart, 2000), pp. 31–58

'Retour à Costa: La primauté du droit communautaire à la lumière du droit international', *Revue Trimestrielle de Droit Européen*, 20 (1984), 425–54

Wolfrum, Rüdiger and Nele Matz, *Conflicts in International Environmental Law* (Berlin: Springer, 2003)

Wood, Gordon S., *The American Revolution: A History* (New York: Modern Library Chronicles, 2002)

Wouters, Jan, Frank Hoffmeister and Tom Ruys (eds.), *The United Nations and the European Union: An Ever Stronger Partnership* (The Hague: TMC Asser Press, 2006)

Wright, Quincy, 'Conflicts Between International Law and Treaties', *American Journal of International Law*, 11 (1917), 566–79

Wyatt, Derrick, 'New Legal Order, or Old?', *European Law Review*, 7 (1982), 147–66

Zuleeg, Manfred, 'Vertragskonkurrenz im Völkerrecht. Teil I: Verträge zwischen souveränen Staaten', *German Yearbook of International Law*, 20 (1977), 246–76

INDEX